If You're Not
Out
Selling,
You're Being
Outsold

If You're Not Out Selling, You're Being Outsold

Michael St. Lawrence

Steve Johnson

JOHN WILEY & SONS, INC.

New York • Chichester • Weinheim • Brisbane • Singapore • Toronto

This text is printed on acid-free paper.

Published by John Wiley & Sons, Inc.

This publication is designed to provide accurate and authorita-
tive information in regard to the subject matter covered. It is
sold with the understanding that the publisher is not engaged
in rendering legal, accounting, or other professional services.
If legal advice or other expert assistance is required, the services of a competent professional person should be sought.

Library of Congress Cataloging-in-Publication Data:

St. Lawrence, Michael, 1960–
    If you're not out selling, you're being outsold / by
Michael St. Lawrence & Steve Johnson.
      p. cm.
    Includes index.
    ISBN 0-471-19119-1 (cloth : alk. paper)
    1. Selling. 2. Success in business. I. Johnson, Steve,
1962–. II. Title.
  HF5438.25.S72   1998
658.85—dc21   97-15013
                         CIP

Printed in the United States of America

10 9 8 7 6 5 4 3 2 1

To Mom, Dad, Cristina, Paula, and Danny
—Michael St. Lawrence

To the most inspirational people in my life, Mom and Dad
—Steve Johnson

Martha and Ruth, thanks for everything.
You two made it all possible.
—Mike and Steve

Preface

This book was written because we believe that the true reasons for success in business are being overlooked in the books and information being published today. We say this because every day, for a combined 23 years, the two of us have been involved in one way or another in a constant study of what it is that successful professionals do differently from everyone else.

More and more of the books that profess to pave the way to increased influence, high-powered communication, and business results neglect the most important factors and concentrate instead on highly technical skills that are interesting, and in many cases even important, but not *vital* in the real world.

In a nutshell, we have been observing, coaching, and selling to people who are motivated to make it, and we've been able to see what really works. We have heard and tried a lot of advice that sounds great but for whatever reason just doesn't produce the desired results. By listening to what these professionals had to say, we have been able to discover what it is that the top performers do that creates their success and we have distilled it into seven fundamentals that you can adapt to your job immediately.

We have found that selling ideas, being persuasive, practicing high-integrity values, and generating quality work and results for your colleagues and customers are the most reliable ways to achieve business success; yet a relatively small proportion of people are really good at doing these things. Because of the enormous focus on technology today, few people are concentrating on developing the fundamentals that will truly determine how far they can climb. Our study has not, like many recent books on communication, motivation, selling, and leadership, been conducted by a team of researchers and analytical wizards who churn out spectacular graphs, statistics, and peripheral insights but who are unaware of the real priorities facing people who are struggling to make it every day in organizations that are competitive and relentless in their demand for immediate results. Although we all seem to be attracted to books that are releasing cutting-edge theories that are new, exciting, different, trendy, and marketed with pizzazz, that doesn't mean that the information will provide the answers we are looking for. In more cases than not, what makes interesting reading is very hard to apply in the real world.

Here is what we have done and continue to do that puts us in contact with thousands of highly persuasive and productive professionals:

- We have personally sold and developed sales and communication training for companies that want to bring out the best in their people for a combined 23 years in the real world, with real prospects.
- We have personally interviewed more than 10,000 people, successful and striving to be, over the last 12 years to determine their individual characteristics and what separates the highest achievers from the rest.
- We have consulted with hundreds of companies from virtually every industry to help them recognize and develop the talents of their people.
- We have conducted thousands of training seminars, convention speeches, and workshops, observing firsthand the application of communication and selling principles in the real world.
- We have managed high-performance teams both in field sales offices and in larger corporate arenas, observing which people are able to get results consistently and why.

Vince Lombardi, when interviewed about his amazing success with the Green Bay Packers back in the early 1960s, said that although football is a complex strategic game, it still comes down to fundamentals: The team that executes the fundamentals better is usually the team that wins. We are finding that there is an extraordinary amount of information on complex strategy and techniques but very little in terms of a boiled-down version of the fundamentals.

In this book you'll find a list of essential skills, abilities, and attitudes that constitute the fundamentals, the approaches you need to take to ensure that you thrive in today's competitive environment and achieve lasting and permanent success. When you've got these fundamentals in place, you'll enjoy some extraordinary benefits for a lifetime:

- You will be more persuasive.
- You will be in control of your future.
- You will be the kind of person that others want to do business with.
- You will be capable of accepting and handling a great deal of responsibility.
- You will be growing and developing at a very fast pace.
- Your work will have a special mark of quality.
- You will be able to solve tough problems and persist when others crack under pressure.
- You will be able to produce extraordinary results consistently.
- Your strongest assets will be your credibility, your trustworthiness, and your ability to make your ideas work for you and for the people you care about.

The OUTSELL factors are dedicated to you because we know how hard it is to achieve the highest level of impact and influence. This is a book written for the professional looking for ideas that can be implemented. Neither of us is an Ivy League professor, but we do have the distinction of having achieved a high level of success in selling ideas, persuading others, and producing quality results. We're eager to share what we've learned with you.

Contents

Chapter One

GET READY TO OUTSELL

Although our book has a sales title, it's not your typical book on selling or how to get ahead. This book is for the professional, whether in sales or not, who has to sell ideas and convince people to take action. This book is for the person who knows that the business environment is competitive and that getting ahead means *being successful,* not just being able to talk about it. We offer no scripts and nothing to memorize, no lengthy forms to fill out, and no analytical data puzzles to wade through. The old wizards of sales have beaten that stuff to death. You don't need any more formulas and prefabricated responses or cute little phrases to plug in at perfectly timed moments in the conversation. You don't need personality-type analysis quadrants to put people into (amiable, analyzer, etc.), because people are unique individuals and should be treated that way. We won't insult your intelligence, so we don't have manipulative language techniques or any "copy me and you'll see" approaches. All of that stuff is insincere and violates our belief that people, including customers and colleagues, should always be treated in a genuine, caring fashion. Last, this is not a watered-down, sanitized book written by a roomful of consultants, dry researchers, and politically correct "languagizers" who have run everything by the corporate attorney. No, we tell it like it is because we've sold for a living for many years. We have had the good fortune to interview, work with, and teach seminars with thousands of top-performing business professionals who know how to sell ideas and get results. We think it is a shame that so many books are stripped of all firepower, controversy, and corporate liability and end up being 250 pages of intellectually penetrating sleeping pills. Our book will not put you to sleep, we promise! The following story sums up our feelings about many of the business theories being published today:

> Deep in the rain forest, a group of explorers came upon a village of natives. In a desperate attempt to win them over (after all, their lives depended on it!), the leader began telling the natives what it was like in the civilized world. "Out there," he said, "we love all the people in our villages."
>
> To this, the natives in unison gave a ringing cry of "Huzzonga!"
>
> Encouraged by this, the explorer continued. "Where we come from there is great opportunity for all!"
>
> "Huzzonga!"
>
> "We are peaceful!" said the explorer.
>
> "Huzzonga!" screamed the natives.
>
> With a tear running down his cheek, the explorer ended his fine speech with "We come to you as friends, as brothers. So trust us. Open your arms to us, your homes, your hearts! What do you say?"
>
> The air shook with one final mighty "Huzzonga!"
>
> Overwhelmed, the leader of the explorers then began talking with the natives' chief. The chief suggested a tour of the village and asked the explorer what he would like to see. The explorer replied, "I see that you have a unique species of cattle here with which I am unfamiliar. I have never seen bulls so big and strong. May I inspect them?"
>
> "Certainly, come with me," said the chief. "But be careful as you walk not to step in the huzzonga."

You'll find a lot of huzzonga out there, but not here. *If You're Not Out Selling, You're Being Outsold* is not going to give you the eternal "secret" of how to make it easier or faster—because there isn't one. "Secrets" sell and they're fun to read, but the bottom line is that people looking for an easier way are secret junkies, and they usually end up shipwrecked on a deserted island at some point or another. A lot of this "attractive" advice is being generated by people who have not had to make that advice work in the real world, but we have. We know which ideas look great on paper, are inspiring, and should work but turn out to be a lot of huzzonga—interesting huzzonga to be sure, but huzzonga nevertheless. Huzzonga ends up wasting our time, sidetracking us, and creating false hopes and expectations. This book is going to cut through all the huzzonga for you. You will not find a quick fix here, because we know from experience that quick fixes don't work. You also will not find any buzzwords or corporate lines of b.s. designed primarily to get the attention of influential Fortune 500 CEOs. This is a book for you if you want the truth about what it takes to reach a higher level of business performance, a level that will put you into the impact zone, the high reward arena where ideas are communicated with power, are accepted, and are acted upon! We are top-performing sales professionals who sell and teach selling in the real world. We will show you how to get there in this book.

Many of you in sales have probably read books on professional selling written by the new army of so-called experts. These books will lull you down the road of inactivity and convince you that your success depends on your ability to analyze, plan, and dissect data; that you will finally hit the big numbers if you'll just fill in the blanks to this preprinted 65-page data analyzer and strategic plan maker for each of your accounts; that all you have to do is load all those 60 million to-do's into your computer database and you won't even have to work—it all just gets done for you! Huzzonga! Hey, we know that planning and studying your accounts is important, especially in large, complex deals, but you don't get invited to those parties until you have mastered the OUTSELL factors. The OUT-SELL factors will put you in a position to get in the game. Are you ready?

Who This Book Is For

Are you an ambitious business professional who desires to be a higher-impact player in this topsy-turvy business world? If so, we wrote this book for you! It all starts with you. If you are convinced that what's inside of you is the ticket to a better lifestyle, more courage, more confidence, and more rewarding relationships, then read on. If you know that only a fraction of your potential has reached the surface, then you're going to love this book. If you believe deep down that your ideas could make this world a better place, if only someone would listen, then buckle your seat belt because we're going to give you an exciting ride. This book is for you if you are certain that your future will be more exciting, fun, interesting, and worthwhile if you could just motivate the world to take action on your ideas. If that's you, then congratulations, *you're ready to OUTSELL!*

What Does *Outselling* Mean?

Outselling means using the seven principles of the acronym *OUTSELL.* Right now, as you read this book, you are performing at the level that your core principles, disciplines, and beliefs allow you to. The principles you have bought into over the years have had a tremendous impact on where you are. Your beliefs shape the way you think and react and have everything to do with the results you get and the way you feel. We'll show you how to go further. When you adopt the OUTSELL principles, you will become stronger, more self-disciplined, and more capable of selling your ideas and persuading people to take action on what you believe in. More opportunities will start flowing your way, and you will find yourself on the road to the impact zone, a place where you can make things happen—faster and with less fuss. OUTSELL stands for

- **O**ne life, one boss: Developing a take-charge-now outlook.
- **U**nder construction: What skills and abilities you must have today.
- **T**ell it with gusto: How to communicate to sell ideas and get results.
- **S**igned, sealed, delivered: How to produce quality and really contribute.
- **E**at breakfast with champions: The best way to network.
- **L**ife's hard; hunker down and reach higher ground: Developing more persistence.
- **L**ive, thrive, and come alive in the impact zone: Finding the more powerful you.

Wisdom is knowledge about certain principles and causes.

—Aristotle

Who Needs to OUTSELL?

As a business professional, you can make your life better if you adopt the OUTSELL principles. You probably have some great ideas, but if no one listens to you or you can't assemble a team to take action on them, you are severely restricted. Whether or not you're in sales, if you're not convincing, you're going to be stuck eating the leftovers while the persuaders are busy feasting on the main course. If you want to be persuasive and convincing, if you want people to act on your ideas, if you want lasting career security, you need the OUTSELL principles.

These days, you must come up with ideas continuously (e.g., how to improve something for your company, your customer) and be persuasive at motivating others to take action. If you're not, then we guarantee you're not flourishing in this rock 'em, sock 'em business economy.

These days, if you're not out selling, you're being outsold. Even worse, you're not having much fun.

Maybe you don't think you're in sales and don't even like the word *sales*. Maybe the following story suggests the way you feel about salespeople and sales:

> A snake and a bunny rabbit were going through the forest and they ran into each other. The snake turned to the bunny and said, "Who are you?" and the bunny replied, "Well, who are you?"
>
> The snake innocently replied, "I am blind and I don't know who or what I am."
>
> The bunny, surprised by what he has heard, said, "I am blind and I don't know who or what I am either."
>
> The snake, thinking the situation over carefully, made an offer, "Let's make a deal. I will touch you and let you know what you are if you do the same for me." The bunny agreed, so the snake reached over and said, "You are furry and cuddly with floppy ears. I know what you are. You are a bunny rabbit."
>
> The bunny was overjoyed and jumped up and down. Next, the bunny reached over and grabbed the snake and said, "You are slithery with beady eyes and sharp fangs. I know what you are. You're a salesperson."

You may not see yourself as being in sales (and you may not be on a commission-based income either), but don't you still need to sell yourself every day in order to be successful? Don't you need to convince people to take action on your ideas? Don't you go to meetings where your input is (or should be) critical? Couldn't you improve the way your department, organization, or company works by being able to persuade the right people to take action on your suggestions? Couldn't you get ahead faster if you were more convincing? We think you could and we'll show you how.

The Business Environment Is Being Transformed

This we know: It's a knowledge economy, and our work world is chaotic, messy, hard to read, and harder still to predict. Our work relies on relationships and things like trust, credibility, and value. Virtually all business professionals spend a significant amount of their time explaining, thinking, problem solving, attending meetings, and suggesting ideas. Business experts say we are heading toward a work world where we, the people who want the good things in life, are probably not making products anymore. Instead, we spend more and more time coming up with ideas and convincing other people to help us get those ideas done. Products may eventually come from our ideas, but the work we do and how we spend our time is increasingly conceptual, more and more an exchange of ideas. The OUTSELL principles outlined in this book are custom-made for a business environment driven by trends such as these:

- Corporate flattening: Fewer layers of management and more power lower in the ranks.
- Manufacturing to service economy: Even manufacturing folks do service work when you get right down to it.
- Knowledge and information age: We have more access to information and need to turn it into productive ideas and improvements.
- Rapid pace of change—no that's not it—frightening pace of change: We need flexibility to adapt.
- Eat-or-be-eaten competitive environment: Job security is gone. Business is too competitive to carry deadweight anymore.
- Value-added, value-added, value-added: What have you done (improved) for me lately?
- Increased pressure to avoid obsolescence: Experience isn't enough anymore to gain an advantage. It needs to be combined with technological capability.
- Superspeed product cycle time: We have to make decisions faster and take more risks. We must stick our necks out more if we want to succeed.

Your success depends on your ability to sell yourself and your ideas. The opportunity is tremendous. All of this chaos and transformation has set the stage for those who use the OUTSELL principles to emerge as winners.

NOW IS THE TIME, THIS IS THE PLACE, AND YOU ARE THE PERSON!

For a moment, consider how lucky we really are! If you had your choice of living at anytime in history where personal freedom, liberty, and opportunity were at their highest level, where and when would you choose?

We know what we would choose—it's right here, right now! When the cosmic forces put this whole thing together and whirled us into the game, we got lucky and drew a great hand. Five hundred years ago, if your family wasn't among the "chosen few," you could forget it. Through all of human history, the access to education, information, and capital has been guarded by those lucky enough to have been born into it.

Today, it's a different world where we all sit. At this moment, there are people who are risking their lives on rickety boats and clawing for a chance, for the opportunities we already have. If you are living in a place where this book is available, then you are sitting on top of a supernova of opportunity. It's exploding all around you. Successful people are emerging faster than ever before. Great ideas with courageous people behind them have more possibilities and potential to grow faster now than ever before. There's more money and financing, more education, more cheap technology, more ways to market, more communication—there's more everything! But you've got to be willing to see the opportunity that's there.

The "System" Is Thriving!

What attitude have you bought into about the "system"? Do you think your government is broken, that the system is falling apart and will ruin your retirement, that your company is forcing you to live an uninspired workday, that it's just too hard to get ahead? If so, you bought the wrong plan, you were outsold by yourself, and you bought some crummy advice. The first sale we all have to make is to ourselves. When you can wake up in the morning, be grateful for the opportunity to compete in the lushest business environment in the history of the world with more freedom, more possibilities, and more access to the playmakers than ever before, then you're outselling the unlucky few, who would like to blame their lack of chutzpah on the government's poorly thought-out economic policy. What a time to be alive! You may have heard the story of Harry and Larry:

> Harry and Larry are twin brothers. Harry is a pessimist and Larry is an optimist. On the twins' birthday, their father bought Harry a bike, a basketball, and a rifle—everything to make him happy. For Larry, he bought a pile of manure.
>
> Upon opening his gifts, Harry said, "If I ride this bike, I might get hit by a car. If I take my basketball outside, someone might steal it. This rifle is dangerous. I will probably shoot someone's window out." He worried

about the terrible predicament these gifts had put him in and turned his birthday to gloom and doom.

When Larry saw the pile of manure his dad had gotten for him, he jumped for joy. Immediately, he began to look through all the rooms in the house. His dad caught him by the arm and asked, "Son, what are you looking for?"

Larry replied, "Dad, with all the horse manure you gave me, there's gotta be a pony around here some place!"

If you think the system stinks, is crooked, and is rigged against you, then you're not going to like what lies ahead. If you are convinced that you cannot make it, that the days of opportunity are gone, and that the economy is sliding and eroding away, then find another book, because we believe that the opportunity for us to succeed is greater today than ever before.

The OUTSELL Experts

You will be hearing from some special people in this book. They are people we have met over the years who are top performers in their fields. We specifically did not interview any stars or celebrities because there is enough advice from those folks already. If you are looking for unique thinking that is intriguing but virtually impossible to replicate, then their advice is for you. Instead, we looked for the kind of people we admire and look up to as role models. We have professionals, managers, and plenty of top-performing salespeople, all of whom are very persuasive and have a history of producing consistently outstanding results. We wanted to share the wisdom of some of the finest people we have met out of the thousands we have had the luck to come in contact with over the years. These people have earned their way through their tenacity, persistence, ability to persuade and convince, and their unique ability to produce that rare quality of self-motivation. We purposefully have not included their company names because we wanted them to feel free to tell the truth with no need to run it by any corporate overseers.

Did You Buy the Right Outlook?

Over time, we all acquire an outlook, one that perhaps gets us the results we want or maybe it doesn't, but one thing is for sure: our outlook has a lot to do with the results we get and the way we experience the events of our lives. Consider the man in this story:

> There was once a man who did not have any formal business training in accounting, engineering, law, or medicine, so he did what most people do in those circumstances—he went into sales. He opened a little stand on a corner and yelled out, "Hot Dog!" Believe it or not, his business started to grow. So he got a bigger griddle, put up a sign that said, "Hot Dog," did some advertising, and his business boomed so much that he was able to put his oldest boy through college.
>
> When his oldest boy came back with a degree in marketing and obviously knew everything there was to know about how to run a business, he looked at his father's business and told his dad there was a recession going on and that he had better change the way he did business, reengineer, and cut back. The dad, certain that his son knew it all, cut out his advertising. Then he took down his "Hot Dog" sign, reduced the size of his griddle, and even stopped yelling "Hot Dog." He went home one day very dejected and his son asked, "What is the matter, Dad?"
>
> The father, sad and dejected said, "You're right son, there is a recession going on out there, and it hit my business awfully hard."

What happened to the hot dog vendor can happen to each of us if we let it. We can become overly reactive to what we hear and see going on around us and stop putting out proactive energy. We first believe the negativity around us and then we start creating negative results that reinforce it. We buy the attitude first and take delivery of the product later. It's so easy to let sneaky little attitude dimmers drift into us. You have to sell and resell yourself every day on principles, attitudes, and beliefs that work and oust the crud that builds up when you're not paying attention. Keeping the gunk out is a never-ending commitment. You can plant a garden with the finest seeds and soil in the world, but weeds will get in there, bugs will start eating, and weather will take its course if you don't put in a little effort each week. The OUTSELL mentality is for you if you can stop thinking about what should have happened or the "it's impossible to make it anymore" attitude that so many people have bought into. They were outsold. They bought the wrong approach. Maybe a psychologist out there has the answer why, but the main thing for those of us who want to realize our ambition is to abandon any beliefs that even hint that we can't achieve the level of influence, impact, and personal power we want. It boils down to our outlook.

Viktor Frankl lived in a Nazi concentration camp and survived to tell about it. He looked back on those years as a valuable contribution to his personal transformation. His ability to learn and grow, even in the most extreme circumstances imaginable, shows how the right outlook can transform the way we experience life. He talks in the following passage from his inspiring book, *Man's Search for Meaning,* about the remarkable attitudes of people he remembered from the concentration camp: "We who lived in the concentration camps can remember the men who walked through the huts comforting others, giving away their last piece of bread. They may have been few in number, but they offer sufficient proof that everything can be taken from a man but one thing: the last of his freedoms—to choose one's attitude in any given set of circumstances, to choose one's own way."

It All Starts with You

By now, you know where we believe all sales start. Whether you're selling yourself, a new idea you've come up with, or a new product to a potential customer, it all starts with you and the principles you sell yourself. You must begin by selling yourself the right attitude. To get and to keep the right attitude, imagine the person you want to become. Forget about possessions and all the material things that come with the picture for a minute—just visualize who you've always wanted to be. Make a commitment to answer these questions sincerely:

- What level of confidence do I want to have?
- What level of influence do I want to possess?
- How persuasive do I want to be?
- How much personal power and proactive energy do I want to have?
- What kind of body do I really want to live in?
- What type of a communicator do I really want to be?
- What is the quality of the relationships I want to be in?
- What am I contributing to others, to the world around me, to myself?

When you have a clear image of the person you want to become, you can sell yourself on becoming that person. You can do it! You can become the person you've always wanted to be if you can make the first sale right now. Sell yourself. Take delivery of the new you. When you can feel it, then you will be energized.

When you have this energy, when you can see who you want to become, you're ready to OUTSELL.

Chapter Two

O ne life, one boss. This is the most powerful OUTSELL principle of all. One life, one boss—it's your life and you're in charge. You're responsible. You hold the key to your own future. You make the critical decisions that shape your day, your tomorrow, and your destiny. You have one life to live and *you* are given full authority to live it exactly as you want to. You must, however, claim that authority and learn to use it. One life, one boss. It's your life. You're the boss. Consider these words:

> Every man dies, but not every man really lives.
>   —William Wallace, from the movie *Braveheart*

The most important word of this quote is *really.* Not just to live, but to *really* live. This is perhaps the greatest challenge of all—to really live each day of our lives to the fullest.

There is nothing we can do to escape the inevitable; all of our lives will eventually come to an end. The quality of the life we are living right now, however, is 100% dependent on how *we decide* to live. We can simply exist, drifting with the current, swept into the momentum of each day, feeling little or no inspiration to improve our lives, or we can tap into an enormous reservoir of energy, potential, and resources and really live! It's the difference between settling for less versus becoming the person we are capable of becoming. Selling ideas and influencing situations is much more a result of our approach to life than mastering the latest, greatest selling tips. I was interviewing Jim, the president of a medium-sized insurance company, several years ago. He was telling me how he decided to form his own business. "I was stuck in a mid-level management job for about 10 years with a very reputable company. I had been passed over for two promotions that I thought I deserved, and I was getting the hint that my career just wasn't going anywhere fast. I guess I started to take it a little personally and realized that my company wasn't really going to guarantee me the future I wanted most. At that point, my thinking changed and I decided to strike out on my own. It was my decision to take more control of my destiny that made the difference. Looking back, I'm sure that if I had had that same attitude while I was working with my employer, I'd have gotten those promotions. It's about being accountable for your own future and expressing to other people what you think will work best, even at the risk of being wrong an awful lot of the time." That's what one life, one boss is all about. Whether or not you decide to live with a one life, one boss approach is one of the most important decisions of your life. Sell yourself right now on becoming everything that you are capable of. Sell yourself on realizing the magic that lies within you. Sell yourself on becoming the boss of your own life that will lead you to your uniquely designed, exciting future. In order to be successful at selling ideas, you have got to be able to differentiate your ideas from the endless other choices people have. It is difficult to differentiate yourself and your thinking if you don't see yourself as being unique in the first place.

Mike Quindazzi, a top-producing sales manager who has seen a lot of salespeople come in and out of the sales business, says, "When I first got into business and looked around, it seemed like there were two kinds of people: the people who took the initiative to get things done and those who didn't. And the people who took initiative seemed to be getting ahead. Regardless of their role or responsibility or title, it was a self directive that they gave themselves that the company didn't give them. And they didn't wait for someone to tell them what to do, they went ahead and did it anyway. It's kind of risky, I guess, because you're going ahead and you're breaking out of the box, but it's also an opportunity, because when you're confident enough in yourself that you're going to achieve something, then even if you step a little outside your boundaries you'll land on your feet. Most people in sales or in an entrepreneurial environment adopt that attitude."

In order to take a closer look at the one life, one boss approach, we're going to break it into two pieces, beginning with the first half: one life.

PART I—ONE LIFE

You Are Unique

Your life is distinct and unique. Like the billions of different fingerprints, all unique in some way, so is your life. It has never been lived by someone else and never will be. It is a miracle or a tragedy waiting to happen. Every new hour signals the possible beginning for the adventure of a lifetime. Your job is unique too. Never before has anyone had the exact same challenges that you face and the same problems to solve. We all write our own history with our decisions, our actions, and our beliefs, and we do it one day at a time.

Nobody has lived or will live the day you are living today. Nobody will ever run across the circumstances you are experiencing right now. No one else on the planet is going to interact with the exact same cast of characters that will cross your path in the next 24 hours.

There is an endless map of possibilities, of destinations, that only you can reach. The question is, which destinations will you decide to get to? One-life thinking means that you sense the unlimited possibilities your future can hold and seize the power that comes from this insight. It all comes down to a decision you make each day—what destination and which future will you decide to reach?

Often, we get fooled into thinking we would be better off if we were more like someone else. We can waste a lot of time putting forth efforts to be like other people, to model their behavior. No matter how hard you try, though, you'll never be as good at being someone else as you will be at being yourself. You are destined to excel at being yourself if you want to. Being yourself is one thing for which you will earn a perfect "10," if your goal becomes to be yourself, instead of being more like someone else. You will never enjoy being like someone else as much as you will being you, if you bring out the real you, the achiever you, the you that gives 100% effort all the time and lives in a state of curious discovery.

Successful, persuasive businesspeople are the people who not only recognize that they have the potential to succeed, but who then, take the necessary steps to realize their potential. You too have unlimited potential inside, you have one life to live, and we want you to find it and cultivate it, so you can ultimately live it. The greatest human experience of all is flowering into who we really are, being turned up to full volume. When you consistently perform at your highest level, you will enjoy being you and will be accepted for being you. There will even come a time when you will be applauded for being you.

It's much easier to put out your best effort day in and day out when you are living your own life and discovering your own special talents. Mike Bowman, a top-performing financial services businessperson explains: "You have to enjoy being yourself, because if you don't, people are not going to enjoy being around you. In many cases, the client is buying you and your expertise, and you have to stand out. One way to do it is to be somebody that people enjoy doing business with." When you put out your best effort at being who you really are, then you have a formula for becoming a very persuasive person.

When we lose sight of this powerful insight, it is easy to begin to put out varying degrees of effort, depending upon how we feel at a given moment. We know we're cheating when we don't give it our best, and the result usually leaves us feeling regretful, defensive, and enticed by the demon of modern society—*mediocrity.*

The mediocre man is always at his best.

—Larry Docimo

Yes indeed, the mediocre person doesn't have to take many risks, because it's easy to fulfill your expectations when they're set low. In fact, over time, the mediocre person finds that even the world around him agrees that his best effort is nothing more than mediocre.

"I get excited because, in a friendly way, in a professional way, it's you against your competition," explains Mark Ferraro, a top-performing sales professional in the building supplies business. "The thing about sales is that there is no second place. You either win or you don't. That struck me as very true. In sales you either get the order or you get zippo! There is no consolation prize or place and show money in sales, because it's all or nothing. That changes the way you have to compete."

To really make it in selling and persuading others, we cannot settle for an attitude of patient mediocrity. We've got to have a more driving sense of urgency, which comes when we realize how unique we really are and how, in this life, we've only got a limited amount of time to bring out that uniqueness.

Often We Don't Feel Unique

Many people don't feel special or unique. They feel part of the herd. In companies today, if you want to reach the higher levels of influence, this belief has got to go. You have got to believe you are unique to feel unique. When you feel unique, you can express yourself in a unique way. The best influencers are unique because they know they have something special inside. Doug Neet, a successful insurance professional explains, "No one cares more about your future than you do, or your money, for that matter. I've always believed that if it is to be, it is up to me. It's up to each of us to make it happen for ourselves."

We feel mediocre or average when we settle for less than we are capable of. It's easy to rationalize away our own, less than 100%, pitiful effort by saying, I just don't have what other people have, I don't have the talent, I don't have the energy, I don't have the good looks, I don't have the intelligence, I don't have the wealthy family, I don't have the Ivy League education, and so on. Remember, it's the people who put the most into their own unique set of circumstances who get the most out of life. A person born with irresistible good looks is in no better position to live a meaningful life than the rest of us. In fact, that person is often lulled into a false sense of importance based on what other people say and think rather than his or her own achievements and efforts. Seek salvation in meaningful contribution, in extraordinary effort, in playing with the cards you have been dealt. In one memorable song, "The Gambler," Kenny Rogers simplifies this powerful insight from a professional gambler's view:

Now every gambler knows the secret to surviving
is knowing what to throw away and knowing what to keep.
Cause every hand's a winner and every hand's a loser.

Your hand is your unique blend of talents, skills, perspectives, and experiences, and it can obtain extraordinary results, meaning, and contributions. You have all you need right now! Your background becomes an asset when you become proud of who you are and how you got to where you are now. When we imitate others, we cannot capitalize on our greatest asset—what's inside.

It's What's Inside That Counts

Once there was an elderly gentlemen who tried to make ends meet by selling balloons on a Chicago street corner. His business had its ups and downs. Whenever business got a little slow, the salesman would release a few of his helium balloons. First a pink one, then a blue one, later a red one. Children would notice the colorful array of balloons and business would pick up. One day a little boy sat across the street watching the balloon salesman. He was intrigued by the flying balloons. Toward the end of the day, the little boy walked over and tugged on the man's coat sleeve. Looking the balloon salesman in the eye, he asked, "Mister, if you let go of the black balloon, would it go up?" Touched by the boy's sincerity, the balloon salesman looked at the little boy and responded with compassion and understanding, "Son, it's what's inside that makes these balloons go up."

We each have incredible potential to achieve things; it's already inside of us. It's just a question of finding it, developing it, and ultimately freeing it to perform. Mike Finizio, a top-producing stock broker in Los Angeles, explains it this way: "My father back in 1971 stumbled upon the tapes of Earl Nightingale, which said you become what you think about. And when he started listening to that tape, I wasn't even 16 yet and I thought my dad had gone off the deep end. But he, through his persistence, started to put that information into our heads osmotically. He paid us to read various books and do reports on them. I learned at a young age that it's my life and I can make it into whatever I want it to be, and I owe that to my father."

We have one chance to do it the way we want to do it. That's the magic of being alive. What can a person really achieve in one life? We can look at some great historical heroes like Ghandi, Helen Keller, Martin Luther King Jr., Margaret Thatcher, Thomas Jefferson, Aristotle, Mother Teresa, and Thomas Edison. All eight of them lived very different lives, but each had an enormous impact on the world around them. They each discovered their own special way of contributing. They found their uniqueness and stretched their potential to the max. They truly *lived* their lives. Day after day they accumulated small victories and they moved forward. They served and worked for the benefit of others, but ultimately they determined their own fate, as do you and I.

And it happens with less famous, but no less extraordinary, people every day. I recently moved to a beach town in Los Angeles. My 10-year-old son missed the deadline for soccer and decided to play roller hockey instead. To my surprise, when we drove up to the tryout location, we found a newly built outdoor hockey rink much like what you would see at an upscale ice skating facility, with concrete instead of ice. The skating surface was brightly painted with boards and Plexiglas around the perimeter. As I settled into the parents' seating area to watch the tryouts, I met a woman who told me the story of John, the commissioner of the league. He started the roller hockey league with just 22 kids and a hand-written note from a junior high school principal saying it was okay for him to use the basketball court area at his public school for practices and games a couple of times a week. Eight years later, the league had grown to 775 kids! John had led the charge and convinced the city to build a municipal roller hockey rink. The league is well organized, disciplined, and flourishing, and it's there because he did it. One life, one boss. John assumed responsibility to get something done because it was important to him. He didn't wait for someone else to do it. He did it himself and as a result is impacting the lives of hundreds of children in a positive way.

There is so much potential locked within each of us. We can all make a difference! We are born with a promise that if we will only assume responsibility for our own lives and stop blaming others, the gate of possibility will open up for us.

Only You Can Do What You're Capable of Doing

What you have the potential to do will be left undone if you don't do it. No one else can pick up your slack. One of the most memorable holiday films of all time is *It's a Wonderful Life* starring Jimmy Stewart. A great truth is at the core of the film's success. As you may recall, Jimmy Stewart plays George, a man who settles into what appears to be an average life raising a family and running a small-town savings and loan. Secretly, though, George longs to live a more adventurous life. He wants to be doing something else, but family, responsibilities, and his own unique set of circumstances prevent him from choosing that life. George stands up to the town tyrant, a man who wants to own everything and chisel away every nickel he can from the residents of the town. When George's world begins to crumble around him, a result of some underhanded activity by the town tyrant, George feels the world would be better off had he never lived. His guardian angel, Clarence, shows up at George's suicide plunge and gives him a magical opportunity to witness what would have happened had he never lived. What he found was that the town he lived in would be in peril if not for the life George had lived. Because of his life and the many good deeds he had done, the world was much better off.

Often, we forget this powerful truth and think that what we do does not make a difference. However, everything we do counts, and each of our actions begins a chain reaction of events that changes the world forever. Who knows how what we do today will influence those around us and gain momentum? Our lives have the potential to make a difference, to change the world around us for the better, and to make a meaningful contribution.

A story you might have already heard sheds light on that special attitude we need to have when the tasks we face seem endless, overwhelming, or of minimal significance:

One early morning an elderly man on vacation went for a walk on the beach. As the sun was rising, he observed in the distance a young boy from a nearby town running up the beach, grabbing a starfish, then throwing the starfish out into the sea with all of his might. As the man approached the young boy, he realized that there were literally thousands of starfish that had washed ashore from the high tide.

"Young man," he said as he neared the young boy, "what are you doing?"

The boy hurled another starfish into the waves and ran back up the beach to grab another one. "I'm putting the starfish back into the water. They'll die if they stay in the sun."

"But young man, there are so many starfish up and down the beach. You can't possibly get them all. How can what you are doing make any difference at all?"

The young boy looked out at the waves, unsure of how to respond. He turned around, walked up beach, picked up another starfish, ran to the water, and gave it a mighty heave. He ran back up to the old man. "It made a difference to that one."

In our concern to do big things, we can easily forget that it's often the little things we do, multiplied day after day, that add up to our greatest accomplishments. I was speaking at a large sales conference in San Francisco for Pacific Bell, and we were having a drink in the bar the night before. One of the senior managers was excitedly telling me about one of his telephone service representatives. "She is absolutely remarkable. She has been working here for 10 years, and when you listen to her on the phone, she makes every single customer feel important, like they are the most important part of her day. Her voice sparkles with enthusiasm and a fresh curiosity and a sense of caring that really gets through to the other person.

She gets the best results of everyone on the team, and when you hear her, you know why." This woman achieves remarkable results one day at a time, one telephone call at a time; you can do the same thing with the tasks you face in your job each day.

What You Have the Potential to Do Makes a Difference

You've got something special to contribute, something significant to produce. There's a light within your life, and only you can make it shine. The important thing to remember is that your life makes a significant difference. What too many of us focus on is the "big picture" of the world instead of the infinite number of little pictures surrounding us that we can have an impact on now!

What you are doing now already makes a difference! Every action counts. The point is to make a difference on purpose.

> Until you value yourself, you will not value your time. Until you value
> your time, you will not do anything with it.
>
> —M. Scott Peck from *The Road Less Traveled*

Only you can live the miracle of the real you bursting forth. And it all comes out when you stop waiting for your one life to begin. It's already going on. The game has started.

Groundhog Day Is Here

There's a fascinating movie called *Groundhog Day* in which a cynical, angry, and frustrated weather forecaster finds himself reliving the most miserable day of his life. He is sent to a freezing small town in Pennsylvania to cover Groundhog Day festivities. He wakes up and announces the main event with a deeply cynical attitude, anxious to get out of town as quickly as possible. However, a snowstorm prevents him from leaving town, so he has to bed down for another night in the same town he never wanted to come to in the first place. When he wakes up the following morning he is astonished to find that it is once again Groundhog Day! The same music is playing on the radio, he runs into the same people in the hotel, the same Groundhog Day celebration is revving up, and his camera crew is once again waiting for him to join them to cover the festivities. It is literally the same day happening over again! This is apparently happening only to him, as everyone he encounters, over and over, seems to be living that day for the first time. Interestingly, although the stage remains the same, he has the freedom to do whatever he wants, and he remembers what happens from day to day, so he can, in effect, realize his gains from the previous days. Groundhog Day becomes his own personal nightmare, as he lives it over and over and over. After what seems like an eternity of suffering, he finally goes to work on himself. Stuck reliving this day, he decides to make the most of it. He reads, studies, and learns to play the piano. He gets to know all the people in the town. He develops himself. He lives that one day, the only day he'll ever have, a thousand different ways. He gives his all to what he thought were hopeless circumstances only to find that he has transformed himself and, in a special way, the town as well. He learned how to make what was the worst day of his life into a day filled with opportunities to make a difference, to contribute, and to develop himself in the process. At last, on the day in which he realizes his fullest potential, he is released from Groundhog Day, wakes up to a new morning, and decides to make his home in that same small town.

Our lives are the same. Whether Monday morning is your own version of a miserable Groundhog Day or the most eagerly anticipated day of your life is up to you. This week could literally be the turning point of your entire career. This could be the week that you develop and sell an idea you've got that begins a whole new outlook and approach to work for you. It's not the circumstances of the day that matter, it's the attitude you bring. You've got one life and, in reality, one day, today, to make it come alive. And it is that sense that your life is special, that today counts, that there is no time to waste or squander that brings the one-life approach into action.

The best way to positively influence the future is to do something that alters it in a positive way today. Learn from the past, study what has happened to you, take what you can, and then move on. It's all about focusing 100% of your energy on today's events. Harness all of your resources to do extraordinary things now!

It Won't Ever Get Easier

"It," the circumstances of your life, will never get easier than "it" is right now. Circumstances are neutral. It's the *experience* of those same circumstances that change as you change. As you become stronger, more focused, more polished, more enthusiastic, the exact same circumstances can transform from the tedious and mundane to the most eagerly anticipated moments of your life. Sometimes, it can feel like our jobs and our lives are going nowhere. *Nowhere* is an interesting word. Break it up and it can just as easily spell *now here*. Opportunity is like that. It's nowhere or now here.

The circumstances you are in today are perfectly tailored to develop the greatest *you* that could possibly exist. Think of it all as the most perfectly designed setting from which the magical you will emerge. For the circumstances to change, you have to change, because your circumstances are ultimately a reflection of the values and decisions you have made in the past.

Often, people who want to be more persuasive and convincing, like sales professionals and professionals who sell, focus hard on learning the techniques of influence, such as negotiation, communication, and personality analysis, but they neglect the most important attitude of all. It is precisely the one-life outlook, which fires up our enthusiasm, urgency, and magnetic optimism, that can dramatically influence everyone with whom we come into contact. People respond when you have the kind of enthusiasm that the one-life outlook generates. It's not just what you say or how you say it, it's the person you are, underneath the words, phrases, and body language, that accounts for the major portion of the persuasive formula.

How to Sense the Right Attitude

There is a special attitude we need in order to truly grasp one-life thinking. We need to sense the greater possibilities that exist for us and break away from the "today's just another ordinary day" thinking that limits us. Imagine for a moment that you wake up tomorrow morning, head into the kitchen, and are absolutely amazed to find your historical hero (anyone you admire—religious, political, military, etc.) seated at your kitchen table with a smile, patiently waiting for you to join him or her. As you regain your composure for what is obviously a once-in-a-lifetime experience, your hero says, "The reason I am here is to arrange for a meeting between us tomorrow morning. Tomorrow morning, you will have 60 minutes to ask me anything you want. First though, you will report to me on the results of your mission. And your mission for today is to go to work and make an enormous, positive impact on your company and your customers."

How would your next workday change if you were to buy this attitude? Can you think of a better way to approach your job?

Living this way invigorates you with a potency and a spirit that is more highly charged, more energized, and more capable of results. The true magic of one life, one boss is that not only do you grow and develop and become more powerful, but your life also gets clearer and less cluttered. You will have less to do at work, but what you will be doing will be much more important and results oriented. You become capable of experiencing your moments with a fresher perspective. This is because the one life, one boss approach elevates your level of thinking and your self-awareness. You'll find that it's not just about how to get richer faster. It's about how to have impact, how to convince, how to persuade the world to move on your ideas and, more importantly, benefit from them.

Discover Who You Are

We define ourselves constantly through our decisions and actions. When we stretch our efforts, try a little harder, and demand a bit more of ourselves, we extend who we are. We discover who we are through extraordinary effort, because it is only through extraordinary effort that we realize our true potential. Too often we cheat ourselves and draw conclusions on the way the world works, what we get for our efforts, and how we should behave in the future based on what happens when we put out less than 100% effort. We start interpreting how the world around us responds to us as a mediocre performing world simply because we are performing in a mediocre way.

I hired a salesperson to work for me several years ago who turned out to be a disappointment. Shortly after he was hired, the two of us were going over his goals. I asked him how he was going to see 15 new prospects each week. "I don't know," was his reply.

"What about the activities we talked about last week?" I asked. "Have you considered them?"

"Yes I have," Rob replied. "But they don't work."

"They don't work?" I questioned.

"I tried for two hours yesterday to schedule appointments on the phone and I didn't get any. It doesn't work."

"Is it possible," I replied, "that you are right now at your absolute lowest skill level in terms of scheduling appointments on the phone simply because you are new at it? Maybe it isn't working because you aren't as good at it as you could be. Perhaps you need to give it a little more time before you make up your mind. We can continue to practice together for a few more weeks while you keep trying and honing your skills."

Rob was reluctant to take any advice and for six more weeks tried a variety of approaches briefly, meeting similar disappointments. He never got good at any of the activities he tried. Based on the results he got with his not yet fully developed skills, he misinterpreted whether or not the task would work. When we draw conclusions concerning the results of new ideas or techniques based on our ability to implement them when the ideas are still new to us, we generally shortchange ourselves.

> One of the most important results you can bring to the world is the you that you really want to be.
>
> —Robert Fritz

Imagine what would happen if a five-year-old child, after being introduced to reading in kindergarten, comes home to find she cannot read Shakespeare and so decides that reading doesn't work. It sounds ridiculous, but this is not far from what we do as adults all the time. How common is it for people (maybe you, maybe someone you know) to join a gym, exercise for a week or two, and, because they don't see the pounds flying off and the muscles bursting out, get frustrated and stop going? What about the person who has a bad experience during a group presentation at work and begins shying away from future public-speaking opportunities?

What are you capable of mentally, physically, and spiritually? What if you made an all-out 10-year assault to improve in all three areas? How far could you go? It's exciting! What kind of a person would a day-in and day-out effort like this create? Would you like to find out? Ralph Waldo Trune spoke eloquently to this topic: "There are many who are living far below their possibilities because they are continually handing over their individualities to others. Do you want to be a power in the world? Then be yourself. Be true to the highest within your soul and then allow yourself to be governed by no customs or conventionalities or arbitrary man-made rules that are not founded on principle."

An ancient Hindu legend speaks of the gifts within each of us:

> At one time all men on earth were gods, but man so sinned and abused the divine that Brahma, the god of all gods decided that this special gift should

be taken away from man and hidden someplace where he would never find it again and abuse it. Brahma had a discussion with several other gods. "Let's bury it deep in the earth," one god suggested. "No, man will dig down in the earth and find it," Brahma replied. "We can do better than that."

"Let's put it in the deepest ocean," another god said. "No, man will learn to dive and find it there someday," Brahma replied.

"Let's hide it in the highest mountains," another god said. "Man will never be able to climb the highest mountain!" Brahma thought awhile and replied, "No, man will climb the highest mountain. I have a better idea. Let's hide it down inside man himself. Man will never think to look there."

We are all unique and gifted, but we cannot find what that uniqueness is until we bring it out of ourselves. When we put extraordinary effort into our goals, our activities, and our relationships, we discover who we really are. The more we pull out of ourselves, by exerting great effort, the more unique we become. Extraordinary efforts unfold the gifts within.

A reporter once asked George Bernard Shaw, "You have known a lot of the famous heroes, politicians, writers, sportsmen, and musicians of your time. If you could be any one of these people, who would you wish you could have been?" Shaw answered, "That is a very easy question. I would wish to be the George Bernard Shaw I could have been, but never was." The greatest possible reward any of us can receive is the desire to become who we really are by putting out our greatest effort.

Every human being has the capacity to shine at full strength, minimal strength, or somewhere in between. When we shine at full strength, we not only accomplish more, we gain more access to ideas, energy, and inner resources. One analogy is to imagine yourself in a field of grass on a very dark night searching for a tennis ball. When you are shining at full strength, it's as if a 1,000-watt baseball-stadium bulb is radiating on that lawn, making it easy to find the ball. On the other hand, when you are shining at minimal strength, it's like being armed with a 1.5-watt night-light. You strain, you squint, and you struggle to find what you are look-ing for. When we put across 75% effort, we simply do not shine with very many watts and, as a result, we act and appear ordinary.

Ordinary effort tends to shield our uniqueness. There is great mystery within each of us. One of the great mysteries is that of finding out who we really are and what we are capable of. We find this when we live each day to the fullest. We must take each day as a challenge to become more. Not necessarily to get more, but to become more.

A Meaningful Life versus a Successful Life

What do you want most, a successful life or a meaningful life? The answer for most of us is probably both. Most of us can answer the question "What does success mean to you?" relatively easily. However, when it comes to answering "What does living a meaningful life mean to you?" the answer is a little more difficult to grasp.

A meaningful life is complete with highs and lows, victories and defeats, and compelling goals that make us give everything we've got. A meaningful life pulls us toward 110% effort. It's about giving everything you've got to a worthwhile goal and improving as a result of that effort. The greatest benefit is often the self-improvement we experience; the rewards are just icing on the cake. When we concentrate too much on the rewards, the methods we use to get them may often short-circuit the parts of our lives that produce meaning. Enter in mid-life crisis, job burnout, exhaustion, feeling lost, and a lack of enthusiasm for living.

Discovering who you are, and developing that to its highest form, is the most dependable and lasting way to fulfillment, happiness, true achievement, and, ultimately, a meaningful life.

You've Got to See It to Achieve It

> The mind is the limit. As long as the mind can envision the fact that you can do something, you can do it—as long as you really believe 100%. It's all mind over matter. All I know is that the first step is to create the vision, because when you see the vision there—the beautiful vision—that creates the want power. For example, my wanting to be Mr. Universe came about because I saw myself clearly being up there on the stage and winning.
>
> —Arnold Schwartzenegger

Great sculpture often takes extraordinary effort to achieve. Michelangelo's masterpiece *David* started as a large block of marble that other artists had considered to be of inferior quality. Michelangelo, however, saw in this raw piece of rock something others could not, and he was willing to toil day and night to slowly bring out the magnificence waiting within. It was his ability to refine what was already there, waiting to be discovered, that created the masterpiece.

There is a masterpiece within you. Yes, you need to apply tools to chisel, refine, polish, and shine it, but it lies within you. Spend more time appreciating and developing the magic that is your life and less time wishing for the circumstances or attributes of others and you will realize your own unique destiny.

It takes great courage to follow your heart. Imagine Christopher Columbus, setting sail in 1492, while all around him warned of the dangers beyond the known world: the sea serpents, the end of the world, an eternity lost. He, however, sensed a different outcome and followed his dream. No less courage is demanded of the enlightened business professional who is determined to convince the world to take action on her ideas. She is risking failure and being wrong because she is willing to stand up and be visible. She is, however, going to discover what she's really made of when she finds the courage inside of her to express her unique perspective with full power. Find what's inside you; it is the greatest treasure of all!

Meaning Is in the Struggle

More and more, it seems people are struggling to find meaning. Successful people in business are chucking it all, moving to Montana, and "simplifying" their lives—getting back in touch, so to speak. It's a common theme of our times, a *trend,* as Faith Popcorn, one of my favorite trendologists, would say.

What is the most meaningful thing that has happened to you in the last 24 hours? How about the last seven days? What about the last month, the last year? Pause a minute to determine your answer. Can you recall a continuous stream of meaningful moments in your life? Or are you finding it difficult to pinpoint anything truly meaningful in the not too distant past? Meaningful connections occur when we give it all we've got. Meaning happens when, for example, we head down to our seven-year-old's bedroom in the evening and grab a book and read a bedtime story with Oscar-worthy enthusiasm and animation. Meaning happens when we stop by the gourmet shop on the way home and go all out to cook an absolutely sumptuous meal for a change of pace. Meaning happens when we refinish a piece of furniture as if we were to present it to God for approval. Meaning happens when we give it our best effort, when we wrestle more out of us than we knew we had. Too many of us are living two feet beneath our ceiling. But when we put out extraordinary effort, we climb through our imaginary ceiling of limitations and view our surroundings from the rooftop. When we settle for comfortable predictableness, we trade away the jubilant excitement of the unknown.

It's one life! Live it! Live it to the fullest. Don't let another opportunity go by to play your part with all you've got. This is where the meaning is. You don't have to be president of the world to live life with gusto. Make a list of great ideas that would work and write them down to share with your company's president. Pick up the phone and ask someone out to lunch who you've always wanted to meet. Shine your shoes tonight as though you were to wear them tomorrow on your wedding day. Throw yourself passionately into what you are doing. Give yourself to the moment. Risk looking foolish. Err on the side of overenthusiasm. Let enthusiasm be your companion and dismiss predictable comfort.

It's not that people lack meaning in their lives, it's more that they are boring themselves to death by doing the same things the same way each day. When you stretch to do your tasks with just that little extra, you will discover who you really are, extend your limits, and increase your potential. This, of course, makes it that much easier to achieve extraordinary results on a regular basis. Sharon Basile, a top-producing salesperson in advertising, explains, "I think you have to take complete 100% responsibility for your results. That's the only way. I take total and complete responsibility because I think my success is up to me! Even when my company lets me down I figure a way to get around that. That's just how you have to be."

One of Theodore Roosevelt's most memorable quotes reflects the one-life approach, the responsibility it demands, and the rewards it brings:

It is not the critic who counts, nor the man who points out how the strong man stumbled, or where the doer of deeds could have done them better. The credit belongs to the man who is actually in the arena, whose face is marred by dust and sweat and blood; who strives valiantly, who errs and comes up short again and again; who knows the great enthusiasms, the great devotions, and spends himself in a worthy cause; who at the best knows in the end the triumphs of high achievement and who at the worst if he fails, at least fails while daring greatly, so that his place shall never be with those cold and timid souls who know neither defeat nor victory.

This immortal quote has inspired countless thousands because of its simple truth that is at the heart of one-life thinking. We must get off the sidelines and into the game and play it with everything we've got. Only then will we know what we're really made of and only then will we know what the world is truly willing to give in return for our greatest efforts.

PART 2—ONE BOSS

Who's the Boss?

Let's take a look at what the one boss part of one life, one boss is all about. First of all, who is the boss? That's a fundamental question we all have to answer. Who's in charge? Who makes the important decisions that impact our future? Who determines our learning and training opportunities at work? At home? Who determines our success? Who holds us back? Who pushes us forward? Who is responsible for what happens to us?

> One person has to be in charge. You can't divide authority and have any left.
>
> —Randall Price

The boss is a person who assumes authority and is in control. We must assume full authority over our own lives in order to create and control the situations we put ourselves into. Becoming the boss means: leaving your excuses behind; resisting the temptation to blame others; undertaking the monumental task of putting shape and structure into your lives through planning; and exercising the discipline to follow the plan.

There Has Never Been a Better Time to Be Your Own Boss

The moment you are breathing in right now is perhaps the best moment ever to take charge of your own life and start driving it in the direction you want to go. Consider that you have lived your entire life to get to where you are right now. Every thought, every struggle, every triumph, every failure, and every sleeping and waking moment have led you to your present situation. It is in this moment that you can take charge! You are more prepared now, in this moment, than you have ever been. You have more experience, more wisdom, more knowledge, and more understanding than ever before. Take charge! Too many people are putting off the day when they will decide to really live, to take charge. It doesn't start when you wake up tomorrow, it starts now. You're the boss.

Sometimes, however, we are like the elephant in the following story, tied to old habits and limiting beliefs:

> A young boy went to the carnival that passed through his town every year. He saw a sign that said, "See a real live elephant for 10 cents." He bought a ticket and was led into a tent that had a large docile elephant in it. The little boy was amazed that the elephant appeared to be unrestrained in any way. When he looked closer, he noticed a thin piece of twine tied around the elephant's foot and fastened to a pole in the center of the tent. The boy walked over to the man working the tent. "Sir, will that piece of twine really hold an elephant? He looks like he could snap it easily if he wanted to."
>
> The man pointed to the elephant and responded, "He could, but he doesn't know it. When this elephant was very young, we put a chain around its foot and tied it to a thick stake set three feet in the ground. The elephant would tug at it all the time but soon discovered that no matter how hard it pulled, the chain would not break. After that, you can use a thin piece of rope in its place because the elephant stops pulling. Even as the elephant grows tall and strong, it doesn't break the rope because it thinks it can't."

What happened to the elephant can happen to you in your career too. Before you can hope to be a truly persuasive person who can really make change happen with the teams you are on, with your customers, and with your boss, you must first break the limiting beliefs that are telling you that you can't achieve what you want most. One of the most important components of becoming the boss of our own lives is the process of challenging our limiting beliefs. These beliefs often stay with us for a lifetime, tethering us to our own pole. When we make a habit of taking control of our lives, we examine what is holding us back, move forward, and break these imaginary limitations.

"One of the things I really believe in," explains Dave Doehr, a highly successful manager and leader in the telecommunications field, "is that you are either going to be a victim or you're going to take control of your life. I don't think enough people really understand that they can take control of their lives, and a lot of it comes from your values. Another piece of it is confidence. You have to believe in yourself to take control of your own life."

You Don't Have to Quit Your Job

In order to live the one life, one boss philosophy, do you have to be in business for yourself so others will see you as the big cheese? Absolutely not. One life, one boss is an attitude, an approach. It's a way of looking at each day as a unique opportunity. It's a way of not waiting for someone else to pave your path. It's seizing control of your time on this planet and using it to steadily improve your efforts and contributions. One boss does not refer only to our work world. It's about being more demanding of ourselves than any boss could be. It's about generating ideas that improve our performance and the performance of the people we work for.

The Boss Sees Security Differently

There is no security on this earth. There is only opportunity.

—Douglas MacArthur

Security is an interesting lure. It can lull us into a sleepy, less effective state of mind if we're not careful.

Nature has a powerful way of assuring that each creature assumes responsibility and stays on alert each day. Animals do not have the luxury of taking security for granted. They are locked into the powerful present and must make each day count. Not long ago, I was on a trip in Africa and, as I looked across the plains in Kenya where so many wild animals live, I was reminded of the words I had seen on a poster somewhere, "Every morning on the African plains a gazelle wakes up knowing that to survive she must run faster than the fastest lion. The lion, on the other hand, must run faster than the slowest gazelle or he will go to sleep hungry or even starve."

Human ingenuity has dramatically reduced for people the type of threat the gazelle faces each day. Although we probably are not going to be killed by a large animal when we leave for work, there is an equally powerful predator out there that can rob us of our direction and enthusiasm. The *security* we have been so successful in creating can become the predator that traps us into a dull, uninspired life. Chip Sollins, president of American Pool Service, sees it this way: "I've always seen myself in terms of having my own business. I think that comes from drive, from wanting to control my own destiny. When you're your own boss, you control your own destiny. Right now, if I say 'Michael, I'm walking out the door,' I can do it, and that's the way I want it to be for me. I think you have to have an entrepreneurial spirit to succeed in sales. To get over the hump and to really make it, you must have that little extra that comes from drive and wanting it. You're never going to make the big bucks until you get it."

Becoming the boss of your own life is about making each day count. It's about achieving the discipline that will not only allow you to survive but to thrive! Like the lion and the gazelle, the boss must be alert each day and earn security one day at a time. Helen Keller put it this way, "Life is either a daring adventure, or nothing. Security does not exist in nature, nor do the children of men as a whole experience it. Avoiding danger is no safer in the long run than exposure."

Think back to your first 30 days in the job you're currently in. Chances are, you weren't sure it was going to work out and you showed up for work with a lot of zip, enthusiasm, and a desire to make a positive impression. Over time, however, it is easy to lose this sense of enthusiasm if we're not careful. Many people simply float along with the current and begin to focus on much longer time blocks like months, quarters, and even years. When we become overly consumed by the long-term view, the potency of being able to truly capitalize on the moment gets lost. Instead, imagine that you are unemployed and that when you show up for work you know that what you produce on that day will determine whether you are asked to come back tomorrow. Work each day with the enthusiasm and desire of your first day. It's a more dynamic way to operate.

I was visiting San Jose on a business trip several years ago and went for a tour of the Winchester House, a historical landmark and tourist attraction. On the tour I learned that Mrs. Winchester inherited an enormous fortune from the Winchester rifle company, the makers of the famous repeating rifle "that tamed the West" we see so often in Western movies. Mrs. Winchester was obsessed with the occult and was convinced that the ghosts of all the people that the Winchester rifles had killed were after her. She believed the only way to hold them off was to continually build on to and extend the home she was living in. For her entire life, she was adding and adding and adding in what appears to be a haphazard, unplanned way, with staircases leading to nowhere, unusual rooms, and entire wings completely sealed off by doorless walls. The builders were ordered to use the finest materials, imported from around the world. She claimed that she got her ideas on what and how to build by holding nightly séances with the friendly spirits that talked to her. She had an enormous staff of maids and groundskeepers, and you can imagine what they must have thought of her. Our tour guide told us that Mrs. Winchester was a very demanding boss and would fire any of her maids at any time, which usually meant when she saw them goofing off or talking behind her back. Someone on our tour asked how she was able to get people to work for her at all, and the guide told us that she had a famous reputation as an employer. She used a unique method of paying wages with all the contractors, maids, and groundskeepers. Each day, when their shift finished, she would pay them what amounted to double the fair standard wages of her day, in cash. With no warning, she might tell one of her employees at the end of a day to not return to work anymore. It was her eccentric way of showing her employees that each day counts, and that you earn your wages one day at a time with no future guarantees.

This certainly would be a difficult system to use today and some might even consider it cruel, but that is not the point. Consider how differently you would approach each day if you were paid one day at time and you had to make each day count. Your emotional reaction may be, "Who would want to have such an insecure future? How terrible!" But look closer. Is it possible that thinking your future is secure, that you can get away with a half-hearted effort here and there is in reality more limiting? What happens when we slack off for a week because we are preoccupied with personal problems or waste a month because we're out of synch? How about the person who just coasts for a year because she was concentrating on other priorities? Is she actually attracting a much less desirable future than if she were putting it all on the line every day? Thinking our future is completely secure is perhaps more dangerous in today's world than thinking we have to earn our way each day or lose it. When you give it your all each day and accept your wages for that day with pride, knowing that you earned them for what you did today, not yesterday, you are on the road to miracles.

There's a healthy state of mind we want to achieve that has nothing to do with the fear that comes when we are anxious about our security. No, we don't suggest you walk around scared that your future is threatened. Instead, assume a mind-set that is filled with enthusiasm and urgency to make something happen today. Be impatient about waiting until tomorrow for something significant to happen. This is a take-charge-I'm-the-boss-of-my-destiny outlook perfectly tailored for the person who wants to influence others in today's world. Don Graling, a consistently top-producing salesperson and manager at a high-tech firm selling state-of-the-art telephone switching equipment, looks at it this way: "In my own career, I've always taken it that I'll always do anything to get the job done. When you say you're in charge, you have to be in charge of all aspects of your job, and that means doing the work that other people don't want to do at times."

Non-Boss Attitudes

In order to be the boss of your own life, you have to get rid of some attitudes that hold you back and in effect give your "boss authority" to someone or something else. The boss needs all of her personal power and cannot afford to give any of it away. The following are some classic non-boss outlooks or attitudes that will short-circuit your progress and personal power in the same way that thin twine can anchor a fully grown elephant to the circus tent.

My problems are someone else's fault
When we feel we are the victims of other people's actions, we trap ourselves. We have given the power of determining our fate to someone else. Several years ago, I was working with a senior manager who had recently gotten a bad review from the president of his company. He felt that the review was unfair and actually let the people around him know how negatively he felt about the company. Because of this, he gave away much of his personal power: The people who worked for him doubted his commitment and his long-term future. Of course, this led to more problems, which he blamed on the company. He became increasingly less effective with his people and his peers.

"I think it's something internal," explains Molly Williamson, a top-producing salesperson. "When you see your own goals and you have control of your own destiny, you live your life a little differently. You've got to realize every day that if you're not happy it's your problem, not someone else's problem."

My daughter was having trouble with high-school algebra. When we saw her grade the first quarter, we asked her what was going on. She said that her teacher was unfair and didn't like her. When we went to school, we found that the teacher had actually given her a better grade than she deserved because of Paula's attitude. The fact was, she deserved to be failing. Paula's grades improved in that class only after she stopped blaming her teacher and assumed responsibility for raising her performance on the tests.

When we feel we can't improve a situation until "they" decide to let us, we get stalled. This is a classic attitude that limits our ability to get results.

Other people limit me

The attitude that we are limited by others is a life's not fair approach. It's like saying, "If it weren't for the way other people view me or the people I have to deal with, I would be more successful." This is an attitude that, unfortunately, is becoming more and more common, an attitude that spawns a lot of litigation and puts people's lives on hold. I was giving a series of speeches in Washington, D.C. several years ago, and there was one particular woman who came to each event. I got to know her pretty well because she always had a lot of questions at the end of the meeting. Her name was Barbara. She worked as a manager of a hair salon for two brothers who owned six salons in the area. Barbara was from Brazil and felt very limited because she didn't speak perfect English. I asked her why she didn't enroll in an English course and she said that the brothers who owned the salon wouldn't pay for it. She felt it was their responsibility. "It's their obligation to support me when it comes to skills that I can use at work," she said. I did convince her to take the classes on her own and ran into her about a year later. She had found a better job working for a better salon and said that she had moved because she had lost respect for her old employer. A person with the "other people limit me" attitude usually lacks the motivation and self-discipline to grow steadily toward his or her goals.

Other people are not doing enough for me

The attitude that other people should be doing more for me is another example of a life's-not-fair outlook. I'm not getting enough help, enough support, enough resources. "Excusitis" is born in this outlook. Usually, people who have this attitude are grossly overvaluing the level of their contributions. Six years ago, I was given a promotion to take over a branch office for the company I was working for, which involved my moving to Washington, D.C. I was much younger than the person I was replacing. The operations manager for that branch was very resentful when I got the job because she felt she was the better choice. However, she had been with the company only two years and had no sales experience at all in what was basically a sales business. In my first meeting with her she gave me a lengthy list of promises her previous boss had not been able to keep for her that she felt had prevented her from doing her job. Although, as I looked closer, her previous boss had actually given her a great deal of resources to get her job done with, it was never enough. As a result, she spent a lot of her time coming up with new ideas on how to convince me to give her more resources, more people, and more authority, and she spent even more time coming up with excuses as to why things were not getting done the way they were supposed to be. The fact is, when she resigned, the department functioned much more effectively without her, with less people.

Yes, we need to get the resources necessary to get the job done, and this is critical when you have a big job to do, but when we've got all the resources we're likely to get, it's time to stop asking for more and make it work with what you've got!

I do what I do because I have to, not because I want to

Some people have the attitude that they are doing something because they have to do it, not because they want to do it. This attitude usually yields very low quality work. People who feel this way are incapable of throwing their heart and soul into their work. They hold back. They produce inferior results and, more importantly, they do not develop themselves to their highest possible level. Don Graling sees it this way, "In sales, especially, you need to be able to take charge of your environment. I think it drives the people above you and the people who work for you. When you're willing to do whatever it takes, then the people around you start to pick up on it. You have to stop whining about the stuff you don't want to do and just get it done." Nola Beldegreen, a highly successful advertising professional, adds, "I've always been a self-starter. I don't like hearing people whine about their jobs. I think if you're complaining about your job and you don't like it then you should move on because chances are there are people who would be thrilled to have it."

I was teaching a management seminar at a large high-tech firm in Virginia several years ago and met a bright young man, Sergio, who was very frustrated. He invited me to meet him for lunch. When we got together, he told me his story. "I don't know what to do," he said. "My boss is not willing to recommend me for the management training program starting later this year and, without it, I know I'll be passed by for any significant promotions. As a result, I'm just not willing to put my all into my job any more." When we talked further, we found that there were a series of disappointments he had experienced with his employer, going back to his first day, when, at the last minute, his boss canceled a meeting with him, giving Sergio the impression that he wasn't very important to his boss. As we talked further, Sergio explained, "I never really put my all into my job because I just never got the feeling that my boss was on my side. I wasn't going to waste my effort."

Many people do not take the training programs or attend the industry conferences they want to attend because their company will not pay for it. In today's world, this is a huge mistake. You are responsible for your future, and that often means you have to make your own opportunities.

I don't have the opportunities that other people have

Sometimes, people feel victims of their past, their lack of education, or lack of connections. As a result they don't invest their time into developing themselves effectively and they end up wasting a great deal of time, taking the fork in the road down the path less worthy of traveling.

I got a call one morning from Rita, a woman who got my name through a mutual acquaintance. Rita owned a small advertising company, and she had hired two new people and wanted some help training them. Rita grew up in "Hell's Kitchen," a very poor area on the west side of Manhattan in New York City and had dropped out of high school at the age of 15. Her family had no money and she was born with a deformed right hand. When I met her, I was amazed to hear her tell me how fortunate she felt to have lived through so much adversity. "It has made me a much better business person," she said. "When people tell me about their problems, I can really listen and empathize because I know what it means to have real obstacles to overcome. I also know that the obstacles in my life have made me stronger and more able to achieve as an adult."

Your background is either a springboard to where you want to go or a brick wall that you cannot see beyond. The choice is up to you. Consider the words of George Bernard Shaw: "People are always blaming circumstances for what they are. I do not believe in circumstances. The people who get on in this world are the people who get up and look for the circumstances they want, and if they cannot find them, make them."

When you let one of these attitudes sneak in and take hold, you are giving up your "I'm the boss" authority. If you're not captain of your own ship, who is? Is it society? The government? Your company? Your family? Your friends? The crazy, chaotic environment we live in? Our parents? The fact is, these elements simply make up the stage we operate on. They are the raw materials of our lives. They are the islands and the seas we sail through, but the ship we are on is ours. We are the captain of the SS *Me*. Let the I'm-in-charge-of-my-own-life attitude sink in and wash away the huzzonga you may have bought over the years that gave to someone else control over your life, the direction you go in, and your potential for greatness.

One Boss Attitudes to Buy Now

As you shed the attitudes that can limit you, it is just as important to gain an outlook that is empowering and filled with growth potential. For a combined total of 23 years we have been meeting with bosses in all types of companies to listen to their problems and help them get better results. The one problem that they would like to solve that comes up over and over, year after year, is how to keep their people motivated. The most exciting benefit of the boss attitudes is that they bring with them the power of self-motivation. David Achzet, a successful sales manager for a large delivery company, explains the essence of the take-charge-now philosophy: "You have to be very tenacious, proactive, and self-motivated. Self-motivated means you don't need somebody to ask you what you're going to do next and what you've got planned. You know what your goals are, you've got your plan, and you're working that plan aggressively with a great deal of urgency. It's almost like a life-and-death matter for me. It's that critical for me to get done what I've got planned to get done, because in the end, it does make a big difference in your results. I treat every day like it's the last day of the month and whatever has to be accomplished on that day has to get done."

One characteristic the boss has above all others is that of motivation. The boss does not wait for someone else to motivate him; he motivates himself. Tommy Giaimo, a consistently top-producing car salesperson in

New Jersey, explains: "When I had the attitude that I was showing up for work and getting paid by the hour, so to speak, I didn't care as much. When you're your own boss, you have to be much more conscious of what you're doing, and you have to work a little harder and spend a little more time there getting everything done."

> Far and away the best prize that life offers is the chance to work hard at work worth doing.
>
> —Theodore Roosevelt

Once you sell yourself on the following ten attitudes, identified by the acronym MOTIVATION, and receive the self-motivation that comes with them, you will become more persuasive and convincing not only with the world around you but with yourself!

- **M**otivated from within
- **O**rchestrates
- **T**akes charge
- **I**nsightful
- **V**isionary
- **A**ccountable
- **T**ells it like it is
- **I**nvigorated
- **O**utside-contractor thinking
- **N**ever quits

Motivated from within

> He who has a "why" to live for can bear almost any "how."
>
> —Nietzsche

The boss knows what a job well done is all about and doesn't need someone else to motivate her to do her best. Doing her best is an expression of her beliefs and goals, not her fear. The more time other people have to spend motivating you, the less likely you are to succeed at motivating others. Persuading other people and selling your ideas is about motivating them. If you can't motivate yourself from within, you'll be much less effective motivating others.

A man who was out driving began having car trouble, so he pulled into a service station just off the highway. He was very leery about going into an unfamiliar station and turning his car over to them, so he watched one of the mechanics work for a while. The mechanic was amazing. He was working on a beautifully restored Mustang convertible. He changed the oil without spilling a drop. He washed his hands before he touched the upholstery and pulled out of the garage very slowly and carefully. The man was so impressed that he said to the guy pumping gas, "Wow, your mechanic does a great job, doesn't he?"

The guy looked over at the garage and saw the mechanic parking the Mustang. "Why not, it's his car."

When we work on *everything* we do the way this mechanic worked on his car then we receive a very special benefit. It's knowing that we gave it our all and also knowing that we are strengthened by challenges that nurture a unique blend of self-confidence the boss has.

Orchestrates

The boss is the orchestra leader of his own life. The way the boss orchestrates is with set standards. Set standards for yourself that elevate your spirit and your intellect. Set standards that liberate your potential! The standards that other people set for you are not going to take you to where you want to go. Their standards for you are intended to take them to where *they* want to go.

When you are in a "providing service" mode, you have to consistently exceed the performance standards or requirements for the service you are providing. That is not what we are talking about here. Standards are your own personal rules and laws that create consistently remarkable results in everything you do.

When your standards are higher than those of the world around you and if you consistently meet those standards with your daily performance, you begin to rise up out of the herd to a position of influence and leadership. The trick is to be more demanding of yourself and also less critical of your mistakes. We must learn from our results, not beat ourselves up because of them. We must learn to accept our failures as indications of the adjustments we need to make and not as omens from above that we are somehow inadequate. Do what you do with more passion than anyone around you and you will slowly but surely raise the bar of your output.

To truly orchestrate, in addition to setting standards, the boss has to also set the schedule. When you look at your future and the results you are trying to achieve, you must take the time to develop a schedule to ensure that all the tasks that need to get done, get done! When you are the boss, you stop complaining that there "just isn't enough time." The boss knows she has no more or less time than anyone else and that the experience of being squeezed for time is a symptom that comes from one of several areas:

- Too many bad habits
- Unclear focus and vision for the future
- Lack of focus on the priorities
- Poor self-development
- Poor sense of vitality
- Too many distractions

You have a lot of hours yet to live in your life, and when you assume the task of ensuring that those hours are invested carefully, you will truly be living the life you want to live. You do this by taking control of your own schedule.

Takes charge
Get turned on about being your own boss. It feels great! Become more motivated to improve, grow, develop, and exceed your past accomplishments. Develop faster than the people around you. The world is competitive. The business environment doesn't make any guarantees. Abundance is there for top performers and it gets taken away quickly from the rest. Some people are going to succeed and others are going to achieve mediocre, often disappointing, results. The boss understands that the environment is competitive and, like the lion on the plains, knows she will go to bed hungry and even starve if she doesn't get out and compete every day.

Insightful
The boss has insight into situations, which he gets by knowing himself first. The boss knows his strengths and weaknesses. The boss is aware of his environment and his resources.

Take out a sheet of blank paper and put your name right at the top. Next to your name in big bold letters write "AS IS." Make a list of the following items:

- Your strengths
- Your job skills
- Your weaknesses
- Your credentials
- Your career shortcomings
- Your enthusiasm about your future
- Your regrets
- Your contributions
- Your successes
- Your failures
- Your physical condition
- Your mental learning pace right now
- Your energy level
- The health of your relationships
- Your assets
- Your liabilities
- Your appearance
- Your enthusiasm level at work, as perceived by others
- Your ability to persuade and convince as a communicator in challenging situations

That's a good start. Be brutally honest. Insight is simply inner sight that develops when you look inside yourself and articulate to yourself what you see.

Once you have finished your list, ask people you know and trust to tell you what they think of you in each of these areas. Listen without agreeing or disagreeing and notice how their perception is similar and at times at contrast with your own.

Visionary
The boss is capable of impacting and of creating the future. In order to create the future, the boss must see it first. To truly be the boss and be in

charge of your own destiny, you have got to discover your vision of where you are going. This vision has got to be compelling, magnetic, and a worthwhile reward for the extra effort and sacrifice you are going to have to make. Later in this chapter we will show you a method to find and ac-tualize your own personal vision, which is at the heart of the boss's end-less fountain of self-motivation.

Accountable

The boss gets a lot of the credit and the boss must accept the blame—that's the way it is. Effective bosses don't make excuses and don't blame others for their mistakes. The boss knows, deep down, that results are his responsibility and that excuses waste time. What the one boss part of this chapter is all about is assuming total responsibility. It's about driving your career, not just riding it. When you feel your career is going places that you don't understand, when you feel your time is being eaten by activities that you don't want in there, then you must do something about it! If you feel out of control, you're riding, not driving. When you embody one life, one boss, you drive your own life.

When employees of large corporations are asked about the corporate message they are getting from top executives, they often respond by say-ing something like, "I hear it, but I don't see it," or "They should practice what they preach," or "They don't walk the talk." Certainly, there are many people in power who "walk the talk," but there are many who don't and as a result short-circuit their ability to influence in a positive way. When you are accountable, you cannot afford to act in a way that is in-consistent with the philosophy you express to others.

The buck stops here.

—Harry Truman

And the buck, or the responsibility for your life, must stop shifting from place to place and has to land squarely in your own lap. Nola Belde-green explains: "I strongly believe in taking responsibility for your own job. If my company is going to put me in the job and pay me to do it, then I'm going to do it and do it right, because if I don't it's not fair to my com-pany—it's not right to my own soul. So whatever I've done, I've always approached it as running my own business. I think that is a big reason why I've always been successful."

Tells it like it is

The boss has the courage to tell the truth in all situations. To be the boss you have got to develop the ability to be honest, painfully honest if necessary, and this *starts* with yourself. If you cannot be honest with yourself, you have little hope of achieving real honesty with others. There is an exercise later in this chapter that will help you construct your own personal constitution, which will serve as a bedrock of strength from which to tell the truth. When something is not right, the boss speaks up. When the boss makes a mistake, the boss tells the truth. When someone does not hold up his or her side of the bargain with the boss, the boss tells the truth. Telling the truth builds credibility and respect even if, at times, the boss has to sacrifice a little popularity.

Invigorated

In a stressed-out, cynical environment, the great bosses always find time to recognize and celebrate breakthroughs and victories. The human spirit is revitalized by celebration. Many people, however, are not feeling this revitalization and are, instead, exhausted by their work and feel worn out. It is impossible to sell yourself with enthusiasm when you are continually tired.

If you look down through historical literature, you will not find many pages devoted to the subject of job burnout, but today it's a common malady. Job burnout is a combination of two things:

1. Minimal sense of completion from day to day
2. No self-directed growth toward personal vision

Job burnout does not come from working too hard. It comes from confused priorities. Imagine the Native Americans living in the Southwest 600 years ago. Do you really think you work harder than they did? Take a drive across the Arizona/New Mexico desert to gain an appreciation for how hard life must have been. They were constantly hunting, moving, on the alert for life-and-death conflict, and suffering great hardships on a daily basis. Imagine one of the tribe's warriors coming in from a day-long hunt and asking to meet with the chief. He enters the chief's tepee and tells the chief that he is burned out, he's been working too hard, and he really needs to take some time off to find himself. We're not sure about you, but to us that sounds utterly ridiculous. Job burnout is a relatively new phenomenon that has arrived on the heels of our increasingly complex lifestyles. These complex lifestyles often confuse our sense of direction and purpose and in turn open the door to a parade of maladies, including job burnout.

Certainly the workaholic who spends 16 hours a day in the office (if such people really exist), seven days a week, is headed for problems. But that is not what a good number of people attending our seminars are complaining of. These are people with ordinary jobs working ordinary hours who find themselves unable to concentrate and throw themselves into what they are doing. They are distracted, tired, and anxious. They want to be doing something else, but they don't know what it is. They are unfulfilled and unsatisfied by their work. They often feel the organization they work for owes them a remedy as a result of their past contributions. In other words, they come to believe that other people around them should "carry" them with their efforts until they return to full strength, if ever.

We were recently in New York City and had an opportunity to see *Phantom of the Opera,* with Davis Gaines playing the phantom. Reviewing the program before the show started, we read that Mr. Gaines had already performed the role of the phantom over 2,000 times. And yet, as members of the audience, it was as if he was performing it with the enthusiasm of opening night. He was spectacular! He brought the role to life and wasn't complaining about how tired he was of playing the phantom for several years, performance after performance. There was no visible job burnout in Davis Gaines that evening.

One of the interesting aspects of competitive sports is that in a relatively short period of time, we can see a project (two of them actually—to win a game) start, escalate, climax, and conclude. A win is recorded, a loss is recorded. We see the start and finish in a neat little package and, whether we like the results or not, there is a sense of completion. We need to bring more of this into our fast-paced, roller coaster-like work world. Often, we get so wound up and involved in multiple tasks and projects that we don't experience the sense of completion that is so important. When we don't feel completion and are, instead, rushed into the next task on a simultaneously running project, we are withholding from ourselves one of the most powerful of all enthusiasm revitalizers.

A good way to become invigorated is by keeping a journal of some sort and recording in it each night before you go to bed or before you leave work the progress you made that day. Record each victory, however small, that was earned. Write out what you learned, who helped you along the way, and what contribution you made as a result of all your efforts. Take it a step further and write a thank-you note to someone who helped you out each day before your workday ends. Not only will this small act end your day on a high, but it will force you to look for the positive things the people around you are doing, a characteristic the boss must do because the best boss celebrates, above all else, the victories of others.

Outside-contractor thinking

What if you were an outside contractor providing the service to your company that you now provide as an employee? How would that change your perspective? Your attitude? Your output? If you knew that in order to win a new contract you would have to post some significant results in a timely manner, would the way you do your work change?

It's easy to settle into the flow and have an "I'll do the stuff that hits my desk efficiently whether it makes a significant impact or not" mind-set. We put major time into minor priorities or, in other words, we major in minors. The boss cannot afford to do this and stay in business for long.

An outside contractor must always strive to provide more service than is expected so they can negotiate better fees later. Entitlement doesn't work with outside-contractor thinking. When we feel entitled to a raise, to a promotion, or to a better assignment simply because we've been there for a long time, we are settling into a mentality that lacks the potency that is so important. We should be striving to always increase our output so that we attract better opportunities, day by day. Each day is an opportunity to earn a ticket to a better game.

Never quits

The extra mile is a quiet place, and it's the place where the boss spends a lot of time. Most people stop way before they get there. It's that post-100% effort zone where we fly right by the competition. Learn to thrive on the feeling that comes from running the extra mile. The extra mile is where the boss belongs; it's where the boss has to be. You need to be able to put yourself on that extra mile with no incentive from others. Mike Finizio sees it this way: "Sometimes we have to do things we don't want to do. I just tell myself, 'cut the crap, you know you have to do it, so just do it now.'"

These ten MOTIVATION attitudes and activities are critical for you to engage in now. You will become the boss of your own life when you start doing the activities that a great boss must do. When you neglect these activities, you diminish your own personal power, and, remember, personal power is at the heart of selling success and influence.

Become the Architect of Your Life

It's easy to let the "flight" of our lives slip into autopilot, slicing through the air, to be sure, but not entirely under our guidance. The problem with autopilot is that it doesn't improvise well or react as effectively to unpredictable emergencies, which is critical when you're trying to realize all of your potential. The other problem with flying on autopilot too often is that over time we might forget how to fly the plane.

Think of yourself, instead, as the architect of your own life. An architect puts together the plans of a building before a single shovel of dirt is turned. The building is constructed in the architect's mind, and the plans are laid out so they can be communicated to all the people who will help turn the idea into a building that matches the architect's original vision. These blueprints allow the architect not only to transfer his vision, but to show others how that vision will be realized. You can have tremendous contractors with the best skills on the project, but if the designs are poorly conceived by the architect, the building will suffer. The plans do two things:

1. They determine whether the people doing the work can maximize their contributions each day toward the realization of the goal. This is dependent on how well thought-out the plans are.
2. They determine the outcome of the total effort by the various contributors to the project. Poor plans equal poor results.

The Empire State Building in New York is a magnificent building, but before one ounce of concrete was poured, an architect had to put that marvelous vision down on paper. The same is true of virtually every notable structure in the world. Your life, if it is to become a magnificent achievement, must also be turned from a vivid vision into plans and blueprints for you to follow.

"One of the most significant lessons I learned occurred when I was going into my senior year in college," explains Molly Williamson. "I was working, putting myself through college, and my boss told us to write down at least six goals that we wanted to achieve by the end of the year. And she said be realistic but be ambitious and of course I threw the realistic right out the window. I had something like 26 units to go before I could graduate but I really wanted to graduate that year so I wrote all these goals down. I wanted to graduate, I wanted to get better grades than I ever had, which meant a 3.7 GPA or better, and I wanted to, if I did that, take myself to Europe. So I wrote all those down and put them in my room, not in a place that I would look at every day, but where I would see them occasionally. I took too many units, worked too hard, and I even stayed at school for Christmas to do an internship that I had to get done. I ended up graduating and I had a 3.95 GPA and I took myself to Europe. So I think goals are so important to write down, not just think about in your head. It's a mystery how powerful they can be."

> To act intelligently and effectively, we still must have a plan. To the proverb which says, "a journey of a thousand miles begins with a single step," I would add the words "and a road map."
> —Cecile M. Springer

What is the plan you are working under? Is there a plan at all? If so, where is it? What is the building (you) that you are creating supposed to look like when the project is over?

Sometimes, in the work world, the project becomes so overwhelming that the plans are forgotten and we fall into a fire-fighting mode, scurrying frantically to put out the flames. We may say we sense the goal intuitively, but we end up reacting emotionally to what is going on around us. It's at that moment that the plan is lost. It's quite common for work environments to devolve to a point that most of the work being done is simply to repair problems, to fight fires.

Can this happen to our lives too? Do you feel as though you are guiding your life to a carefully thought-out destination, or are you waking up and dealing with whatever comes down?

What if your goal was to build a cathedral of a life as opposed to a shack designed only to protect you from the elements? How would your activities each day change? Build a cathedral! It's worth the effort for what it will make of you inside. Then you get to live in the cathedral, which is not a bad place to live!

It comes down to having a plan for your life. If you don't have your own plan, chances are you're living as a part of someone else's. When a person has a clear plan for his or her life, it is much easier to gain the co-operation of others to fulfill that plan. Certainly, we all need to contribute to the success of others, but if we do not work at putting plans together for our own lives, we will float aimlessly from task to task feeling, in the end, frustrated and underappreciated.

We often make the planning process far too complex. It's as simple as setting your sights on the person you are trying to become and visualizing what that person is good at doing and then, day by day, scheduling activities to ensure that you will acquire those abilities, habits, and skills. Your plans begin with your personal vision of where you want to go and conclude with concrete activities for you to perform today.

Vision-to-Reality Flow

The vision-to-reality flow is a simple way of understanding how long-term vision is turned into reality. This easy-to-use process is designed to not only help you achieve your dreams, but to build your character so that you may indeed reap your own magical destiny. A great poet captured the power of the vision-to-reality flow with these words:

I bargained with Life for a penny,
And Life would give me no more,
However I begged at evening,
When I counted my scanty store.

For Life is a just employer,
He gives you what you ask,
But once you have set the wages,
Why, you must bear the task.

I worked for a menial's hire,
Only to learn, dismayed,
That any wage I had asked of Life,
Life would have willingly paid.

—Anonymous

The most important thing we must do as the boss is take responsibility for creating a life that we want to live. What many of us really want is to be able to bring about in the real world what we have created in our mind. *This is the greatest selling skill of all.* We want the ability to make happen the things that we want to make happen. Forget the simple, "positive thinking is all you need" baloney, because attitude is not enough. Here's how it really works.

Our personal vision can become reality or delusion based on five distinct factors. Keep Figure 1 in mind as we go through the five layers of the progression from vision to reality.

Here are the five steps:

1. Articulate our *vision* for the future.
2. Decide the values and beliefs that will create the person we want to become, which we call our *personal constitution.*
3. Break the vision down to achievable *goals.*
4. Make and break the *habits* that will support the goals.
5. Plan *activities* that build the right habits and achieve our goals.

As shown in Figure 1, the first step we start with is vision. When we start with our vision, then we are sure to align the other four steps in the right direction, so that once we get the planning done, our plans will lead us to the top step, which is achieving our intended vision. This simple system is a very reliable way to achieve your dreams.

Step 1. Vision

The first step is to envision a compelling, magnetic picture of who you are becoming, of you functioning at your highest level, and of you producing extraordinary results. Create a mental snapshot of your destination, of where you want to go. This snapshot should be a clear picture of you being the best you can possibly be, not copying someone else, not in competition with someone else, but you, chiseled, polished, and operating at your highest possible level. This vision needs to be clear and preferably written down. Doing this step can literally transform your future. Tommy Giaimo explains it this way: "The attitude I've had is that my company provides me with the tools, the phone, the desk, and the supplies, but it is in essence my own business. Because of that, I have to look at the big picture first, not just today or this month, but what do I have to do so that on

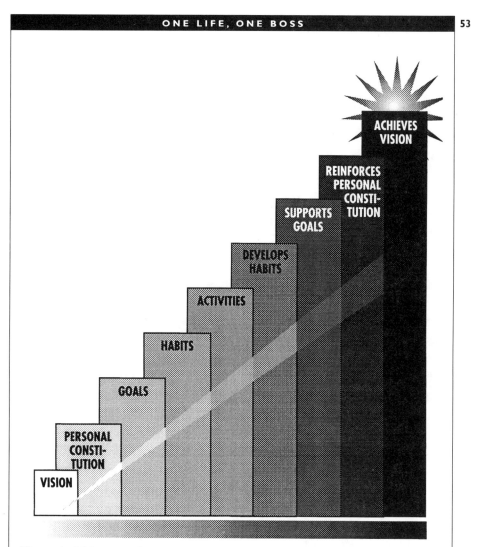

Figure 1. Vision to Reality Flow

down the road I'll be successful. I think in terms of being in business for myself, and that means I have to see what I'm trying to build, before I start building it."

About 10 years ago, I was working in Manhattan when I learned the story of Eugene Lang and his remarkable sixth grade class. I was conducting a sales workshop in a classroom located right next to Grand Central Station, as I had a hundred times before. One of the class members asked me if I knew that Eugene Lang worked on this floor. I had seen his name on the door of a company down the hall from mine, so I replied "yes." "Isn't he the guy that was on *Sixty Minutes* that promised all the kids in that Harlem school a college education?" she asked. "I'm not sure," I replied. The following day I called up a friend of mine who worked at CBS and verified that it was indeed the same person. What happened was that in the 1970s the mayor of New York had asked several successful people to go into the underprivileged school districts of New York and speak to the younger kids about opportunity and what they could achieve if they were willing to work for it. Eugene Lang was one of these people, and the results from his visit were so remarkable that *Sixty Minutes* did a very well-received feature piece on it.

Running into Mr. Lang one day in the hallway, I introduced myself and asked him if I could buy him breakfast and hear his remarkable story straight from the source. He told me that the school he visited was in a very poor area of Harlem and, while he was speaking to the kids, who were not paying much attention to him, he, on the spur of the moment, offered to back up his vision of opportunity by promising each kid in the class a college education if they would only qualify for it. This offer was being made to a class where less than 30% of the kids would graduate from high school, let alone go to college. The response from the kids was indifference because they didn't believe him. It wasn't until they took the kids down to the bank and showed them the money in their accounts that they started to believe that Mr. Lang would indeed keep his word. The project involved setting up extra support for the kids, but Mr. Lang said that what transformed these kids behavior was *believing* in a better future for themselves. That was the key. That vision helped them to navigate the challenging roads they had to cross. The result was that 65% of those kids went on to graduate from college: a remarkable story about the power of vision.

Your vision needs to be exciting and achievable. A sample personal vision might read like this:

My vision is to live in a nice house in a safe neighborhood with outstanding schools where I can raise my family. I see myself as a top executive in a large advertising company in New York. I will be happily married to a woman I love, admire, and share similar values with. We will nurture and support our children to become the best at what they want to do. I will be in top physical condition with energy and vitality. I will have completed my MBA at New York University. I would like to travel occasionally to different places in the world and speak fluent Spanish and German.

The key here is to *write it down!*

Step 2. Personal constitution

The next step is to articulate your personal constitution, which is nothing more than a list of your values and beliefs that when followed will build the person you are trying to become. Just as the Constitution of the United States laid the foundation for unprecedented growth and prosperity, your well-thought-out constitution can serve the same purpose for you. A personal constitution enables you to build and become the person you most want to be while you strive to reach your vision. The values and beliefs give you rules and boundaries by which to live your life and will ensure that you do not make the mistake of failing as a human being while achieving your material goals. For instance, you may have as part of your vision the desire to be financially successful. If you achieve that success by dealing drugs, then you are most likely going to live a very limited life. A personal constitution might look like this:

- I will be honest in my dealings with all people.
- I will not cheat or steal in any way, whether it be with business associates, the government, or my competitors.
- I will study the Bible and live in accordance with its principles.
- I will take the time each day to learn something new.
- I will value my health and fitness and strive to live in a physically fit body.
- I will be assertive while being considerate of the feelings of others.
- I will build my career by always striving to provide outstanding service to others.
- I will save 20% of all the money I earn and invest it.
- I will spend quality time each day with my family.

There are certainly more items you could add to the list, but this should give you the idea. The personal constitution is often missing when people engage in goal-setting exercises, but it is the step that allows your character to grow as fast as your assets. When it's all said and done, your character is your most important asset anyway. Henry David Thoreau put it this way: "Live your beliefs and you can turn the world around."

Step 3. Goals

Your vision is next broken down into goals that are easy to grasp. "I wake up each day and thank God for yesterday and thank God for getting me into today. And it's my job to turn myself on by just setting some personal goals of what I'm going to accomplish today," explains Paul Thomas, a successful sales manager. The goals we set help keep us motivated and, as Paul puts it, "turn us on." Goals are improvement road marks that can be measured and, more importantly, turned into action steps. Michael Jordan talks at length about the power of goals in his short, but inspiring, book, *I Can't Accept Not Trying.* On goals he says, "Step by step, I can't see any other way of accomplishing anything." Here is an example of some written-down goals, based on the vision already outlined:

- To weigh 195 pounds with no more than a 13% fat content ratio.
- To read 24 books a year.
- To earn $150,000 a year and put $15,000 away for retirement and another $15,000 into short-term savings a year.
- To spend distraction-free time with my family every day.
- To be promoted to vice president in 24 months.
- To complete a meditation/relaxation program and practice the techniques daily to reduce stress buildup.

Certainly, this person could have more goals, but it is a start. Every one of these goals is measurable and will contribute to the actualization of the vision. The goals help you to stay on track and stay more in control of the direction of your life. "When you set simple goals for yourself, you feel more in control of your own life," explains Don Graling. "As a result, people don't bother you as much when things go wrong. When you're in control, you feel more self-confident, and that's what goals can give you."

When you don't have a plan, it's easy to forget the most important details. Consider the story of the woman who decided that a pet might help her deal with the loneliness of her single life following the death of her husband:

A woman went to the neighborhood pet store and considered a number of pets, including puppies and hamsters. Finally, she settled on a parrot after the owner of the store assured her the parrot would talk to her.

The next morning, she was back at the pet store to complain that the parrot wouldn't speak. The shopkeeper sold her a mirror saying, "Parrots like to see themselves. Put that mirror in the cage where the parrot can see its own reflection and, sure enough, he'll talk." So the woman took her mirror and put it in the cage.

The next day she was back at the store and told the owner the parrot still wouldn't talk, so the owner sold her a ladder and said, "Put that ladder in the cage and your parrot will walk up and down and, sure enough, he'll talk."

The next day she was back and told the owner that there was still no response from the parrot. The owner sold her a swing and said, "Put that swing in the cage and your parrot will swing back and forth and be so happy that, sure enough, he'll talk."

The next day, she came into the shop with a very sad look on her face. The store owner asked her what was wrong. "Last night, my parrot died," she replied.

"I'm so sorry to hear that," the owner replied. "I just can't understand it. Did the parrot say anything before it died?"

"Oh yes," she replied. "Just before he died he said, 'Don't they sell any food at that store?'"

Without goals, it is so easy to forget to do what's most important first. You may think this story exaggerates the point, but think again. How many people have a desire to be wealthy but "forget" to save a portion of what they earn each month? How many people have a desire to achieve great things in their career but never sit down and write out a game plan of how to do it? Goals give us focus. Here's another story to illustrate our point:

A rookie jet fighter was trying to land his jet on an aircraft carrier in very bad weather. There were clouds, rain, and waves, and it was difficult to focus on the yellow stripe, let alone land the jet. He began to get nervous and to sweat and shake. He was losing his confidence in his ability to land safely. Behind him was an experienced veteran pilot who began to coach him. He told the rookie to focus only on the yellow stripe, because if he did that, everything else he was focusing on would fade and therefore not be a barrier.

When we focus in on our goals, all of the barriers and obstacles fade.

Step 4. Habits

The habits we form either support or hinder the person we are becoming from achieving the vision we have created for ourselves. To effectively work with habits, we must first identify the habits we already have that take us away from our vision. Then we must identify the habits we need to build. We start first by removing a habit that must go before we add anything new. This yields a side benefit of simplifying our lives and removing clutter. Here is a sample of how this might look:

Remove: Putting off distasteful tasks until the end of the day.

Add: 20 minutes of planning first thing in the morning.

Remove: Spending more in a month than I earn.

Add: Setting up automatic payroll deduction for both savings plans.

Remove: "Winging it," when it comes to selling ideas to my boss.

Add: Thinking through all ideas I present to my boss from her perspective first.

Remove: Missing dinner with my family when I am in town.

Add: A family outing/activity every weekend that we all can enjoy.

Remove: Waking up only 20 minutes before I have to go to work so I am rushed.

Add: 20 minutes of meditation/relaxation every morning.

Remove: Allowing my coworkers to distract my focus.

Add: Reviewing my goals with my boss each week.

Remove: Not planning my sales presentations in advance.

Add: Reviewing my presentations for tomorrow before I go home today.

The French entomologist Jean-Hentre Fabre conducted a wonderful experiment that illustrates the powerful impact of habits. The experiment used processinary caterpillars—wormlike creatures that travel in long undulating lines, one after another, at the same pace and cadence, giving no thought to their final destination. If you've ever been to the circus and seen elephants marching around the ring with the trunk of each elephant interlocked with the tail of the elephant in front, you get the idea. In essence, they simply follow the leader and don't care where the leader is going. Dr. Fabre placed a group of these caterpillars into the rim of a large round flowerpot. He carefully set it up so the leader of the group was nose to tail with the last caterpillar in the slow circular parade around and around the rim of the flowerpot. Even for Dr. Fabre, it was hard to tell which was the leader and which were the followers. In the center of the flowerpot, he placed an abundant supply of food. The caterpillars were circling around the food with nothing to prevent them from breaking their circular chain and crawling to the center of the pot where the food was. The caterpillars inched around day after day in a steady circle like an unbroken chain. After seven days, they began to die one-by-one of starvation and exhaustion. The abundant supply of food was only inches away but out of reach unless they broke the habit of following the caterpillar in front of them.

Habits are like that. They can make us blind to greater possibilities if we're not careful. They can also help us to achieve our goals if they are habits we acquire on purpose rather than habits we're stuck with.

Before we move on to activities, think carefully about the words of this unknown author:

I will push you onward or drag you down to failure. I am completely at your command. Half the things you do you might just as well turn over to me and I will be able to do them quickly and correctly.

I am easily managed—you must merely be firm with me. Show me exactly how you want something done and after a few lessons I will do it automatically. I am the servant of all great men; and alas, of all failures, as well. Those who are great, I have made great. Those who are failures, I have made failures.

I am not a machine, though I work with all the precision of a machine plus the intelligence of a man. You may run me for a profit or run me for ruin—it makes no difference to me.

Take me, train me, be firm with me, and I will place the world at your feet. Be easy with me and I will destroy you. You know by now, my friend, that I am your habits.

Step 5. Activities

Finally, we are ready to identify activities and incorporate them into a calendar or daily structure that will ensure that we attain the right habits to support the goals toward creating our vision. When we have our direction this clearly articulated and mapped out, we can focus on the moment, because the task we have chosen has already been identified as the best possible activity to engage in. In addition, focusing on preplanned tasks is easier to do and more energizing. "To keep my energy level high, I try and keep myself focused on small tasks," explains Mike Bowman. "I focus in on my tasks one day at a time. It's easier to stay pumped up about a day than it is to get excited about a month."

Planning what activities to do is most effectively done in two steps:

1. While carefully reviewing your goals, make a master list of activities that will support the habits you are trying to build, along with the approximate time needed to accomplish each task. It is best to plan the master list for an entire week.
2. Once the master list is complete, transfer each task to a calendar divided into daily time blocks, so that these activities receive as much, if not more, attention as the more commonly scheduled items on your daily calendar.

Figure 2 shows an example of a master list of activities. Planning in this manner ensures meaningful progress that yields extraordinary results. Remember, the boss covers all five bases: vision, constitution, goals, habits, and activities.

Don't Just Get Things Done—Contribute!

The time management gurus of our day have bluffed us into thinking that the key is to organize ourselves so we can quickly and efficiently get it all done, squeeze more into our calendars, combine a little quality time here and there, and, poof, we're effective! It is precisely this kind of thinking that strips us of our ability to find meaning and joy in what we are doing. It's not about getting more done. It's really about getting less done, but getting it done at a much higher quality level, focusing more on purpose, and, as a result, being able to contribute more. Who wants to figure out how to be efficient at doing what is of little value in the first place? Learning to organize and complete more unimportant stuff than anyone else is not a lofty goal.

Instead, take a hard look at what you're doing now and ask yourself these questions:

- What contribution am I making right now?
- What contribution am I capable of making right now that is of significantly higher value?

ACTIVITY	GOAL/HABIT SUPPORTED	AMT. OF TIME	SCHEDULED FOR	✔
Re—work professional goals	More focus at work	3 hours	3/17 @ 2pm	✔
Lunch with VP Finance	Broaden my contacts	2 hours	3/27 @ 12:30 pm	
Finish one book this month	Education and Reading	10 hours	7—8 am each morning	
Listen to German tapes	Learn new language	7 hours	To and from work	
Three gym workouts	Physical	6 hours	Mon/Wed/Sat.	
Open a new IRA account	Financial	1 hour	3/21 @ noon	
Finish cost red new idea	Work goal	4 hours	4/3 @ 3pm	
Family hiking trip	Family quality time	10 hours	3/29 all day	

Figure 2. Vision and Activity Planning Guide

- How can I turn every mundane activity I am engaged in into a challenge of epic proportions?
- How can I do each task, however routine, better than I have ever done them before?

It's not about checking off items on a to-do list. That is not lasting satisfaction or the way to a meaningful existence. Your actions have true meaning when you stop thinking about the value of checking off items and start thinking about the value of experiencing yourself doing them with every fiber of your being. Give yourself the ride of your life. Do important things well. That is the way to fast forward your life and to increase the sense of meaning you'll take to bed every night. Experience yourself well outside your comfort zone for a change.

Attitude Is Not Enough

So much has been said and written about the power of a positive attitude and, true, a positive attitude does count. Without it, your energy level will diminish. A positive attitude is uplifting and that perhaps is its greatest value.

But a positive attitude is not enough. It's not near enough. There is nothing more annoying than spending time around someone who has a buoyantly inflated positive attitude with no real demonstrable actions or achievements to back it up with. It feels phony and contrived. It's attitude combined with extraordinary effort that completes the formula.

An optimistic attitude will not beat the results of a good plan and skillful effort. It just won't. The potency of being able to throw your best effort into your task at hand, regardless of how you feel, is impossible to describe. You experience not just a positive attitude but an invincible attitude. Your will becomes more powerful than your emotional urges. It's the attitude of no excuses. Because many people feel they have to psyche themselves up first, spend time getting a positive attitude before they get down to business, they end up facing roadblocks. What we're saying is, let's forget attitude at first (though optimism does feel good), let's get rid of the excuses we make that allow us to put a half-hearted, rationalized effort into the tasks we engage in from day to day. It's attitude plus accurate planning plus skillful execution that yields the highest level of results.

You've Got One Life and You Are the Boss!

Robert Schuller capsulized the benefits of the vision-to-reality flow powerfully and succinctly:

> Sow a thought and you reap an act, sow an act and you reap a habit, sow a habit and you reap character, sow character and you reap a destiny.

This chapter gives you the tools to get started, but the tools will not work if you don't work them. Schedule some time to work through the five steps of the vision-to-reality flow right now. Realize that it will probably take you several sessions to complete all five areas. This action plan is the blueprint of the life you truly want to live. Don't be like the processinary caterpillars, performing the same tasks day by day because they're familiar regardless of whether they're effective. When you can look back at the end of the day and check off the calendar activities that come out of your vision-directed goals, then you will live the life you want most. Be the boss, take control. Do it now and reap a unique destiny that is waiting for you.

The purpose of life is a life of purpose.

—Robert Byrne

Chapter Three

s the "person" you live in under construction and improving or in danger of being condemned? A key to outperforming the competition is how quickly you learn and improve the most important tool you've got—you. The more you learn, the more you earn. It's that simple, provided you learn the right things. Are your mental skills sharper today than they were a year ago? How about your energy level, your stamina, your strength—are they improving? Is your sense of meaning and inner peace improving from year to year? The following story illustrates how the under construction principle really works:

A frustrated minister was working at home in his study on his sermon one Friday afternoon. "I can't come up with a single original idea," he muttered to himself. Suddenly, his 10-year-old son burst into the study, full of enthusiasm. "Are you ready to play ball, Dad?" he asks.

His father, concentrating on his sermon, ignored his son. "Dad," he persists, "You promised we could play catch tonight. Can we play now?"

The father set aside his papers and looked at his son. "How was school today?" he asked.

"We studied geography today, Dad."

"Really," the father replied. "What did you learn?"

"We learned about the world and where all the different places are, like China and France and Argentina. The world is a really big place, Dad!"

"It sure is," the father replied and glanced at the newspaper on his desk. Coincidentally, a full-page advertisement showing a large picture of the earth as seen from a satellite was showing. "See, look at this," the father said, pointing at the picture of the earth. "Would you like to do a puzzle?" he asked his son.

"Sure, Dad."

The father tore off the page of newspaper with the picture of the earth and began to rip the picture into small pieces, thinking it would take his son a long time to put the self-made puzzle together because the picture of the earth would be difficult to piece back together. This would give him time to finish his sermon. He handed all the small pieces to his son, who went into the kitchen to work on the puzzle.

Five minutes later, the boy burst back into the room his father was working in. "I'm done, Dad," he said.

"You're already done?" the father asked, astonished at how quickly he had finished, and he stood up to go see the newspaper picture all pieced together on the kitchen table. "I'm amazed at how fast you did the puzzle, son. I figured that picture of the earth would be very hard to put together. How did you do it?"

"It was easy, Dad. On the other side there was a picture of a little boy that was a lot easier to put together. I figured if I got the little boy right, then the world would turn out right too."

"Let's go play ball, son," the father smiled. "You have given me the idea I've been looking for."

That's the way under construction works. By focusing on getting your own skills and abilities "right," you impact your world at the same time. When you grow and develop steadily in the skills that support your life blueprint, the circumstances of your life will respond with positive change. Under construction is a principle that focuses you on improving the one element of your life you can truly control—you!

Under construction is an approach to self-improvement that looks at the total you. This principle will not only help you to grow, but it will help you to achieve more and, most importantly, to enjoy the ride. Under construction is a principle that integrates the three primary areas we need to grow and improve in from birth to death—physical, mental, and spiritual. When we continuously develop in these areas, we improve both today and tomorrow for ourselves and the people around us. What makes living in the world today so exciting is the unparalleled opportunity for personal growth. Under construction is a principle you must sell yourself on so that you not only recognize the opportunity, but harvest it!

THE 5:00 QUESTION

The ride home from work, whether it be a stroll from the den to the kitchen or a torturous commute on crowded freeways or stuffed commuter trains, is a real moment of truth. That's where a most important sale is made. This is a sale you need to make to yourself. You are either going to make a decision to goal achieve or stress relieve. Is the "free time" you have before and after work something you look forward to as "Wow, this is my time, my time to build a better me and a better life"? Or is it more, "I'm exhausted, how can I do as little as possible and just rest? I can't believe all the stuff that is piling up at home. I don't think I can get to it today."

After 5:00 thinking is either "round two, let's grow" or "life is harsh, I need some sleep!" The impact of a lifetime of accumulated decisions to approach round two as simply rest and relaxation time results in a continuous shrinking of energy, opportunities, and breakthrough experiences. On the other hand, using those hours to construct a better life unearths a hidden treasure, waiting to be opened.

We've talked a lot in this book about the beliefs and attitudes we sell ourselves and how these "sales" are what really determine our overall success in our careers and our lives. Whether or not you sell yourself on living the under construction principle is perhaps the most critical of all the sales you will make today. What are you going to do when you get home?

If you want to become absolutely unstoppable as a persuader, as a convincer, and as a persistent, never-say-die communicator, begin by making the sale every day at 5:00 to get under construction, to build yourself and your future, to achieve goals, and to really live your life at a higher level!

When Charles Wilson was president of General Electric, he was asked by the president of a small midwestern company how his experience as president of a large company could apply to the president of a very small company. Wilson answered by describing a job he had when he was a child. He had worked for a dairy, and his job was to fill the milk bottles. The bottles were different sizes. Some were a pint, others half gallons, and still others were a gallon. They all had different-sized necks. On his way home from a 10-hour workday, he asked himself what he was learning. The answer was that no matter what size the bottle, the cream always came to the top. In a competitive, no-excuses business environment, the cream always rises to the top and rises fast. And when you apply the under construction principle to yourself, you become the cream and rise up no matter what circumstances you are in.

Part of the reason so many people today feel run down and stressed out is because they are neglecting their own self-development. When we don't invest enough time in under construction, we end up having to work much harder to achieve fewer results. This is because our ability to create results is directly tied to how much we learn and develop. You should be able to create results much faster at age 40 than you can at 30. If, however, you can't, then you'll have to make up for your lack of ability with more time. You'll have to put in more time to get fewer results. It's a crummy trade-off. Keeping up becomes exhausting. Under construction is the way to generate more free time over the long haul. The under construction principle will also build you into a person who is truly capable of enjoying that free time without the limitations that saddle so many of us later in life.

Lack of Credentials Is Not an Obstacle!

Credentials, or the lack of them, can be viewed as a curse or a blessing. You might feel that you would be better off today if you had a more advanced degree from a prestigious university, or more specialized certifications and credentials in your profession. Sometimes, people actually limit what they believe their future can bring them because of missing credentials. Certainly, credentials are important. However, a lack of the highest credentials is not necessarily an obstacle. When we say to ourselves, "I can't get ahead because I haven't got an MBA," or "The school I went to wasn't good enough to get me into the kind of company I would like to work for," then we become victims of our own thinking.

Instead, we need to look as objectively as possible at the credentials we do and don't have. Then we apply the under construction principle to get us to where we want to go. Don't beat yourself up for the credentials you don't have. Instead, use the next five years to make up for it! The credentials you do or don't have today are not going to limit you if you get serious about under construction. What limits us today can literally be our springboard tomorrow. Under construction thinking allows us to do something now about what was limiting us in the past.

Credentials Are Not Guarantees Anymore

Christian Haig, governor of Mississippi, went to a barbecue after campaigning one evening. After his first serving of chicken, the governor was still hungry, so he went back to the food line and asked for a second piece of chicken saying, "I'm famished. May I have another piece of chicken?"

The person serving the chicken replied, "Only one per customer."

"Do you know who I am?" demanded the governor.

"No," was the answer.

"I'm the governor!"

"Well," said the server, "I'm the lady in charge of the chicken."

The walls of authority are dropping every day. The credentials of yesterday don't always carry the weight that we think they should. More and more companies are adopting open-door management approaches. Even medical doctors are finding themselves being challenged by more knowledgeable patients demanding more information and shared decision making.

Perhaps you already have some powerful credentials. Maybe your résumé is impressive. Credentials will get you into the game. They are, in a sense, the tickets to the ballpark. Too often, however, we think that they should also be guarantees of success, like entitlement certificates. That just isn't the case anymore. Credentials do not ensure lasting credibility—that has to be earned. As the knowledge base expands faster and faster, the credentials you have today may become less and less relevant.

"Somehow, you have to make yourself unique out there in the marketplace," explains Don Graling, a top-producing salesperson and manager. "You do this by getting as many unique experiences in your life as possible. Education can do that for you. I went back to school after I got my graduate degree in economics to get another graduate degree in accounting. I thought that would help me in my business and build my credential base. I've found that you can never stop educating yourself. I always found it important to go to different seminars and classes to move ahead. You meet a lot of fun and interesting people at those events. Whenever I feel I'm in a rut, I look toward outside educational opportunities to try to work myself out of it. Go to courses outside your normal environment that aren't necessarily job related."

Credentials can become obsolete fast. They must constantly be renewed and updated. Either update and improve them or risk losing the value they once represented. If you don't update them, you may find that the credentials or tickets that you have earned will be to a game that has already been played. The game will be over and you will be on the court after the win or loss was already recorded. Continuously updating our skills improves our capabilities, which is more critical now than ever before because of the pace of change.

Change Is Too Rapid to Stand Still!

Maybe there was a time when the pace was slower, when security was real, when getting ahead meant putting in your time, we don't know. We're still pretty young and we just didn't live through it. Nowadays, life moves quickly and the only way to combat it is to adapt. The insulation that was reportedly so beloved to generations gone by is now a liability. The more insulated you are, the more a target you become when the fat choppers start swinging their axes. Our knowledge-based economy is placing an increased value on learning. The price of standing still is very high. If you are not on a steady improvement plan you are losing ground. Fast-paced change demands fast-paced learning. Your ability to acquire valuable skills and knowledge faster than the people around you is your ticket to financial success.

The beauty of under construction, and why this principle is so timely, is that when we learn and develop we also diminish our resistance to change and increase our ability to adapt. That's what we need right now in this fast-changing world. And this ability to adapt to what is going on around you is also a fundamental skill when it comes to selling ideas. The more we know, the more connections we can make between ourselves, other members of the world, and the often unsettling paradoxes that characterize modern living. In a typical idea-selling scenario, we need to be able to understand the person we are speaking with and adapt to their perspective before we voice ours. The under construction principle will show you what you need to do to grow in the most useful ways. More importantly, you'll discover how to become energetic and inspired enough to do so. The following well-known story talks to the responsibility we all must assume when it comes to developing our abilities:

Many years ago, a wealthy man, about to leave for an extended trip, called for his three servants to give them his instructions before he departed. To the first servant, he gave five talents, which at that time was a form of currency, like dollars, and said, "Take care of these talents, good servant, while I am far from you." Then, he turned to the second servant and gave him two talents, saying the same words. Finally, he looked at the third servant and gave him three talents, with the same words of advice.

After three years, the wealthy man returned. He called the servants to his side. The first servant greeted his master and said, "Master, you delivered me five talents and I traded with them and made another five talents." The master smiled broadly and said, "Well done, good and faithful servant. I will make you ruler over many things."

The second servant approached and said, "You gave me two talents and now I give you two more." The master replied, "Well done, good and faithful servant. I will make you ruler over many things too."

The third servant came up to the master, trembling. "Master, I know you to be a hard man, reaping where you have sown, and I was afraid. I hid your three talents you gave to me in the ground." And he gave the three talents to the master.

"You wicked and lazy servant," replied the master. "You ought to have at least deposited the talents in the bank and I could have gotten some interest." With that, the master threw the unprofitable servant from his castle into the darkness alone.

Life, like the master in the story, can be ruthless with us if we do not continually invest back into ourselves and develop our talents. Is it unreasonable to expect that we should all be improving, all the time? When you were in third grade, did your parents expect you to make it to fourth grade the following year? Or was it more like, "Well, I guess you were just too tired to grow this year. It's okay, let's spend some more time at this level and see what happens next year"?

Ridiculous, isn't it? But how many of us are living that way as an adult? A recent statistic showed that the average college graduate reads 0.9 books a year. That's less than one book a year for the most educated strata of America. Take a walk through a bookstore today and marvel at the number of titles dedicated to virtually any topic we can think of. Less than three percent of the population has a library card. And it's free! Then there are the thousands of books on audiocassette to listen to in the car.

For some reason, many of us equate non-work time with rest. Many different surveys have come out over the years claiming that the average adult watches between three and five hours of television, on average, per day. Add that up and you've got at least 45 days worth of time being funneled into television each year. That's almost one full day a week! It's ironic that so many people are spending a significant portion of their lives watching other people succeed on television, while they feel stuck and frustrated in their own lives. When we neglect the under construction principle, we slow down considerably.

What About the Busy People?

On the other hand, there is a big group of us that are so busy, we seemingly cannot squeeze any "personal" self-development time into our nonworking lives. What is it that we are so busy doing, anyway? Is it possible that all the motion and activities we are so busy with are in reality doing little to move us forward? There is nothing wrong with being busy, but when we're too busy to invest time back into ourselves, then we've really got a priority problem, not a "too busy" problem. The bottom line is that if your life is so crowded, rushed, and crazy that there is no time left to build a more exciting future, then you have done a crummy job of planning, and your priorities are probably in need of a serious review.

The time you spend preparing and doing the things that will pay off when the game starts will help you to yield better results when it counts.

It seems the large creatures and the small creatures got into a dispute about something that seemed important at the time. They argued back and forth and decided that the only way to settle the dispute was to do it the old-fashioned way. So they decided to have a football game. Both teams squared off for the opening kickoff, and the first half was a disaster for the small creatures. Nearly every player on the large creatures' team—the elephant, giraffe, bull, rhino, and even the donkey—scored a touchdown, and the score was 55-0 at the half. The small creatures headed for the locker room dejected and demoralized, a defeated team. The coach of the small creatures, realizing the terrible predicament he was in, did everything he could to regroup, reorganize, and inspire his team. He even called in a motivational speaker!

Right after the kickoff of the second half, a new player for the small creatures, the centipede, came bursting out of the locker room and onto the field. He entered the huddle and said, "Give me the ball. I'll score a touchdown." So the quarterback, bruised and battered from the first half, handed the ball to the centipede on the first play, who sprinted around the end and ran 70 yards for the small creatures' first touchdown.

On the next play, the centipede made a tackle, forced a fumble, and recovered it, scoring another touchdown. For the rest of the third quarter, the centipede was a one-man wrecking crew, intercepting passes, running for touchdowns, and making fantastic plays continuously. At the end of the third quarter, the score was 55-55, tied up!

As the team gathered together on the sidelines before the fourth quarter, the coach looked at the team. "Who is scoring all those touchdowns?"

The centipede stood up. "It was me, Coach."

"You're playing fantastic," the coach said. "But I've got to ask you, where were you in the first half when we were getting trampled?"

"Well, Coach," the centipede replied, "I was in the locker room getting my ankles taped."

Often, busy people are too frantic, too involved in the game, to take the time to get their ankles taped and truly prepare for the most crucial challenges of their lives. They race from activity to activity, but they never really accomplish much.

Simple activities can provide great opportunities to grow and develop and discover new things. Activities such as listening to tapes in the car, reading biographies, having lunch with new people at work, helping our kids with their homework, or walking the dog at night can be turned into dramatic self-improvement habits if we want them to. Self-improvement is not only about what we do, it's about how we do it. By doing nearly the same things we are doing now in a new way we can engage a whole new level of self-discovery, learning, and problem-solving. This is where the value of the blueprints we introduced in Chapter 2 come in. They allow us to weed out time-consuming activities that yield little results.

It's What Under Construction Makes of You That's Most Important

A remarkable film entitled *Rudy* tells the true story of a young man, Rudy, who has a lifelong desire to play football for the University of Notre Dame. He doesn't possess much natural football ability; he's small and he hasn't done well enough in school to be admitted academically. He's got some significant roadblocks, I think we would all agree.

Rudy's desire was so great that he moved to South Bend, Indiana, where Notre Dame is located, got a part-time job assisting the university football stadium grounds crew, enrolled in a nearby junior college to improve his grades, and worked out to stay in shape, holding tight to his dream of playing football for Notre Dame. He commited every waking hour to the task of qualifying to get into the university. He eventually did get in and even made the football team practice squad, but what was most remarkable was the person he became through this struggle to reach his dream.

With only one game left in his senior year, Rudy had yet to actually suit up for a real game. He was only used on the practice squad. The other players, who had seen Rudy give his all day after day on the thankless practice field, petition the coach to let Rudy suit up for the last game of his senior year. The coach agreed, more as a reward for his persistence than a strategic move to improve the performance of the team. Rudy was only on the field for two insignificant plays at the end of that game, but when that game was over, a remarkable thing happened. His teammates lifted him on their shoulders and carried him triumphantly off the field, heralding him as a champion. Rudy was carried off the field as a salute to the man he was, not to his athletic ability. The struggle to reach his dream had made him into a man who was admired by those around him. Without the unique challenges he was forced to confront alone, Rudy would have been just another college football player. The fact that he had significant barriers that he had to overcome set the stage for him to accomplish the greatest possible feat. And that challenge was to take *himself* to the highest possible level of development he could.

The hidden beauty of this story is that after that final game was over, Rudy got to take that remarkable human being he had created with him! Like Rudy, when we put ourselves under construction to increase our talents, skills, and capabilities, we simply can't lose what we gain on the inside. It's our own prize to keep forever. Who you become as a result of the intensity of your own personal struggle is an end in and of itself!

The true reward of under construction is what we gain on the inside. The conditions of the world will always ebb and flow; sometimes we are in the right place to harvest, other times we are not. But what we gain on the inside because of our carefully thought-out efforts is the most satisfying of all of life's rewards, and the more we have inside that we can share with others, the more influential we become. You are the prize you get when you sell yourself on living the under construction principle.

Robert Riples, after doing some careful analysis, came to a startling conclusion about the value of ordinary iron. In a famous article he published, Riples wrote, "A plain bar of iron is worth $5.00. This same bar of iron, if made into horseshoes, is worth $10.50. If made into needles, it is worth $355.00. If made into pen knife blades, it is worth $3,285.00 and if made into balance springs for watches, that identical bar of iron becomes worth $300,000.00."

We are the same. As we develop into the person we can be, our ability to create remarkable results grows, and the way the world values our contribution grows in the same proportion.

Who Can You Become?

Where you are today is hardly the limit of where you can get to with the added boost of the under construction approach. When we approach our barriers the way Rudy did, they become the launching pad to a better life. Sometimes we think that we are limited because we've only got this level of education or that level of certification. What a bunch of baloney. Where you are today is the best possible place from which to launch the rest of your life. Where you are now is not limiting, it's perfect! You will find, if you engage in the task of developing yourself to the highest possible level, that where you are today will become an incredibly valuable asset someday. Remember, the limits you feel today will become the roadmarks toward your greatest triumph if you are willing to overcome them.

Nature has a beautiful way of illustrating the growth process. Take the Chinese bamboo tree for instance. The seed is planted, watered, and fertilized and, for the first four years, there is no visible growth. However, during the fifth year, the bamboo tree will grow 90 feet in six weeks. The question is, did the tree really take five years to begin growing? Not at all. Although growth was not visible, the tree was actually experiencing tremendous development during those first four years, which made it possible for it to stand sturdy and secure in the fifth year.

Under construction is much the same way. At first, the investment you make into your "roots" seems to yield little visible benefit. However, once a critical point is crossed, great possibilities can literally shoot up in front of you.

A close friend, Vince, worked for about five years at a popular children's television network. During that time, he was continuously creating proposals for new shows that he would then pitch to various producers, investors, and possible collaborators. Heartbreak after heartbreak followed with lots of near successes, but no big sale. Nonetheless, he kept coming up with new ideas at night after work, refining them, and enlarging his contact base until finally, with all that experience behind him, a producer latched onto him. Now, he's got a major hit with one show he's writing and several more coming down the pipeline. An overnight success? Hardly. By working to perfect his writing and proposal pitching skills night after night, year after year, Vince learned the skills that would eventually put him over the top and bring opportunities his way. Without the preliminary self-development, though, it is doubtful that those opportunities will appear for Vince, or any of us.

UNDER CONSTRUCTION REQUIRES VITALITY

Under construction requires discipline, and discipline requires energy. It's difficult, if not impossible, to grow and develop when you don't feel good. Many people, maybe you, too, have great intentions and make commitments from the heart but lack the energy to get off the dime and follow through. It's amazing how many people are walking around in a state of half exhaustion! How can we possibly be thinking about making today the greatest day we have ever lived when we are essentially tired from the moment we wake up until the moment we go to bed?

One of our clients told us an interesting story about one of their salespeople. He works on inside sales on the telephone, his customers love him, and he does a very effective job. The company has an outside sales position open that represents more money and opportunity, but they have not given him the job because he is so overweight. They are unsure of the impression he would make on customers. Is it right? Should the company feel this way? Maybe not, but that's the way it tends to work in the real world. When we do not look like we exude vitality, it can actually hinder us from opportunities we might have attracted based on our accomplishments.

The component we need that is perhaps the most valuable possession of all is *vitality*. When we feel a strong sense of vitality, we are more able to enjoy and invest ourselves into our day. Learning, which asks us to put more effort into our free time, requires vitality. Would Vince have been able to develop all those program ideas at night without vitality? It's virtually impossible for us to look forward to the opportunity building time we have after 5:00 if we feel listless, tired, and drained. To make the most of the after-5:00 challenge, we need energy and vitality. If you don't have it, that is where you need to start. You need to build it up. This is not going to turn into the latest diet and exercise book, we promise, but we do hope to help you see how simple it really is to increase your vitality.

Most people do not lack great dreams, they lack the energy and resolve to pursue them. Just maintaining their lives, just keeping up, becomes so taxing and so exhausting that there is nothing left. Athletes use the term *second wind* to describe a state they enter into after that initial feeling of tiredness. The second wind kicks in, like a reserve boost of energy, as we push past our initial exhaustion. Many people in their adult lives never experience the second wind when trying to develop to their highest level, because they don't have vitality to get past the first wind! A low-vitality life is no way to live if you want to enjoy the greater destiny waiting for you.

Vitality Is the Fruit of Under Construction

Vitality feels great! It allows so much more to happen. Vitality is the "wire" through which we experience the world. With a crummy, rusty, low-quality connection, all of our senses are dull, our thinking is foggy, our actions lack potency, and our appearance is muted. With vitality, our clarity increases, our appearance shines, and the ease with which we perform tasks that might have, in the past, shut us down, is remarkable. Vitality is, to be sure, the number one benefit of under construction.

You probably recall Aesop's fable about the goose and the golden egg:

A farmer visited the nest of his goose one day and found a glittering yellow egg. He was tempted to throw it away, but a second thought caused him to take it home and look it over more carefully. Much to his surprise, this strange egg turned out to be pure gold! Morning after morning, he gathered one golden egg after another from the goose, becoming very rich. The richer he became, the greedier he got until, one day, he became impatient with the gradually accumulating wealth. Hoping to get all the gold from the goose in one shot, he butchered it, only to find the goose empty.

Often, we become greedy in the same way with our free time. We stop investing daily into serious learning and self-development and kill off the golden goose in our own lives, which is, of course, our increasing ability to create value. The goose that will indeed lay your golden eggs is nurtured through living the under construction principle. Vitality is the window to the impossible, to miracles, because with vitality, we have more energy to invest into ourselves.

When you've got vitality, a whole new world of possibilities opens up to you; not only will you become aware of more opportunities, you'll have the gumption to act on them! As you develop your vitality to a higher level, you attract supporters, competitors, colleagues, and coaches of a higher caliber too. And when high-vitality, under construction people get together, stuff starts to happen!

What Is Vitality?

Liken vitality to the amount of watts you have in your lightbulb. The more watts you can put in your bulb, the more you can illuminate the paths of your life. Vitality is like that. When you have it, problems become easier to see and to solve. With vitality, exercise is easier to do, and making healthful choices changes from being a sacrifice to a joy. Activities that in the past were frustrating and exhausting become exciting and challenging. We enjoy the journey, the destination, the whole thing. We were in a strategic thinking session several years ago with some high-powered colleagues. The meeting was into the second day and really stalled in the afternoon. Everyone looked tired, and the problem solving was turning into problem creating. Gerry, a lower-ranking invitee, somehow had energy reserves no one else in the room had. He stood up and asked the group if he could lead the meeting for awhile. Relieved, the team agreed with his suggestion. Gerry quickly summarized what was going on and introduced several new ideas that were immediately adopted. His infusion of energy and enthusiasm, at a time when everyone needed it, became a turning point in his career. After the meeting was over, Gerry was invited back and eventually promoted and it no doubt had a lot to do with the boundless energy he displayed that day. Sometimes, life asks us to go through experiences where we need a 5,000-watt halogen bulb-sized burst of energy. Vitality can give you that burst.

People are attracted to vitality and are influenced by it. When you have it in abundance, you will find opportunities to improve yourself, your career, and your relationships. Vitality is a magnet. When we lack vitality, however, we have to struggle to be heard, fight to get in the door, and climb the mountain to get a chance to compete with the big boys. What an ironic fact it is that people with low vitality actually attract more low-vitality people to them, which, of course, sap what little vitality they have.

Have You Got an Empty Battery?

Maybe you think influence is about the way you choose, put together, and express language. You might believe that being convincing and having impact is strictly a verbal phenomenon. Well, it's not. Your energy level has as much to do (maybe more) with the way you influence the people around you as do your communication skills. To be a powerful influencer, you need a full energy supply, a full battery. When you have enough so that the people around you start to, in a sense, feed off your energy, you are influencing. If, on the other hand, you are the vacuum in the room that sucks up the energy of others, chances are you are the one being influenced or, even worse, repelling others. Under construction builds a more powerful reserve tank of energy and vitality for you to use. It also helps you to avoid problems.

"I think that staying in shape both mentally and physically has given me a lot of the stamina and endurance I've needed to make it to the top," explains Mike Finizio, a top-producing stock broker for years. "It's also given me an out for the frustration and pressures during the day. I've been working out since I got out of high school and it has helped me tremendously. I think that the discipline transfers to the way I work, which is why I've been able to consistently be a top producer."

When energy is flowing freely through you, you will reduce the likelihood of repair later down the road. The reason for this is that operating at a cleaner, higher energy level actually lightens the load on your system. That's the interesting paradox. You lighten your load when you increase your vitality. Living without much vitality is a lot of work. Increase your vitality and you will access more energy; use less of it and enjoy the ride a whole lot more.

VITALITY AND THE BIG THREE

A lasting sense of vitality is the result of consistent development in three key areas. You can't neglect one for long without limiting your overall vitality. They work together. When you develop in all three areas, you create a synergy effect so that one plus one plus one doesn't equal three but can equal 10.

These three areas are also the key areas you need to organize your under construction development around. Under construction, when approached in the way we're about to describe to you, is the most effective way to build vitality, and it is designed to increase your vitality now!

Let's make it as simple as possible to get started. You can look at under construction in terms of these three primary areas of development:

1. Mental
2. Physical
3. Spiritual

If you grow in all three of these areas each day, there is no telling what you can accomplish with 60 to 90 years of really living. Think of these three areas as the three great treasures of life:

1. To have a mind that is creative, well educated, resourceful, and able to solve problems. To be able to understand what is really happening and make good decisions.
2. To live in a body that has lots of energy, feels good, and has strength and stamina. To have strong resistance to disease along with balance and coordination.
3. To feel a sense of meaning, truth, and peace from within. To feel connected spiritually, with nature, and the people in our lives. To live values that uplift us and the people around us. To enjoy giving to others.

Mental development is the acquiring of knowledge and skills that allow us to accomplish our highest goals. It's an understanding of our problems and how to solve them. It's the ability to determine a plan and find the resources to accomplish it. It's the ability to penetrate beneath the obvious to deeper meaning and insight.

Physical development is easy to understand. Ultimately, in this area we want to build a body that feels good and has endurance, energy, and strength. We want a body that doesn't fall into disease easily and that holds up well over the long haul.

Spiritual development is the identification of our highest values and the ability to live in accordance with them. It is the cultivation of inner peace through our relationship with God. It is the understanding that all of our actions count and that what we give to others is our greatest accomplishment. Our spiritual development opens us to the wonder and magic of being alive.

Mental Under Construction

Let's look at the first of the three under construction development areas, mental development. The knowledge you have and your ability to use it to make a valuable contribution is what determines your value. In this environment, we need to be on a fast-paced learning curve now and, quite possibly, for the rest of our lives. Accept this reality and begin to enjoy the art of learning useful things that help you make a more valuable contribution.

We're living in a world where knowledge is valued above all else. There are people who can earn over a thousand dollars an hour (and others much, much more!) simply because of the value they bring to a project or problem. Why? Because they have specialized knowledge and the ability to use it in a way that creates dramatic value for the people they work for. It's not about control or tyranically forcing things to happen; it's about creating value, and that takes knowledge. Simply put, this is a great time to be alive if you are willing to develop your mind.

Another key piece of the mental development puzzle is the cultivation of effective self-talk. There is an endless conversation that goes on inside each of us, the "inner dialogue" as Carlos Castaneda, author of several books about his association with a Yaqui Indian sorcerer named Don Juan Matus, puts it. The quality of that conversation has an enormous impact on how we feel and act. "Your attitude is like a rose garden," explains Mike Quindazzi, a top-producing sales manager. "It may be beautiful today, but if you don't take care of it and water it and pull the weeds out, the roses are going to die off and the weeds are going to grow. Keeping a positive attitude is like that. You have to constantly weed out the bad stuff and nurture the good stuff."

Learning breaks paradigms that limit

We all develop beliefs and ways of seeing the world that many people call paradigms. The term has been popularized by some highly visible management gurus like Stephen Covey and Joel Barker. The paradigms we form can actually limit our possibilities. For instance, if 15 years ago I wanted to build a better telephone, but my belief system held tight to the notion that the handheld part of the phone must be connected to a cord that runs to the base, then I would have worked for years at perfecting a phone that no one would want. Why? Because I would have completely missed out on the wireless innovation. All the improvements I would have made to that corded phone would have been useless because people prefer buying cordless phones. That is an example of what a limiting paradigm can do. We have paradigms in all areas of our lives, including our relationships. At times our paradigms help us, and at times they don't.

"Self-improvement, I believe, requires change," explains Chip Sollins, the president of American Pool Service, the largest pool management company in the Washington, D.C. metropolitan area. "How you choose to self-improve doesn't matter, as long as you continue to change and adapt. I used to be a hot-head. I had a temper. For me to self-improve in that aspect I realized I needed to change or I would not be able to get better results and grow my business. By changing, not reacting always with my temper, and being a little more understanding, it has gotten me a lot further. I've been able to motivate people much better as a result."

A fast-paced learning approach helps us to break limiting paradigms much more quickly. Let's say you decide to become fluent in Spanish and work hard at it for several years. As a result, you plan a trip to Mexico City. Your experience of the city and the people you meet will be completely altered by this new knowledge of their language. Your new skill in the language will dramatically enhance your ability to understand the Mexican culture and, more importantly, it will increase your ability to function effectively in a city that is new to you.

When we adopt a fast-paced learning lifestyle, we quickly become aware of and move past our limiting paradigms. We don't get stuck for as long a time and can actually become perceived and valued by others as creative and innovative simply because we have less-restricting blinders on than the people around us.

Learning helps us to understand and accept the people and conditions around us. It makes us less paranoid of people who are not like us and helps us capitalize on this diverse world we live in. We become interested in others, not afraid of them. This can help us to be much more persuasive and develop better rapport with a wider variety of people. We develop a broader perspective, become more interested and interesting, and become less ignorant. These are all fabulous characteristics if you want to go after the big prizes in life, prizes like influence, affluence, and high-quality, supportive relationships. It's worth it. Get unstuck. Learn faster. Make the 5:00 decision. Read for 30 minutes today.

What are you reading?

What is the quality level of the stuff you read on a regular basis? Can you notch it up a bit? The average person, if they read just 30 minutes a day, would read over 18 300-page books a year. Do you think that would make a difference in your intellectual power over time? What if all 18 of those books were of the highest quality, such as challenging novels, classic works of literature, or respected publications on business, health, fitness, and relationships. What if you took notes, reviewed those notes, and implemented them? That's fast-paced learning. That's under construction. Before you go to bed, read something that will contribute in a meaningful way to the knowledge you need to have to do a better job at what you will be doing tomorrow. Read something that will bring you more insight, like a classic novel. Listen to a tape on the way to work tomorrow that will help you discover more of your potential!

For the person who wants to be an expert at selling ideas, consider the following topics as areas to continuously read in:

- Biographies of successful people
- Articles and books tracking and reporting business trends
- Psychology books on relationships that help you understand how people really work
- Popular business books that make the best-seller lists
- Leading management thinking, approaches, and trends
- Quote books that pull together a wide variety of stories and anecdotes
- Well-written novels, which improve your ability to use language

The more you read the better, but it doesn't take much more than 30 minutes a day to become a well-read person. Even a moderately paced reader will complete at least 15 books a year just by reading 30 minutes a day! Think of what a difference it would make over a five-year period if every day you pumped 30 minutes of quality knowledge into your brain!

Mike Finizio explains: "You have to turn yourself on and motivate yourself, but you can cheat too. You can cheat by listening to other people who are very successful in the field. I never consider myself to be the best because there is always room for improvement. So I will continually go to things like toastmasters or listen to motivational tapes. I go through the Nightingale Conent brochure each month and pick out a tape that I think may help me. I find sometimes that after listening to 12 hours of tapes that I only may get two or three good ideas from all the tapes. But those two or three ideas can bring in some tremendous returns. A lot of people just won't go through it, to shovel through all that snow to find just two or three ideas, but I will. When I'm in the car, I listen to it constantly. I think that has helped me considerably, and my family is 100% behind these types of motivational classes and education."

Input on Purpose

Think of the experiences you have during the day as being the input that is going into the creation of who you are. Make sure that at least some of this input happens on purpose. Was the physical input (food) you fed yourself of the highest quality you were capable of finding, or was what went into your body today more a formula for creating blobulitis? Did quality information touch your memory banks, or were you feeding it titillating distractions instead? What are you taking in? What is the quality of your input? Are you still growing? Would you prescribe the quality of the information you are digesting for a person who is intent on developing to the absolute highest level? Is there any other level to shoot for? Why settle for less?

When Alexander the Great was a boy, his father searched for the best tutors in Greece. He hired special teachers to work with young Alexander on music, science, mathematics, and even hired Aristotle as his tutor in philosophy and politics. By age 30, Alexander the Great had conquered the known world for the Greek empire. Do you think there is a relationship between Alexander's learning pace and his ability to achieve? Like Alexander, to accomplish great things tomorrow, we need to take the right steps today.

Physical Under Construction

The current state of our physical body is relatively easy to measure and, to a large extent, it determines the amount of energy we have. Are you in a strong body that has flexibility, stamina, and balance? Can you knock off 25 push-ups right now? How about ten pull-ups? Can you run a couple of miles? Can you go for a five-mile hike and enjoy it? How about a ten-mile bike ride? No one's asking you to run a marathon or compete in a triathlon, but is your body reasonably well fit in terms of strength, stamina, flexibility, and balance?

Or is your body generally stiff, weak, aching, and lacking stamina? If so, your body is limiting you and limiting the opportunities that flow your way. It could also be limiting the impact your message has on others and even be repelling people and opportunities. A poorly fit, unhealthy body will lower your quality of life and, in general, it just feels uncomfortable to live in. When you feel that way, imagine what happens to the way you communicate. It's hard to smile with enthusiastic abandon when stuff hurts.

Three years ago, I was speaking at a convention, and I was following a man, Michael, who was presenting before me. He was at least 75 pounds overweight and had an expression on his face that appeared to be masking pain of some sort. "How are you?" I asked, shaking his hand. "To be honest," he replied, "my back is really hurting. It's been bothering me for a couple of months now." He seemed to be out of breath and was definitely not "in the flow." When I watched him on stage, I noticed that his energy level was very low and it had a very quieting effect on the audience. When he came backstage after his presentation, I shook his hand again and he said, "Wow, that really takes a lot out of you." I had an opportunity to meet with him several times over the next two years and he was always the same—tired and sore. I remember one meeting where we were putting together a new advertising promotion, and he was part of the team. He seemed unable to concentrate for long periods of time, always fidgeting and trying to get comfortable in his seat. As a result, he was not a very inspiring person to be around. There are a lot of people like Michael who are continually suffering because their body hurts. It's hard to solve vexing problems when the body is always crying for more and more rest.

Your body really wants action, movement, and the opportunity to express itself physically. As you raise the quality of your physical body, you improve your mental power, too. "I find that I tend to bottle things up inside, which generates a higher stress level," Paul Thomas, a successful sales manager, adds. "When I stay involved in some type of physical activity, I can get it out. It makes a big difference in the way I work. I'd say it's a key element of my success."

That's not to say there aren't some very influential people who are out of shape, because there are. The question is, however, is the quality of their life on the way up or down? We're really after a combination of quality of life, meaning, and influence. That takes a steadily improving physical vehicle that powers you into opportunities instead of providing you with excuses.

Physical development keys
Here they are, folks, the big mystery, the three components that determine the lion's share of the feeling of vitality you experience from a physical standpoint:

- What you eat and drink
- How you exercise
- How you rest and relax

We're not going to launch into a fitness program here, but let's cap all of this by saying that moderation is critical, common sense is valuable, and nonfanatic discipline is essential. Get some commonsense advice from a person who has vitality. Go to a trained fitness expert at a local gym. Get a couple of books that exude common sense, and most importantly, look to yourself for some inner wisdom. You'll find it's not that hard to figure out. Usually, in a single paragraph, this is what most people discover:

> I need to eat a stimulant-free diet (sugars, caffeine, drugs, etc.) that is rich in fruits, vegetables, grains, and low-fat proteins. I need to drink a lot of fresh water, keep alcohol intake down, and get about 30 minutes of exercise a day. I need to stretch out every day, and if I alternate aerobic workouts with strength building every other day, I can't miss. I need to get at least six solid hours of sleep every night and maybe a restful 15-minute break a couple of times a day.

Do this and your vitality level will probably go up. Cut the crap, cut the excuses. It's your life. Live in a body that feels good and helps you achieve your God-given potential.

Imagine that you had a million-dollar racehorse given to you. What would you do with him? What would you feed him? What would you give him to drink? How much exercise would you give him? When would you put him to bed at night? You probably would do everything you could to maximize the horse's performance, but what about yourself? If you would treat a horse with the most well-thought-out care, why not do it with yourself. Don't you hold the same incredible potential inside waiting to be released?

About five years ago I was going through a relentless series of business trips that put me in a different city every week for about a year. I completely fell off my normal exercise regimen and felt totally exhausted and fatigued. I blamed my low energy on the travel, and it certainly was a contributing factor. By luck, I ran into a guy on the road at the end of that year who traveled even more than I did. I asked him how he dealt with the accompanying exhaustion and he laughed at me. "I've never felt better physically in all my life," was his reply. I asked him how he did it and he explained that all it really took was 45 minutes a day to either jog or hit the hotel gym. I became aware of all the excuses I had come up with for putting off exercise and realized that they were just that, excuses. I took his advice and within a month I felt great, even though my travel hadn't lightened up at all. I learned a valuable lesson about exercise and vitality and how easy it is to let excuses slip in and derail the train.

"I think health and exercise are so important," explains Tommy Giaimo, a consistently top-producing car salesperson. "If I let myself go for a couple of months and don't go to the gym, I can feel it. I feel kind of run down. I've found that you really do have to eat right and keep in shape to stay on top of your own game."

Typically, what most people say when they consider beefing up their exercise regimen is, "I would love to do it, but I don't have the time." If that's you, then we strongly suggest putting your exercise activity at the beginning of the day before the day starts to take on a life of its own. You'll create your own personal victory first thing in the morning, you'll get it out of the way, and it is the time of day that is easiest to control in terms of unexpected interruptions and schedule screw-ups.

I was on a plane recently and was browsing through an in-flight magazine. On the cover was Jerry Rice, the superstar receiver on the San Francisco 49ers football team. The article explained that at 33 years old, Rice was already way past the typical "prime" for an NFL player. What the writer discovered, however, was that Jerry Rice, who should have been at the end of his career, is faster, stronger, mentally tougher, and performing better than guys 10 years younger. Why? Commitment and discipline. The writer observed Rice's workout regimen to try and determine the secret of his longevity and a career free of serious injuries. What was the secret he found? Simply this: Jerry Rice works out harder than anyone else in the league. Every year he increases his strength, endurance, speed, and power. His daily regimen of sprints and power drills frightens off even the most conditioned athletes who often visit with the intention of "hanging" with Jerry Rice but soon find shortly into the workout that keeping up with Rice is easier said than done. Jerry Rice will probably go down as the greatest wide receiver in NFL history because of his discipline and commitment to physical under construction.

Do you and I need to get to that level of fitness? Probably not, but we can, like Jerry Rice, gain access to a much higher level of vitality and accompanying performance if we pay strict attention to our exercise needs.

Make rest and relaxation a necessity, not your primary goal

"Thank God it's Friday," is an interesting saying that is pretty well representative of an attitude that values having fun more than making a contribution. Why is it that two days off on the weekend can create so much excitement and positive anticipation? What makes the prospect of free time on the weekend so relieving?

Rest must become preparation for the next event, not the goal itself. It's maintenance, not the reason for being. We all need to rest and relax, and we should rest and relax well, in spectacular fashion, so that we are truly prepared for whatever comes next. Often, however, our relaxation time is anything but restful. As a result, we are exhausted for what we consider the contribution part of our lives and are too often in a frame of mind that says "I'm going to tolerate this rather than leverage it!"

Over a period of time, all sea-going vessels accumulate barnacles. Barnacles are marine organisms that form a hard shell attached to a ship's surface, fouling up the ship's bottom. The accumulation of small individual barnacles on a ship's bottom can add tons to the ship's weight, creating a tremendous drag as the ship glides through the water. This reduces the ship's efficiency and can add huge costs to the ship's operation. At regular intervals, the ship must be dry-docked to have the barnacles scraped from its bottom. When you feel inefficient and tired because you aren't getting the right kind of rest, it's like carrying around a load of extra barnacles. Those barnacles, that tired feeling, can prevent you from coming across to others with the level of punch you need.

Rest is not recreation. We need rest in order to fully enjoy recreation. Often, we mistakenly confuse the two and end up having a lesser experience doing both. How much sleep do you need to really feel refreshed in the morning? Find out and make sure you get it every night.

Get the appearance you really want

From a purely selfish standpoint, wouldn't you rather live in a body that looks and feels the way you really want? You deserve to, provided it is the body that is the best possible version of *you*. We should not strive to be the image of someone else, but simply the best possible version of ourselves. Earn the appearance you really want. What can compare to the feeling you get when you step to the front of the boardroom, ready to make a presentation, knowing that you look great, your clothes fit, you feel energetic, and nothing is hurting? When you are in shape, you look great in clothes, and you can wear clothes that make you look and feel great. Create a comfortable body to live your life in!

Spiritual Under Construction

This is a touchy area for many people. Typically, when we conduct goal-setting seminars, most people feel that they are not growing and have not grown for years in their spiritual life. Perhaps because spirituality is often shrouded in mystical gobbledygook, it is hard to get a firm grasp on. However, some very simple daily practices can create a dramatic effect on you spiritually. When you develop a stronger sense of your spiritual center and have a greater sense of inner peace, you'll be better able to deal with the daily stress of change, time constraints, having to do more with less, and so on.

Don, a businessperson I truly admire, runs a business in Chicago. He has grace under pressure, and in business situations he is able to stay composed, even when people around him are falling into emotional turmoil. Having observed him over several years and marveled at his profound balance and equanimity, I asked him how he does it. He told me that it comes from his inner sense of spirituality. You may know someone like Don, but you probably know a lot more people who aren't like him at all—people who sway with every emotional wind that blows. You can develop more composure by paying more attention to your spiritual development, and this in turn can really help you in business.

A good place to start is to read something uplifting from one of the great spiritual texts (the Bible, Bhagavad Gita, Koran, Tao Te Ching, etc.) at night before you go to bed. Read only a small section and take time to think about its meaning. You may even want to keep a journal of spiritual insights nearby that you can jot notes and special thoughts into. Writing down your thoughts and beliefs about God is a great way to increase your sense of spirituality.

Another worthwhile activity is to do something good for someone each day with no thought of remuneration or reward. Simply do it for the joy of giving to another human being. Whether it's writing a quick thank-you note to a coworker who helped you out today, or telling the manager of the restaurant about the good service your waiter gave you, or saying something positive (and true!) about someone behind their back, you'll find that these positive contributions will impact the way you feel. Volunteer time regularly to a local youth development program or donate some time to serve at a local homeless shelter. There are countless opportunities each day to give to others selflessly.

Perhaps the most powerful of all spiritual activities is the cultivation of inner calm, peace, and, ultimately, quiet. Prayer and meditation are the most popular ways to quiet your thoughts and sense your bigger purpose. Living in accordance with your highest values doesn't hurt either. If you did the one life, one boss blueprint, then you already know what those values are.

A walk in the woods or a visit to a tranquil place can reconnect you with nature and your spiritual center. At lunchtime drop by a church and spend 20 minutes by yourself. Don't neglect your spiritual development, because it is the rock of strength that we all come to lean on from time to time.

There is a story by an unknown author about a dream he once had. In the dream, he was walking down the beach beside the Lord. As they walked, above him the sky was reflecting each experience of his life. When he reached the end of the beach, he looked back and saw the two sets of footprints extending down the way, but suddenly, he noticed that every once in a while there was only one set of footprints. And each time he noticed the two sets of tracks turning into one, there was above reflected in the sky a series of events that were times of great trial and suffering in his life. Upon realizing this, he turned to the Lord and said, "You promised that if I walked with You, You would always be by my side. Why did You desert me in times of my greatest need?"

And the Lord listened with compassion and said, "My beloved child, I wouldn't desert you when you needed Me. When you see only one set of footprints, those were the times in your life that I carried you in My arms."

It is from the well of our spiritual nature that we all must draw during life's most difficult moments. It pays to increase the size of the well a little each day.

WHAT HAVE YOU LEARNED RECENTLY?

Take out a pen and paper. Make a list of all the significant things you have learned this week. Difficult? Take a whole month if necessary. Still difficult? How about the whole year. If someone asked you to make a speech today on the most important lessons you have learned this year, what would they be?

Shouldn't there be meaningful learning taking place each week? Each day? Are we being unreasonable when we say you should be able to tick off some meaningful progress each day before you go to bed? How about a journal that asks you for your learning breakthroughs each day? What is reasonable to expect in terms of progress each week? Can you chart some progress? If yes, congratulations! If not, why not? Get started now.

5:00 Opportunities

One thing for sure, as you approach your post-5:00 challenge, the one thing you don't want to do is bore yourself to death. Shacking up with three hours of business books is not what we're talking about. Consider all of these alternatives:

Mental
- Enroll in a class at a local junior college.
- Read a biography of someone you admire.
- Read the latest "on trend" book on your profession.
- Enroll in a conference or convention that will help you grow.
- Learn a new computer program.
- Take a guitar or piano lesson.

Physical
- Take a walk each night with a loved one.
- Go dancing or take a dancing lesson.
- Climb a nearby hill and enjoy the view.
- Hit some golf balls.
- Go to the gym and work out.

Spiritual
- Read a spiritually oriented book for a few minutes a day.
- Take a yoga class.
- Close your eyes and relax for 30 minutes a day.
- Take a walk by the lake and enjoy the sunset.
- Stop by your place of worship.

All of these things can be considered under construction activities. Be creative. Do something that puts you into a learning/discovery mode and, more importantly, pour yourself into it. When you're in an under construction activity, you have to eliminate distractions and focus all of your concentration on that activity. If you're thinking about something else, anxious to get that activity over with rather than giving it 100%, then you are cheating. Remember, the real learning comes from the effort.

Time Efficient Under Construction

Are you ready for the ultimate concept in time management? Here it is. Find activities that knock on the doors of several goal areas at once. We'll call these compound activities. For instance, tomorrow call up the highest-ranking finance person in your company and offer to take him or her out to lunch. Tell them that you would like to learn more about their ideas on how to make your department more profitable. In this case, you're combining learning (an accounting person's perspective) with relationship building, with finding ideas you can use to achieve results. Let's say you need to work on your relationship with your 10-year-old child. Why not go on a bike ride together tonight, pack a snack, and have a mini-picnic, which, of course, is a great time to talk and pal around. Or how about you and your spouse developing the habit of going for a 15-minute walk every night just before bed. On this walk, let each person talk for half the time about what they perceive to be their most significant accomplishment of the day with absolutely no interruptions. No criticizing allowed! The walk ends with each person complimenting the accomplishment or sharing some encouragement with the other. Imagine what a couple of months of these walks would do for your relationship.

With compound activities you improve several areas of your life at once. You can get exercise, work on a relationship, and improve your verbal skills all at the same time.

The next time you go to lunch with a colleague, develop a list of ideas that would help cut costs in your department and submit them to your boss together and possibly even offer to spearhead their implementation. Give up running one night for a change of pace and for some fun and relationship building, take a dance lesson. Then follow it up with a night of high-energy dancing. Why not sign up for piano lessons with your eight-year-old? You've probably always wanted to be able to play, and what a great way to learn—with your child! The two of you will share that marvelous skill together for the rest of your life. Exercise, family time together, healthy food, fresh air—the benefits flow to you quickly when you learn to use compound activities.

Time management isn't exclusively about how to organize your appointment book, it's about how to accomplish results, how to make things improve for yourself. We are, as a business culture, overly focused on to-dos and underfocused on value. There are miracles waiting to happen in that 5:00-till-sleep window. Make them happen! Before you go to sleep each night ask yourself if you did the following:

- Increase your value?
- Increase your stamina?
- Increase your strength?
- Increase your flexibility?
- Increase your mental power?
- Increase your vocabulary?
- Improve your memory?
- Deepen your spiritual roots?
- Improve your ability to observe, notice, and listen?

Learn to experience true joy as you feel yourself expanding in these areas.

Did Your Learning Curve Drop Off (Sharply) Along the Way?

"I think we have to first recognize what we have inside that needs to improve," explains Nola Beldegreen, a highly successful advertising professional. "We have to notice what doesn't feel right to know what we need to improve. When we feel something isn't right inside, that is an indication that we need to work on it."

Kindergarten through high school was level one. College and graduate school, if you did it, was level two. More importantly, though, we all eventually get to level three, which is probably where you are now. And what's fascinating is that you can overcome a deficit in level two by getting to work in level three.

You are now on an advanced, self-directed, lifelong learning program. No one is going to enforce it but you. Learning has become an elective. Has your learning curve dropped off because you're not working at it any more?

No one is saying that you have to come home and study for seven hours a night. There are many ways to learn. What we are talking about is how you approach and invest in your free time that you have bought into. Is it goal achieving or stress relieving?

Overtime Happens at Home

Overtime is a pretty neat concept. You get paid time and a half or even double time when you stay late and clock in some extra hours. This is exactly what happens when you buy the under construction principle. You will be clocking overtime at home. You will be increasing your value, increasing the joy you get out of life, and increasing the likelihood of positive opportunities coming your way. Guess what that will do to your energy and enthusiasm?

It starts today, now, right now. Stop worrying about the tomorrows you will never live. Throw yourself into developing you. Do it now, because you'll get another chance tomorrow when tomorrow becomes today. Learning to function in the now is the way to wrestle out of yourself more of who you really are and the magic of who you truly can be. It all starts when you make a plan, when you go through the vision-to-reality process, when you identify the habits you need to remove and the habits you need to build and start putting them into your daily schedule as priority number one every day.

Take today as a personal challenge. Go to bed knowing you have constructed a better you as a result of today. Find out what your best effort is really all about. Don't take under construction halfway anymore. Go for it. Just do it!

It's Evolution, Not Revolution!

So how do we get to this exalted state of mind when it seems light years away? You start where you are. For example, right now, you're reading this book. How could you read this book with more of a commitment to get the most from it? Do you have a highlighter in one hand? Do you have a notepad out? The whole point is that it starts right now, not in five minutes, five hours, five days, five years, or five decades. Right now! Soon, you'll put the book down and be off to the next activity. The mistake we often make is to labor too much over the selection of what we're going to do rather than approaching whatever we happen to be doing with a stronger under construction approach. Want to watch TV? Surf the channels and find something that is really interesting. Take notes! Watch actively. Certainly we do need to plan the right activities, but you can and must start with whatever you're doing now. That's the key. The opportunity is right here, right now. Focus on today. Make today the objective, not tomorrow. Don't think about when you'll start, just start with whatever your next activity is. Put more of yourself into it. Do it as though God were watching, waiting to applaud you for your spectacular performance.

Mark Ferraro, a top-performing sales professional, explains: "As a human being, if you don't learn, you don't get any better unless you grow and improve. It's part of the growing process. I got it fairly young that learning is something that is nonstop. I've heard it from people I admired my whole life. The old guy in the office that's the most successful always says, 'I never stopped learning.' Self-improvement to me has always meant improving and getting better."

One of the most inspiring truths about improvement and performance is that you don't have to improve 100% to get 100% better results. Small improvements in performance can yield enormous benefits. Consider major league baseball. The difference between a lifetime .280 hitter and a .300 hitter in terms of prestige, recognition, and fame is enormous. Nearly all lifetime .300 hitters, such as Babe Ruth, Willie Mays, Ted Williams, and Rod Carew, make it to the Hall of Fame. That is not necessarily so with .280 hitters. You would think the difference between the performance of these two groups would be enormous, but when you do the math, the difference in performance is actually very small. A .300 hitter only gets one more hit in every 50 at bats than the .280 hitter. That's just one more hit in about 10 games! This holds true in many other arenas: the proposal that won out by just a hair, the horse that wins by just a nose, or the golfer who wins the tournament by only one stroke. What we find is that the top performers in any field are not twice as good as everyone else, even though they may be enjoying twice the benefits.

Is the salesperson who gets the order twice as good as the competition? Not always. Maybe she is only a little better than her nearest competitor, but she gets 100% of the order and her competitor gets nothing! That's the way it is in business. When you're a little better than your competitor most of the time, you do a lot better than they do.

Dave Doehr, a highly successful leader in the telecommunications field, explains: "You're going to come across your little gold nuggets every once in awhile. Whether it's from someone you see in the office, or something you hear on a tape, or something you see on video. And you're probably going to sit back and say, wow, that's a great idea and that could really work. But where the rubber meets the road is in the implementation and practice of what you learn. That's what separates the achievers from the wannabes. You have to practice the little things you learn every day that add up to a big improvement over time."

Become the Boss Again and Take Control

Where do you need to grow and develop? Take out your life blueprint and activity planning sheets and write down some activities that can jump start your learning curve and put you under construction. Put those items into you calendar. It's the putting into the calendar step that most people never get to. Don't con yourself into believing that you're too busy to squeeze in a little under construction activity. You've got all the time in the day to grow!

Chapter Four

Tell it with gusto is OUTSELL principle number three. This is the art of communication, which covers both what you say and learn through interaction with other people. Once you've got the one life, one boss principle in place, which gives you responsibility for your own life and the ability to become the architect of your future, and once you are under construction, which means you are growing quickly in the areas that really pay off, then it's time to tell it with gusto, because the quality of all of your relationships is a direct result of the quality of your communication.

Virtually all surveys given to senior executives to determine which business skill is most important reveal that communication is the number one skill. You simply cannot be persuasive, manage well, lead others, participate effectively in teams, or build strong customer relationships when you can't communicate. When I lived in Washington, D.C. I had a salesperson working for me named Beth. She was continuously complaining that she couldn't get any help and support from our administrative team. The rest of the salespeople were very complimentary of the administrative assistants, but not Beth. When I observed Beth working, I noticed a lot of things on her desk, such as letters, faxes, and proposals, that could be given to the administrative team to do. I asked her why she didn't hand them off. "It takes too much time to explain what needs to be done, and how will I know that they'll do it right?" was her reply. When I asked the administrative people what they thought of the situation, they explained that when Beth asked them for help, her directions were always unclear and overly simplified. She would use phrases like, "you can figure it out," or "it's not that difficult, here just do your best." As a result, the work would come back to Beth not fitting her expectations. Instead of working on her ability to communicate, Beth decided to do all the work herself, which meant more hours, more stress, and less selling time. Over time, I noticed that this same skill deficit carried over to the way she interacted with customers, with colleagues, and with her boss. She was very motivated and had a good work ethic, but Beth never achieved any more than mediocre results because she didn't work at developing herself as a communicator.

There are millions of people like Beth who are limiting their future because they do not take the time to become outstanding communicators. But you, after reading this chapter, will not make the same mistake.

GOOD COMMUNICATION CREATES IMPACT

What can compare to the feeling of communicating well? It is the hidden treasure of life that the greatest feeling of all is when we can make ourselves understood by our fellow human beings—to be able to play our song with passion and enthusiasm and have it well received. We often neglect this. On the other hand, one of the most frustrating things of all is the inability to communicate: when you just can't get your point across, when people don't understand. It's frustrating and taxing. When you've got a great idea for a customer but you can't get that customer excited about it, your value to that customer is not where it could be. When you are unable to bring life to your presentations, whether they be to your boss or to a buying committee, you won't be tapping your true potential.

You're not alone or isolated when you can express yourself. You feel a part of the never-ending interaction that is taking place because you are making connections and seeing your ideas understood, accepted, and acted upon. Your ability to communicate determines how the world interacts with you. People are inviting, friendly, and interested when you can communicate. If you are difficult to understand, people will show stress when they are around you. If you are clear, concise, and interesting, however, you will find an enthusiastic audience for your thoughts and ideas.

Often we feel isolated trapped and misunderstood. This is because we have not been able to communicate so that others truly understand us. We must take responsibility for how well others understand us and how eager they are to make us an integral part of their professional or personal lives. How often do arguments and misunderstandings end unresolved with the familiar phrase, "you just don't understand me"? It doesn't have to be this way for you. You can not only develop the ability to express yourself so others can understand, but you can learn to listen in such a way that other people find it relatively easy to be understood by you.

Tell it with gusto will show you the true communication fundamentals that can transform you as a communicator if you are willing to take the development of your skills as a communicator seriously. It's important. It's critically important for the person who wants to sell ideas with impact.

Have you bought the belief that you are not an exciting communicator? Are you convinced that you are not very persuasive? Do you believe you have a poor memory for quotes and interesting stories? Are you not as effective as you would like to be in front of groups because of nervousness and uninspiring delivery? Do you believe you are not a very good conversationalist? If you answered "yes" to any of these questions, then you have got to sell yourself right now on the belief that you can dramatically improve as a communicator. That's sale number four.

No one reading this book is predisposed to be a poor communicator. This is perhaps the easiest of all the seven OUTSELL factors to improve in quickly for the average person because we all have so many opportunities each day to work on our communication skills. Each day we go through a number of communication situations that can easily be turned into a skill-building adventure.

Sell yourself right now on the belief that you have the potential to be an exciting communicator, because you can. Great communication skills are essential if you want to OUTSELL in the impact zone. If you really want to be a high-power influencer then you've got to be able to not only communicate, but say what you have to say with gusto!

Gusto means expressing your message with pizzazz, with excitement, with enthusiasm. Gusto doesn't mean loud and obnoxious. There are times when telling it with gusto means soft or serious. It's more an intensity level than it is volume. When you express yourself with gusto, you have impact on your listener. Tell it with gusto means to bring vitality into the communication interactions you have each day, to be inspiring in the way you express yourself, and to help others to be better communicators, too.

What a relief it is to be in a business meeting with someone who brings life to the meeting with a relevant outlook, humor, and bold ideas. A person like that can improve the performance of everyone else around the table.

I was at a dinner party not long ago when the song "New York, New York" came on the stereo, sung by Liza Minelli. The room was infused with new energy. That's telling it with gusto! It's bringing what you have to say to life so that it is interesting and exciting to listen to.

Can you think of anything that has a greater impact on the way we experience our lives than our ability to communicate? If you are reading this book because you want to be better at getting your ideas across persuasively, credibly, and with impact and pizzazz, then grab your notebook, highlighter, and pen, because tell it with gusto is about the art of being a distinctive, memorable, and powerfully positive communicator.

Too often, people settle for a mediocre skill level when it comes to communication. We'll work like hell to get in shape or put in extra hours at work, but ask the average person (even ask the motivated non-average person!) what they did today to grow as a communicator and you will probably get a blank stare. What did you do today to significantly increase your communication impact, clarity, power, expressiveness, humor, and ability to make what you are saying interesting, memorable, and thought-provoking?

We're here to inspire you to become a great communicator so that you can become a communicator who inspires others. You can be a communicator who enjoys all the interactions of life and relishes the opportunity to help others be understood.

Think of the impact Winston Churchill had on England during the darkest moments of World War II because of his powerful speeches proclaiming that "we will never, never, never give up!" Great communication can change the lives of others, as did Lincoln's immortal Gettysburg address. A whole generation was moved by John F. Kennedy's words, "Ask not what your country can do for you, but what you can do for your country!" And it happens with less famous people every day, like the seventh-grade science teacher who turns on a class of 12-year-olds to the wonders of chemistry, or the project manager who with a few choice words during a meeting leads a team of engineers toward a breakthrough insight.

Become a Great Communicator: Your Happiness Depends on It

A huge amount of your happiness comes from your ability to communicate. Forget for a moment about the results and rewards that flow to the great communicators; let's just look at the little things we stumble upon every single day.

Every day, you exchange projects, new work, and interesting challenges with the people you work for and with. With each exchange, there is communication that can either enhance or diminish the quality of all that you do. When you are able to clearly understand what people are saying to you, you'll make less mistakes in their eyes. When you are able to be clearly understood, you'll get much more accurate assistance from others.

Imagine how much fun you would have if you were able to tell 10 humorous stories on the spur of the moment. How about if you were able to express your ideas in a meeting at work with more conviction, animation, and power? What about being able to come home and engage the people you love in a lively interaction about what happened during the day rather than the same old "life never changes much" dull conversation? How would you like to have the ability to put other people at ease and eagerly engage in conversation at a social gathering, party, or business lunch? How would your experience of the days change if you were able to speak to people in such a way as to inspire *them* to be more interesting, insightful, animated, and fun to listen to?

Good Communication Saves Time

There are very few time-saving strategies that I am aware of that will save you as much time as good communication. In Chapter 2 we talked about the architect who draws up plans for the construction project. How well those plans are communicated to the construction workers determines to a large extent how efficiently the project of building goes. The construction workers may be highly efficient workers, but if they misunderstand the plans because of poor communication, they will efficiently accomplish that which should not have been done at all.

When communication is not clear, it wastes your time and the time of the person you are speaking with. Consider the two people in this story:

It was the boss's birthday. He was an affluent man who had everything, so his employees decided to buy him something truly unique. They bought him a penguin! The next morning the boss called one of his employees into his office. "Please take this penguin to the zoo today," he told him, and the employee left with the penguin.

Later that afternoon, the employee came back to the boss's office with the penguin. The boss looked up from his desk, surprised. "I thought I told you to take this penguin to the zoo."

The employee looked at the boss, confused, "I did take him to the zoo and he enjoyed it so much that we're going to Disneyland tomorrow!"

This is the kind of useless activity that results from poor communication. How much time do we spend each day on activities that would have been unnecessary or possibly streamlined had we been able to communicate better? This wasted time takes us away from more important tasks, like working on our long-term vision, creating new ways to sell our ideas, and creating value for our company and customers.

Recently, we were printing a new brochure for our company. We worked with a graphic artist who had terrific technical skills but was a bit quiet and had difficulty expressing himself. He felt his work spoke for itself. We loved his designs and told him to print them with verbal and written instructions about various shades to be used. When we got the brochures, we were shocked at how the colors were much darker than what we had seen in his office. He was too. He said that he had failed to communicate clearly enough to the printer what needed to be done. As a result, he ate a $5,200 printing bill and had to invest more time getting it right.

Good communication skills solve problems, minimize errors, and, in the work environment, create more focused, profitable action.

Good Communication Improves Relationships

Much of the fun of work is experienced through our relationships with other people. When the relationships are supportive, enriching, and challenging in a positive way, our experience of the hours in the day is transformed. Communication plays a big role when it comes to the quality of our business (and personal) relationships. Our ability to say what we mean, listen, understand, and respond with clarity, conviction, and enthusiasm chisels away at the sculpture that ultimately becomes the relationship. Certainly, there are other very important factors, such as attitude, honesty, values, integrity, and so on, but without good communication skills there are bound to be a lot of unnecessary misunderstandings.

What happens when we say one thing to a customer and he or she hears something quite different? Perhaps a person with a new idea says, "I've got something new I'd like to show you," but the customer thinks, "You mean you've got something new to sell me" and replies, "We're busy right now. Please get back to me in a few months." An opportunity gets lost because somewhere in the interaction there was an ineffective transfer of enthusiasm, excitement, and information that would inspire the listener.

The same thing can happen in our personal lives, too. Fifteen years ago, I met my wife. She had recently moved to New York from Colombia and spoke very little English. My high-school Spanish was all but forgotten, so in the first few years, we were constantly miscommunicating with one another. We both had a poor vocabulary in the other person's language and no understanding of the endless nuances that characterize the way we phrase ourselves in our native language. I can reluctantly recall a long series of misunderstandings that were due simply to the fact that neither one of us really understood what the other person was saying. Little things would get blown up into big disagreements. Over the years I have seen the results of what happens as the quality of our communication steadily improved. A big part of that improvement is a direct result of the patience it took both of us in terms of making sure to understand the other person's point of view.

Good Communicators Can Wake People Up and Leave a Lasting Impact

A question I often ask of the audience at conventions I speak at is, "How many people have in the last six months seen an interesting, well-delivered presentation at work?" Rarely in a group of 500 or more do more than a few hands go up. I follow that question with, "How many people would agree that at least nine out of 10 of the presentations they see at work are boring?" Usually, everyone will raise a hand and occasionally both hands! I've been asking this question for at least five years and have seen the same response throughout. This is not a scientific survey, but it is accurate nonetheless from our viewpoint. When someone who can really communicate is in the limelight, it is a pleasure for the listeners. It wakes them up, brings energy into the room, and grabs people's attention.

Have you ever been driving late at night, feeling a little sleepy, and had a song come on the radio that you really like? It's amazing how we can get a burst of energy that can last well after the song is over. Great communication is like that. When listeners are interested and their attention is engaged, exciting things can happen.

The same thing can happen with a great theatrical performance. I was in New York not long ago and went to the theater to see a new Broadway show called *Smokey Joe's Cafe.* I was tired that night, but 10 minutes into the show I was mesmerized and filled with a buoyant energy that lasted hours after the show.

It can happen with books, too. I was recently in the emergency room of the hospital with a friend who was having kidney problems. I had to wait about two hours and was thoroughly bored. My friend had thrown a book into his bag before going to the hospital, and I picked it up and opened it. The book was *All I Really Need to Know I Learned in Kindergarten,* by Robert Fulghum. Within minutes I was laughing, filled with wonder, and at times tearful. This simple collection of stories is nothing short of a magnificent example of clear, powerful communication that can move the reader.

You, too, can have a powerful impact on your listener. Like many other skills we discuss in this book, it is a learned art and an art worth learning. You are reading this book because you want to have more influence and increase your impact and the ability to sell ideas and communicate, so the ability to tell it with gusto is a must-have item in your tool kit.

CONCENTRATE ON LISTENING FIRST

For some reason, when we think about communication, most of us initially think about the way we express ourselves. No doubt, this is a solid piece of the equation. The other half, though, and the half that has as great an impact on the quality of the communication that takes place (if not more!) is your ability to listen. Good listening skills will generate four significant benefits for you as a communicator:

1. You will learn faster.
2. You will improve the communication effectiveness of others.
3. You will create a receptive environment for your ideas.
4. You can tailor your message better.

Listening Is Learning

When you ask interesting questions that put people into a more animated, insightful mode, you learn more, faster. When people start sharing with you at a deeper level, you will have real attention-grabbing experiences and hear interesting stories that will fill you with new ideas. The more dynamic you can make the people around you, the faster you learn and the better time you have when you're around them. In business, you make the person speaking to you more aware of their own needs and concerns. In addition, your ability to recall your experiences will improve dramatically when what you hear is more interesting and engaging.

When you are sincerely listening to what another person has to say, you are in a learning mode. You are soaking up impressions, ideas, insights, and expressions. Too often, we tolerate listening rather than maximize it. Many people complain of a poor memory when, in effect, they more accurately are suffering from poor listening skills. When you listen deeply to other people you will fast-forward your learning pace.

Listening Impacts Others Too

On the most basic level, listening is becoming quiet enough to allow another person to speak. "I find people talk to me longer than they talk to other people," explains Nola Beldegreen, a success in advertising, "because they know I'm not in there trying to sell them, but I'm asking questions and I'm so attentive listening to them. Most people say they like to listen, but in reality they end up doing all the talking. People like to be listened to. In business, we're people dealing with people. We're not machines dealing with machines. We're people dealing with people, and you have to plug into that person and the way to do that is to make it a goal of yours."

The deeper level of listening, however, is generating in the person who is speaking a more exciting and enthusiastic message by asking insightful questions, showing genuine interest, and having an enthusiastic response. We can make other people much more interesting through better listening.

Listening Generates Receptiveness for Our Ideas

Great communicators have always understood that in order to truly influence a person with their ideas, they must first create a receptive environment for the ideas to be heard. Socrates, through his teaching style in ancient Greece, originated what is known as the Socratic method, which uses questions, instead of lecture alone, to transfer knowledge. The right questions create a more receptive and interesting learning environment. Listening is the way we prepare the soil for the seeds to grow. Often, people simply toss ideas (seeds) onto soil that is no more receptive (fertile) than an asphalt parking lot, and they end up frustrated and discouraged that their well-thought-out ideas, ideas that would work, are not accepted.

Of the "influence management" literature that has been written over the years, 90% hinges on the understanding that people become more receptive to our ideas when we demonstrate an interest and openness to their concerns first. We'll say it again: *People become more receptive to our ideas when we demonstrate an interest and openness to their ideas first.*

This simple truth can transform the way you communicate and the results you get with people if you will not only read it, but chew it up, digest it, and let it seep into your pores! It's not enough to just understand the concept; you've got to act on it or else a lot of the other ideas about communication we'll be showing you in this chapter will be useless.

"My philosophy is this," explains Mike Finizio, a top-producing stock broker. "At first you are not smart to the person you are trying to convince. You will be smart when you listen to them and find out everything about them. You may think you know everything, you may have gotten straight As in all your training classes, but it won't matter, because you are not smart yet, not until you really spend time with that person and find out what it is they want, fear, and hope for."

Many people, however, are overly eager to seize control of the conversation and start talking. They don't realize that this is the quickest way to alienate their listeners because often, what they are saying is not as relevant as it could be if they would take more time to understand the person they are speaking to. Remember this story when you feel the urge to proclaim your brilliance before you understand the perspective of the person with whom you are speaking:

A hungry mountain lion that came out of the hills attacked a bull and killed it. As it feasted on its kill, the lion paused from time to time to roar in triumph. He would stand and let everyone in the jungle know he was king. A hunter in the area heard the commotion, found the lion, and shot him dead. The moral of the story is: When you're full of bull, keep your mouth shut.

In most cases, when we are trying to be convincing, we are full of huzzonga until we listen to the person we are trying to convince and get smarter first.

Your Message Can Become More Effective When You Listen

The following insight gets to the heart of virtually every good selling process that is being taught in corporations today. When you listen first to the people you are trying to understand and eventually persuade, you become familiar with their language, their individual fears, and their concerns. That familiarity allows you to adapt and tailor your message effectively. You learn what to emphasize and what to ignore, where the hot spots are, and what is of little interest to your listener.

"I'm always amazed at how little most salespeople know about the people they do business with," explains Nola Beldegreen. "They know hardly anything about them as individuals, yet they expect this person to buy, to spend hundreds of thousands of dollars with them. They don't even know how this person thinks or feels. They have no idea what this person likes in their life. They might like vanilla and you keep giving them chocolate because you don't know what they like. This is very important. You have to know what their favorite flavor is."

Everyone is motivated differently. When you understand what it is that does motivate a person and learn to tap into it, you can expect action to follow.

A man lost his valuable hunting dog and placed an ad in the local newspaper offering a $500 reward. He waited several days and got no reply at all. Frustrated, he called the newspaper office. "I want to speak to the advertising manager," he said into the phone.

"She's out of the office," the receptionist replied.

"Well, then, let me talk to her assistant."

"He's out also."

"Okay, let me talk to the editor."

"The editor is out of the office too."

"All right, let me talk to the editor's assistant."

"Sorry, he's out too."

"You mean to tell me there is nobody there?" the man asked.

"Nope," replied the receptionist.

The frustrated man asked, "Where are they?"

The receptionist replied, "Well, they're all out looking for your dog!"

In this example, the $500 reward was the motivating factor, but you'll never know what it is that motivates the person you are speaking to with certainty until you learn to listen effectively first. Dave Doehr, a highly successful leader in telecommunications, explains, "As a manager, most of what I sell people on now are ideas and concepts, and I've found that if you're going to be persuasive, the first thing you have to do is get into the other person's shoes. If I can understand their position from their shoes, then I've got a much better chance of getting them to see it from mine. You've got to know their position first."

Listening? Maybe You Find People Boring!

Hey, listening is great and you may have a sincere desire to be a good listener, but what happens if everyone you listen to is dull, boring, and uninspiring? Whose fault is it? When people are boring you, who is to blame? Is it possible that you have become as boring a listener as the people around you have become as talkers? Do you ask interesting questions that challenge people to think, to stretch, to open up? Or are you rather passive in your listening? Sure, some people are painfully difficult to listen to, but they are, in reality, a relatively small group.

Larry King, the legendary talk-show host is considered by many to be one of the greatest conversationalists of all time. He is able to speak effectively with virtually anyone, from any country, on most any subject. He writes about communication in his book *How to Talk to Anyone* and cites as one of his basic attributes of good communication the principle of "take an interest in the other person."

After teaching hundreds of classes on communication and observing thousands of professional men and women interact in the classroom and on the breaks preparing and delivering presentations, going through communications exercises, and conducting problem-solving meetings, it is generally easy to spot the person that the class will come to see as the natural leader. It's usually the person who is genuinely interested in what others have to say. The key word here is *genuine*. When a person develops a genuine interest in others they bring a lot of value to the people they are listening to. They give them the feeling that what they have to say is valuable. When you give a person the gift of feeling important in a sincere way, you are naturally going to be in a position to be a powerful influencer.

To really listen, it takes a curious attitude combined with a willingness to get personal without being offensive and nosy. It's a delicate balance, but not that difficult to find if you work at it. Curiosity begins when you take the focus off yourself and put it on the world around you.

A lot has been said about this thing called active listening, as though it is a formula of well-timed head nods, smiles, and encouraging verbal grunts! Well, that's about 1.1% of what it really means to be an active listener. The beauty of being the listener is that you can truly control the flow of the conversation, the direction that it takes, and the level of intensity and seriousness as well. Most of us, however, are rather passive, preferring instead to be on guard for the moment where we can jump in and say something. Herein lies the biggest problem in human communication. Most of us are too eager to speak to be good communicators. We have got to master and, more importantly, learn to enjoy the active element of listening in order to be as persuasive as our potential will allow us.

The key to enjoying listening rather than just getting good at it and tolerating it as a "necessary evil" is in the way we ask questions. It's developing an outlook that says, "I'm going to find out what turns this person on and ask questions that let her talk with excitement so that I can really enjoy this conversation!" It's about challenging the person you are speaking with. It's about being a little provocative without being offensive.

Get Rid of Distractions

Often, we find ourselves wishing we were somewhere else right in the middle of a conversation. Our eyes start jetting around the room, our ears tune into a nearby conversation, and we tune out the person we are with. Two single friends of mine, Gene and Larry, went out for a drink at a popular bar not long ago. I was listening to Larry's description of the evening. "Going out with Gene is always a tough experience because he's always paying more attention to the scenery than the conversation. When he sees a pretty girl he'll poke me in the arm and point her out, and it went on like that all night. The next morning when I woke up and took my shirt off to get in the shower, my arm looked like a bruised-up 10-day-old banana."

Paying more attention to the surroundings than the person you are speaking with is a great way to alienate people and throw out vibes that repel everyone in the room. Instead, be the one person in the room who is transfixed by the conversation you are in, oblivious to what is going on

around you. Treat each person, each conversation, with a level of atten-
tiveness that vaporizes outside distractions, and you'll be shocked at how
quickly your influence index shoots up.

On the other hand, if you are a person who is easily distracted, you are
going to prevent people who want to help you from developing a relationship with you. Not long ago, we were hired to help improve sales for a
brokerage office in Los Angeles. The sales manager was a very nice guy,
but he was always distracted whenever we would get together to help him
solve his problem. As a result, our time together was always unfocused,
interrupted, and the environment was rushed so that true understanding
and problem-solving couldn't be nourished. It's hard to believe that his
problems will change much until he is able to focus on them and solve
them one at a time with uninterrupted concentration. And you have probably had to deal with people just like this in business. Imagine how difficult it is to develop good relationships when you are constantly distracted.

Many years ago I noticed an interesting effect, which I've witnessed
countless times since, that enthusiastic listening has on business meetings. I was in a meeting with about six other people and was listening to
an idea that I found very interesting. I guess it showed in my facial expressions and body language. As a result, in this meeting, the person presenting the idea started to spend most of his time looking at and speaking
to me to a point that near the end of his presentation, it was as if we were
having a one-on-one conversation. Now, in meetings, I try and show support and enthusiasm as a listener and find, more times than not, that the
person who is talking will develop rapport with me and will become more
animated as a result.

Another form of distraction is filtering a person's message to the point
of being unable to really understand what they are saying. When we do
this we are often listening in order to respond instead of to understand.
We jump to conclusions too early and assume we know more about the
person who we are communicating with than they do. This quickly alien-
ates the other person and fractures rapport. When rapport is lost, forget
about influence. Observe the two people in the following story:

> Once, there was a man, Bill, who had a cabin in the mountains. Every Sat-
> urday morning he would climb into the cockpit of his black Porsche sports
> car and drive to his cabin on a very dangerous road filled with blind curves,
> unguarded drop-offs and tricky turns. But Bill was not bothered by danger.
> After all, he had a great car to drive, was an excellent driver, and knew the

road by heart. He was coming up to one of his favorite blind curves. He slowed down, shifted gears, and put on the brakes in preparation for the turn that was about 200 yards away. All of a sudden, from around the turn, came a car screeching out of control. The car nearly went off the cliff, but at the last second its driver pulled the car back onto the road and swerved into Bill's lane, back into its own lane and back into our Bill's lane again. "My God," Bill thought, "I am going to be hit," so he slowed almost to a stop. The car came roaring toward him, swerving back and forth. Just before it was about to hit Bill, at the last moment the car swung back into the other own lane. As the car screeched past him, a beautiful woman stuck her head out of the car and shouted "PIG" to him as loudly as she could. "How dare she call me that!" Bill thought. He was incensed by her accusation. In reply, he yelled at her "SOW!" as she careened down the road. "I was in my lane. She was the one all over the place," he said to himself. Then he began to get control of his rage. He smiled and was pleased that at least she didn't get away without his stinging retort. "I got back at her," he thought smugly. And with that he put the accelerator to the floor, raced around the blind curve, and ran into a pig.

When we form conclusions too quickly based on a less than complete understanding of what our communication partner is saying, we can make the very same mistake.

Stop Interrupting

> There is an art in silence, and there is an eloquence in it too.
>
> —Cicero

A big enemy of rapport and good communication is interruption. The average conversation is a fast-paced game of "how can I cut in and say what *I* want to say?" It's as though a nanosecond pause to take a breath is a reason to interrupt and gain the conversational spotlight.

I was working with a division of American Express several years ago on a project to improve customer service. I met with the vice president in charge of the telephone service unit and gained some interesting insights on the destructive power of interrupting. American Express measured each complaint call carefully in that unit, and they had, through analysis, determined that the average person with a strong complaint can really lay into the customer service representative for about 25 seconds before they run out of gas—unless they are interrupted. If the customer service representative interrupted, even politely, before the customer got finished expressing their aggravating complaint, the length of the complaint was likely to go on for another full minute after the interruption.

This same phenomenon is true in most human interaction. The average conversation consists of a blistering series of cuts, stops, and starts initiated by people eager to get to the end of what the other person is talking about and into what they want to say. When we give the person we are talking with the feeling they are not being heard and understood because we constantly interrupt, they develop an even stronger urge to talk more and become even more assertive in interrupting us.

Why not be different? Allow the people you talk to get to the end of their thought before you add to the conversation. Ask an extra question or two before jumping in with your comment. Practice the one-second rule, which says that you only speak in a conversation following one second of pure silence. That discipline will allow you to give people the feeling that they are not being rushed. They'll slow down and stop interrupting you as much too. When you are locked into conversation with someone who still interrupts you mercilessly, simply excuse yourself or explain to them that you appreciate their curiosity but find it hard to communicate when you can't finish your sentences. The one-second pause technique is fabulous if you want to be a great listener.

About five years ago, I learned a powerful lesson about listening. I was giving a talk on interpersonal skills, and the topic was listening. A friendly woman in the front row of a filled 300-seat auditorium asked me if I thought I was a good listener. I was a little on the spot and thought for a moment. "I think I am. I've worked hard at it," I replied.

"How do you know?" she asked.

That question stopped me dead in my tracks. Driving home from the talk I thought about it and determined the only way to really know is to ask someone you speak with frequently. They know. At dinner that night, I turned to my 13-year-old daughter and said, "Paula, I'm going to ask you a question and I want you to be completely honest with me when you answer. Do you think I'm a good listener?"

I knew I was in trouble when she paused, judging the weight of what she was about to say. "Well, Dad, not always," she said.

I felt blood rushing to my face. "Well, what I mean, Dad," she continued, noticing my reaction, "I mean you ask us a lot of questions and stuff and you do listen and let me talk a lot, but . . ." she paused again, looking for an accurate choice of words. "Well, a lot of times I can tell when you are listening that you are thinking about something else, like work or something, and you're not really listening. You're distracted."

I was devastated. All those patient years of encouraging her to talk! I could hardly believe what she was saying. I thought back over the last several days to remember if Paula and I had had a disagreement that she was now getting back at me for. I searched for a reason to prove her wrong.

I looked over at my six-year-old son for help. "She's right, Dad, you do that a lot."

It was then that I realized listening requires us to give the person we are speaking to our undivided attention—mind, body, and soul. People notice.

"As a manager," explains David Achzet, a manager for a large delivery company, "I have to really listen before I try and persuade people. I have to know their thinking, their values, goals, and desires. Once you understand that, it becomes a much easier process to persuade people. The most important thing to know is what's in it for them, for the person you're trying to persuade. If you're trying to propose something to them that doesn't bring any value to them in their eyes or mind, then you're not going to be able to persuade anybody to do anything. So, the first real fundamental step is to listen and really understand what the person you're talking to is saying. Next, once you think you understand what they're saying, repeat it back, and get confirmation from them that you've understood properly. That will generate even more variations because sometimes the person you're talking with doesn't always clearly communicate. So once you play it back to them, then they get a chance to clarify their message even more."

How good are you at listening, at eliminating all distractions? There's one sure way to find out. Ask some people that you interact with regularly. Ask your family, your friends, and colleagues that you trust, and listen to what they say. Be open, ask for suggestions, and, above all, be nondefensive. This is feedback that will help you build self-awareness.

Be Observant

Listening is being observant, it's noticing the entire person you are communicating with, it's taking in their complete message. A lot has been said about eye contact and, yes, it's important, but don't lock on so tightly to those little black spots that you miss the body language, the facial expressions, the mouth of the person talking to you. It's much more interesting to observe curiously (not analyze mind you!) than to simply maintain effective eye contact. Once again, too many people have attended programs that hammer on about the virtues of eye contact to the point that they are practicing eye lock. This makes people nervous and can even create unhealthy stress in both people. Take it all in. Challenge yourself to notice more. Try to remember what each person you speak with is wearing. Notice the jewelry of the person you are talking to. Take a look at the print on the tie. What is unique about the eye color of the person you are talking to? Soak it up!

You can increase the depth of your relationships by becoming interested in others rather than finding fault in them. Everybody has something unique to contribute, as this story illustrates:

A store owner was tacking a sign above his door that read, "Puppies for Sale." Signs like that have a way of attracting small children and, sure enough, a little boy appeared under the store owner's sign. "How much are you going to sell the puppies for?" he asked.

"Anywhere from $30 to $50," the store owner replied. The little boy reached into his pocket and pulled out some change. "I have $2.37," the little boy said and continued, "Can I please look at them?"

The store owner smiled and whistled, and out of the kennel came Lady, who ran down the aisle of his store followed by her five teeny, tiny balls of fur. One puppy was lagging considerably behind. Immediately, the little boy singled out the lagging, limping puppy and said, "What's wrong with that little dog?"

The store owner explained that the veterinarian had examined the little puppy and had discovered it didn't have a hip socket. It would always limp. It would always be lame. The little boy became excited. "That is the little puppy that I want to buy."

The store owner said, "No, you don't want to buy this little dog. If you really want him, I'll just give him to you."

The little boy got quite upset. He looked straight into the store owner's eyes, pointed his finger, and said, "I don't want you to give him to me. That little dog is worth every bit as much as all the other dogs, and I'll pay full price. In fact, I'll give you $2.37 now, and 50 cents a week until I have him paid for."

The store owner countered, "You really don't want to buy this little dog. He is never going to be able to run and jump and play with you like the other puppies."

> To this, the little boy reached down and rolled up his pant leg to reveal a badly twisted, crippled left leg supported by a big metal brace. He looked up at the store owner and softly replied, "Well, I don't run so well myself and that little puppy will need someone who understands."

Sometimes, we need to really put ourselves in another person's shoes and forget our initial reaction or impression of them in order to really understand what they are saying. This is what empathy is all about.

Multiply the Value of the Speaker

You can make the people you interact with much more interesting if you ask them interesting questions. People often appear dull because we are not challenging them to talk on topics that bring out their more interesting sides. This is the key to creating more interesting and useful conversation.

Consider these questions the next time you meet someone new:

- What's the most interesting project you've ever worked on?
- What was the biggest traveling hassle you've ever been through?
- What do you find to be your biggest business challenge?
- How did you get into the work you are doing now?
- What is your favorite hobby? How did you get into it? What do you like most about it?
- If you could take two paid years off to study anything you would want, what would it be? Why? How did you get interested in it?
- What are your career goals?
- What changes would you make in your company if you were totally in charge?
- If you could speak to anyone who has ever walked the face of the earth for one hour, who would it be? What would you ask them?

Not long ago, I had a dinner meeting with a manager who was one of our customers. Before that dinner, he seemed overly reserved and restrained in the way he expressed himself. During the dinner, I started asking him questions about some of the challenges he had had in his life during the last year. He revealed that it was one of the most stressful years of his life due to the loss of a loved one, some serious turnover on his sales team, and the constant pressure of meeting goals that were very challenging. He opened up and shared his fears, anxieties, and pent-up frustration. He seemed relieved to get it out and talk to somebody about it. I have noticed that since that dinner, he has developed a lot more confidence because he is beginning to feel more in control again.

When you ask good questions and really listen, you give people an opportunity to transcend their problems. There are people that you touch every single day who would really benefit from a little attention from you. You can help people blossom with your ability to listen. Why wait? Start today.

Wake people up with your curiosity. Curiosity is powerful! Be a challenging listener and you'll be shocked how easy it is to become truly interested. When you look at the faces of some people trying to listen (fresh from a listening strategy seminar, no doubt!), you get the feeling they are exasperated, experiencing inner pain, and forging their internal fortitude and tolerance. That's not the way it should be. Make people around you more interesting by bringing out the interesting side of them. And, yes, virtually everyone does have a fascinating side. "What do you find fascinating?" is a great question you can use with someone almost anywhere. Often, we play it too safe with questions. If we ask, however, simply curious to discover the answer rather than agree or disagree, then we find that everyone has a more passionate side, a side that is stimulating to listen to. It takes courage to stop fulfilling the dull expectations of others. Step out of your normal box. Be different.

Master the Artful Summary

An important communication technique to master is the ability to summarize not only what you are saying but what you are observing in what others have said. Conversation often needs a summary to get it back on track. Meetings need constant summaries in order to keep them on schedule. A good summary capsulizes what is being said into bullet points. You can change the focus of a conversation by summarizing and redirecting. Let's say you are meeting with someone who keeps going on and on and on and you can't get them to stop. At some point, call time out and say, "Bill, just so I am clear on what you are saying, may I summarize what I've heard so far." Add your summary, ask for agreement, then steer the conversation to a direction you would like it to take with a question like this, "Now that we've established these three points, let's move the focus in a different direction. What are your feelings on . . ."

"A great communication technique I use," explains Molly Williamson, a successful sales professional, "is to summarize what I think I heard the other person say. That is the most incredible, easy tool that I've ever come across. For instance, 'Did I understand that you said that you feel this way? Is that exactly how you said it happened? I want to understand exactly what you're saying.' You can see people's shoulders go down and just breathe again because they know they've been heard because you're reflecting what they just said."

When you work on summarizing, you will increase your ability to be an attentive listener. You cannot summarize without paying close attention to what is going on, and that is the hidden secret of why summarizing works so well. It shows others that you are paying attention, often closer than they are. I was at a strategic planning meeting when the CEO of the company I was working for ended his opening remarks, which had gone on for 20 minutes. He asked the rest of us for feedback and I said, "Based on these five points you made . . ." and went down my list, "it looks to me like we should go in this direction." He turned to me and said, "Can you give me a copy of those points please, Mike?" I had helped him organize his thinking and had learned a valuable lesson. When we can make sense of what others are saying and organize it for them through a summary, we are paying them a valuable compliment.

When making a formal presentation, you need to summarize your message every 10 to 15 minutes to refresh the listener's attention and should always summarize before your closing remarks. The mark of an experienced speaker is when the audience is able to summarize the key points of the speech almost as accurately as the speaker did.

ENOUGH ON LISTENING; ON TO SPEAKING

There does come a point in any persuasive dialogue when you will need to deliver your ideas and, regardless of what you may have heard anywhere else, this is a must-have ability. You need to punch your ideas out with gusto in order to reach the highest level of influence. Let's talk about what it takes to shine when the spotlight is on you.

The Four Expression Inhibitors

There are four inhibitors that diminish your ability to express yourself with maximum impact:

1. fear
2. stress and anxiety
3. low energy
4. constrained delivery

First, we'll look at each of these inhibitors, then we'll suggest some ways to overcome them.

The fear inhibitor

Fear can cause the other three inhibitors, but, more importantly, it can prevent communication from even taking place. Fear can cause us to not even show up for the game. We can react to fear in one of two ways: We can retreat or we can charge ahead. When it comes to expressing yourself, you have got to sell yourself on the belief that overcoming your fear is the only way to go. Stop playing it safe. Get involved in some activities that can put you face to face with your fear. Take more risks today with the people you communicate with.

These are the three characteristics of fearful communicators:

1. *They don't participate well.* These people hold back in meetings, avoid the spotlight, and avoid visibility. They don't take the risks that can lead to success and influence.

2. *They participate in a muted way.* These people, when they communicate, seem to be talking through a foggy cloud. They lack enthusiasm and intensity in their communication and don't speak with the level of conviction that they feel inside.

3. *They play it safe and imitate.* These people say what they think other people want to hear, even when those thoughts aren't their own. They are afraid of being wrong in other people's eyes. The problem here is that these people will increasingly bring less and less value to the table as they become more and more imitators and not originals.

The stress and anxiety inhibitor

Stress, or the way we react to stress, can have a similar impact as fear, but stress is more likely to diminish our effectiveness in high-pressure situations if we let it. Here are the four characteristics of people who suffer from stress-inhibited communication:

1. *Preoccupied.* They are thinking about events other than what is happening now. More concentration is given to the future or past than the present moment, which causes them to think about negative consequences and outcomes.
2. *Lower caliber of concentration.* Extreme stress can severely limit attention span and ability of the individual to concentrate. Often, people preparing for a major presentation are not even able to prepare until the last minute because the mere thought of the stressful situation makes them feel unable to tackle it. This last-minute preparation usually produces less-than-astounding results.
3. *Physically uncontrollable reactions.* Sweaty palms, high-pitched voice, stiff gestures, and distracting nervousness characterize these people. These reactions distract the listener and display a lack of self-confidence.
4. *Muddled thinking and havoc with memory.* These people draw blanks, forget key points, and are unable to be clear, concise, and convincing. They seem unconvinced themselves, and the logic of what they are saying gets disconnected from the primary message they are trying to communicate.

The best way to deal with stress—there is no way we have found to eliminate it—is to channel it positively. Let stress be a charge of enthusiasm into your system. Great stage performers often say that prior to their performance they feel a lot of stress, often uncomfortable stress, and they also say that it is a good sign. It is precisely that stress that allows them to lift their performance to a higher level. This can happen to you, too, if you let it.

The low-energy inhibitor

Low energy is frequently the cause of dull, uninspiring business presentations. Low energy may result because the person speaking is low energy themselves or unable to notch it up a bit to suit the occasion. The low-energy communicator may actually be confident and comfortable, but boring. This is why the under-construction approach is so critical. To be a high-impact communicator, you need energy. Under construction will slowly but surely build your energy and personal power to a level that will enhance your communication, instead of inhibit it. It's difficult to be a high-energy communicator when you are a low-energy person.

History is littered with people with great ideas but no ability to express them. In his autobiography, *Iacocca,* Lee Iacocca explains, "I've known a lot of guys that had great ideas but couldn't explain them to a board." He goes on to say that developing his speaking skills was one of the major keys to his success, and not a skill he was naturally good at, either.

The constrained delivery inhibitor

To be a good communicator, we need to have flexibility and fluidity when we express ourselves. Our voices need to be able to increase in volume and recess to tones of a whisper. We need to be able to speed up and slow down and to speak in different voices so we can, at times, play the characters that can bring a point to life. Having only one way to express yourself doesn't allow you to adapt to others and apply good interpersonal skills.

Stiffness limits the range we can cover as communicators. When our voice is stiff, our gestures will probably be stiff as well. When put into pressure situations confident people will often stiffen, become overly cautious, conservative, and, as a result, dull. A stiff communicator strips the listeners of energy in a similar way as the low-energy person.

Learn to Flip on the Switch!

Now that we've spent some time reviewing what happens with poor communication, we need to look closely at what we can do to improve and to avoid these mistakes. First, we need to be able to flip on the switch when we need it, to crank up the message. If we are operating at a 5 energy level (on a scale of 1 to 10, 10 being highest) most of the time, then in those critical communication situations, we need to raise it to 7, 8, or even 9 or 10 at times. This is called range, and you've got to develop it. The desire to develop it comes first, and, once you have the desire, the rest will come relatively quickly.

"Being a persuasive person has a lot to do with the packaging and way you carry yourself," explains Chip Sollins, president of American Pool Service. "What you say, how you believe in what you say, and your self-confidence determine how persuasive you are. My own personal passion is what makes me a persuasive person. Last night I had 20 minutes at a meeting to make my presentation, and I believe in my company so much that I exude that belief. And I get people to believe in it by my believability and my own passion. I sweep them in with my own excitement. I've never lost a contract when I go in and sell it myself because of that belief. It always works."

There are defining moments in our lives that come frequently at times, at other times infrequently. It is in these moments that we need to be able to stand tall, flip on the switch and tell it the way we see it. When we do that we are taking bold action, and bold action is the mark of leadership.

Communicate the Truth

There are people who seemingly have all the ingredients to be powerful communicators but never really get there. They often come up short in one crucial area: They develop the habit of overstating or exaggerating the truth and, as a result, their message is not credible. It's like the little boy in this story:

> Little Johnny always came to school upbeat and positive. Every Monday at Johnny's school, they had a sharing time in class where the students would share something positive about their weekend. Little Johnny always had great things to say, and one day when it was his turn, he was grinning like he had walked through a swinging door on somebody else's push. He stood up and said to the class, "Me and my daddy went fishing this weekend and caught 75 catfish that weighed 15 pounds a piece!"
>
> The teacher said, "No way, I don't believe it. What if I were to tell you on my way to school today I came up against a 1,200-pound grizzly that was about to attack me. Right before he got to me, an eight-pound dog jumped on him, beat him up, and sent him off running into the woods. Would you believe me?"
>
> "Yes," Johnny replied, "That's my dog!"

It's possible to be optimistic and positive without stretching the truth and destroying your credibility. When you develop a reputation for changing the facts a bit to suit your taste, all the techniques in the world will not help you. Instead, commit yourself to telling it the way it really is, even if there are short-term consequences.

Some of you may recall the frightening Tylenol scare back in the 1980s when somebody decided to poison the pain relief capsules in Tylenol bottles and put them back on the shelves in stores to be bought by unsuspecting consumers. It was refreshing to see the CEO of the company that made Tylenol stand up immediately and recall all Tylenol bottles in an effort to protect consumers. Many people thought that bold action would actually create a negative public relations incident with people switching to other brands. In fact, this immediate and truthful action proved over time to strengthen the Tylenol name, improve sales, and has certainly been a story shared at many a business conference on the ideal way to handle a consumer crisis. When you face a crisis you, too, need to be honest and up-front and communicate those feelings as quickly as possible, because it is the right thing to do. In the end, when you do the right thing, you have nothing to be afraid of.

Listen to Inspiring Communicators

Who do you consider to be a good communicator? Maybe you can find some tapes of speakers, preachers, teachers, or politicians whom you admire. Listen to their style and how they make their points. Listen to the stories they tell and then practice telling them. Sometimes you have to tell a story a dozen times before you can really tell it well.

The network news anchors are usually very good communicators. Observe the way they phrase their words, the time they take to pause, and how slight intonations of voice can communicate much more than words alone.

When you watch a daytime talk show, notice how the mood and energy of the host impacts the guest, the audience, and you, the viewer.

Many inspiring communicators have audiocassette programs available. If you live in a large metropolitan area like Los Angeles, Washington, D.C., San Francisco, Miami, or Chicago, you probably spend a considerable amount of time in your car, because these are the five heaviest traffic areas in the country. Turn this traffic time into productive time and listen to the great communicators.

Talk about the Books You Read

Remember back in fourth grade when you had to give a book report? The same activity can dramatically increase your ability to articulate complex ideas in a simple way. With the next book you read, arrange to meet with someone and try to explain the key points and what you got out of it. Talk about what you agree with, what you disagree with, and what you learned that you can use. You can do the same thing with movies and, occasionally, with television shows too.

I like to run by the beach where I live in California. Often, when I run with my partner, we talk about the latest books we've read, and I find it very challenging to explain what I found to be the true meaning of the book. It forces me to think deeply about what I want to say and to organize my thoughts. As I articulate my thoughts it brings the meaning of the book to a much higher level and, as a result, my retained knowledge increases. It also makes the run go more quickly.

Learn Another Language

Learning a new language is another way to improve your communication skills. Although it is quite a commitment, look at the benefits. You'll dramatically expand your memory skills and your understanding of words and how they work. You'll be able to communicate with many people whom you will never reach in your native language. What a boost to your confidence it will be for you to be skilled in more than one language. This could also open up international business opportunities for you in the future.

Build an Outstanding Vocabulary

If you want to excel at selling ideas, then you must master the art of using language. The more word choices you have, the more precise and concise you can be. Shakespeare is reported to have had an active vocabulary of over 10,000 words, yet the average adult uses less than 1,000 words in 80% of their communication. Imagine how much better you could be at expressing yourself accurately if you could increase your active vocabulary by 50%. Here's an easy way to do it; just learn one new word a day. That's it, just one a day. Open the dictionary to any page and look for an interesting word you don't ordinarily use. Don't look for words that no one but you could possibly be familiar with, because that will turn people off. Look for a word that you're familiar with but that you don't ordinarily use. Put it on a three-by-five card and make a couple of notes about its meaning. Put it in your pocket, near your money, or in your wallet, somewhere to remind you during the day to use it. At the end of the day, put the three-by-five card with the others you have used and review them from time to time. Over a period of years you will build an extraordinary vocabulary and will have a much greater ability to choose and use words that get results.

Keep a dictionary by your side when you read. Look up words you don't recognize and, again, write them down on three-by-five cards as indicated above.

Throw Yourself into Your Message

To influence, to be convincing, to impact people beneath the logic level, you have got to develop the capacity to throw yourself into your message. Too often, we hold back, leaving our listener unsure that we really believe in what we are saying. People who put their all into what they are saying are more interesting to listen to, more entertaining. I was listening to Bob Farrell, the founder of Farrell's Ice Cream Parlors, explain the secret of their success. It was one of the most inspiring and motivating speeches I have ever heard. His talk was so moving because he threw himself into it with such enthusiasm, and I'll never forget his message. He related that at Farrell's, every birthday had to be treated with absolute importance because every kid was there on the most important day of their year with the most important people in their lives. The "Happy Birthday" chorus had to be sung by the employees knowing this was the only time this child had this year to celebrate his or her birthday. It is with this commitment to serving each customer that Farrell built his ice cream parlors. And we need to put that type of enthusiasm into our message.

When you are entertaining, you can capture and hold people's attention, which is the gateway to influence. If what you're saying is worth saying at all, it's worth saying with gusto. Sink into your message with all of your might! Be passionate!

To get a feeling for what it really means to dive into your message, rent a couple of Jack Nicholson movies like *One Flew Over the Cuckoo's Nest, The Witches of Eastwick,* or *A Few Good Men* and observe how he relishes every word he speaks. He's a master of gusto-filled communication and is thus able to play powerful characters.

Be Physical, Emotional, and Logical

Having well-thought-out ideas that make sense and are communicated to appeal *exclusively* to our logical nature is not always the most effective way to communicate. We may kid ourselves into thinking that being logically sound is all that matters, because this is generally the safest way to communicate. But, like many things in life, the path with the least risk is also the path with the least rewards. Satisfying logical concerns is important. Getting the numbers right and correctly analyzing all the data is important, but this is just the foundation when we master the higher art of communication. The real influence happens when you use that foundation as your support and then communicate with emotional power and express yourself with physical freedom. Concentrate solely on logic, analysis, and data and your message will most likely be stiff, dull, and uninspiring. You'll lose people's attention and come across as overly technical. It is more powerful to inspire than to convince, to excite rather than explain. Set higher goals for yourself when you speak. Accomplish more than just relaying information. Influence with emotion and the full expression of your physical self!

Incidents and Analogies Are Important

What makes people painfully dull and uninteresting is not only the message itself, but the way the message is expressed. Most people depend heavily on their opinions and an approach that says, "Believe me because I checked it out and this is my opinion." This approach would probably work well for Einstein or Ghandi, but you and I need a lot of credibility before our opinions will carry the kind of weight that is necessary when we rely exclusively on unsubstantiated opinions. This is only one of several methods we can use to influence people, but we shouldn't use it too frequently because it isn't the most powerful way to influence people—not even close.

A much more powerful way to make a point is to draw from your own life experiences to illustrate your ideas. You can use the experiences of your life as the primary source of your most persuasive ammunition, and the beauty of it is, you already know them! We can package a point in an incident that is more interesting to tell, more interesting to listen to, and a better launching pad for a memorable point, too. Notice how in the next two examples an incident can bring communication to life. Both examples are a way of me trying to convince you of the same point.

Example 1:
One of the things I would like to convince you to do is to be discreet in what you say and where you say it. You never know who could be lis-

tening in and how they could influence your results. If you do this, you can avoid embarrassing moments.

Example 2:

　　Early in my selling career, I was on a call with another salesperson, going to see a gentleman we had met several times already, but were unable to close. It was an appointment first thing in the morning and we strode into the building where his office was, joking about some idiosyncracies of the person we were going to meet. This fellow was a fanatic about neatness. His office could easily have been an executive model showroom. It appeared as though every item on his desk had been neatly measured and placed to create perfect geometry and symmetry. It was hard to imagine the guy actually working in there, for it seemed to us he spent all of his time arranging stuff. We hopped in the elevator and an older woman stood quietly in one corner. We continued talking and joking. "I remember the last time I met with him," I said. "I accidentally nudged something on his desk out of its place and he immediately put it back exactly where it had been. It seemed to unnerve him." My colleague shook his head in disbelief. "I swear to you it's true," I continued. "When you show him our proposal, accidentally move something on his desk and see how he reacts." We laughed together and the elevator door swung open. To our surprise, the woman who was on the elevator with us stepped off and into the same office we were going to. She walked back into the hallway while we stopped at the receptionist. A moment later, the very same woman appeared from the hallway and escorted us back to her boss's office. Needless to say, we didn't make the sale and were never invited back! I urge you to be discreet, especially when joking about others.

See the difference? As a reader, what is your experience of the two examples? If you could see me tell it with all of the facial expressions and gestures, then you can magnify the impact times two. This is what we mean by using incidents. Why just express an opinion when you can bring that position to life with a real-life example that people can relate to? The human level is where emotion resides, emotion that when you tap into it is the most persuasive power of all. When you are speaking from experience, your emotion comes out because you can throw yourself into what you are saying. This impacts the listener in a way that is unique and powerful.

Many years ago, Charles Laughton, the famous English actor, was touring America, giving Bible-reading demonstrations. He was a Shakespearean actor with considerable dramatic skill.

Once, after reading in a small midwestern community in a large rural church, Laughton's audience was totally and completely silent. It was almost as if God had made a special trip and was there amidst the congregation. After what seemed like an eternity, a man about 70 years old stood up and asked for permission to read the Bible. It was granted by the pastor and, as the old man started to read, it was apparent he was no Shakespearean actor. He did not have the voice, the elocution, or the diction of the great Charles Laughton. As he read, however, it became completely obvious to everyone present that if this had been a Bible-reading contest, the great actor would have finished a distant second. When the evening was over, a reporter went to Charles Laughton and asked what his reaction was to the old man's reading. Laughton thought for a moment, looked at the reporter, and said, "Well, I knew the script, and I knew it well, but the old man knew the Author."

The power that the old man in the story was able to tap into, the power of really knowing the message through personal experience, gives an extra boost of credibility and enthusiasm. This is exactly what happens to each of us when we speak from experience and use incidents more frequently.

To be able to use incidents effectively, you need to first take an inventory of the memorable experiences of your life. Here is an exercise to help you accomplish just that. Think back for a moment and on a blank sheet of paper make the following lists:

- List several significant learning experiences from your business career.
- What sacrifices have you made in order to get to where you are today?
- List the five most significant accomplishments of your life, along with a memorable incident that happened along the way to each accomplishment.
- What challenges have you had to overcome to get to where you are today?
- Who are the people who have had the most positive impact on your life? What was the most memorable thing that happened with them?
- What were the most meaningful experiences you have had and what specifically happened?
- What were the most important decisions you have made in your life? Why were they so important?

- What are the things you have done that give an indication of your character?

With each item on the list, make notes about the incident that most clearly illustrates what happened. Then, make notes about the point of the story. Now, you are ready to practice telling the incident. Practice with people you meet every day, because when you use incidents to express your opinions and point of view, they'll be much more interested in what you have to say. Try it and you'll see how this simple technique can literally transform the way you communicate.

Let's imagine that you need to make a point with a customer of yours about the extra value they receive from you and your organization. Why not think of an incident that you lived through where you learned firsthand the importance of not cutting corners? Or, the next time you have to make a group presentation, start off with an incident that clearly illustrates the main point you want the listeners to remember. Time and time again, we find that a listener will forget most of the facts and virtually all of the data from a group presentation. What they do remember are the stories, anecdotes, analogies, examples, and incidents—so use them!

When you can quickly recall the experiences of your life and use them as part of your communication package, you will become much more interesting. Many of us, however, have forgotten, at least temporarily, many of the important incidents of our lives. To be a great communicator, you need self-awareness, and you build self-awareness by gaining a fuller understanding of all of the events that stand out in your life. Take an inventory of all these events and write them out. To be a great communicator takes work, it takes self-mastery. We call this step taking a life-experience inventory.

Once those lists are complete, reflect on how truly unique you are. No one has ever had exactly that combination of experiences in the unique sequence with the extraordinary characters that you have. You are interesting, you really are. If you have the courage to start using your experiences as the base of your communication material, you'll find yourself becoming much more engaging and exciting to your listeners.

Here's how to tell great incidents. First, don't take too much time setting it up by saying things like, "I'm going to tell you a story that is very meaningful to me and points out the following things . . ." Just dive right into it so it's more like this: "I was walking down Broadway and I looked up and saw a woman standing on the roof of . . ." The more you set it up, generally the less engaging the story will be. Second, know the point you want to make and tell the story so the point is self-evident. The point should be so clear that the listener, if asked "What was the point of this story?" would be able to say pretty close to what you would say. Third, remember it's the detail and the movement of the story that captures the listener's attention. The more attention you have, the more potential for the point to really sink in. Touch the senses with your words. Bring the story to life with detail, characters, color, and movement. Finally, don't kill the story by taking too much time to make your point. Make your point quickly and succinctly. Boil it down to as few words as possible. Make it compact and easy to say and even easier to remember. Make your point crystal clear.

Spice It Up Occasionally

Those of us desiring to be exceptional communicators need to have various spices to throw in to make our message taste and feel better going down. By spice, I mean you need to learn some inspiring quotes, poetry passages, and classic stories from history that illustrate key principles you believe in.

"The significant problems we face today cannot be solved at the level of thinking we were at when we created them," said Albert Einstein. I have used that quote hundreds of times to emphasize the need for change and improvement, a theme that never seems to go away. "What good doeth a man if he gains the whole world but loses his soul?" is another example of a quote that will help make the point that you've got to do the right thing in all situations, no matter what.

An inspiring quote, well-placed in a letter, speech, or casual conversation can have a strong positive impact on your listener. You don't have to know many, just a few that you can use from time to time. It says so much about you as a communicator when you are able to use quotes, and it makes you more interesting too.

President Lincoln at times ran an open-door White House, even at the height of the Civil War. Believe it or not, it was possible for the average citizen to show up at the White House and get in to talk with the president. Lincoln explained to a reporter, who had asked how he was able to afford the time, an interesting facet of his communication style. He said he was able to do this because the time it took to meet with these people was not long, usually less than five minutes. He would start the meeting by asking the citizen what was on their mind. Usually they had a question or a comment to which they wanted him to reply. Lincoln then responded with a story that usually took less than two minutes, which satisfied the visitor.

Lincoln told the reporter that as a practicing attorney he found that stories were very effective in persuading juries. He and several other attorney friends of his would get together every week in a local pub and practice their stories with one another. He said that training proved to be invaluable. The ability to relate his ideas around an interesting story that has a point was what Lincoln found to be a successful way not only to communicate quickly, allowing him to have a constant stream of visitors, but to also communicate effectively.

Lincoln knew that a well-told incident or story is one of the most effective ways to influence the thinking of listeners, so he worked to master them. What nearly all good communicators do is spice up their communication with interesting stories, anecdotes, examples, and analogies that keep the listener engaged, but that also convey powerful points that are persuasive, convincing, and, most of all, memorable.

There are many reference books, with new ones each year, that have famous inspirational stories and poems that are often just the touch we need to spice up our communication. Go to any large bookstore, ask for one of these books, and browse until you find something you like. Like Lincoln, once we learn to tell a few powerful and meaningful stories, we can dramatically reduce the time it takes for us to make a powerful point. In communication, less is always more, and the quicker you can make your point in dramatic fashion, the more likely you are to influence your listener. Often, when it takes too many words to convey the message, we lose the attention of the listener. Poems, inspirational stories, and quotes are the spices you need to add to your tool kit to be a well-rounded communicator.

Sometimes, just packaging the message with a little extra flair can make all the difference. Sharon Basile, an advertising professional, explains: "I put a little sizzle in my proposals by packaging them in a special way. For instance, I might wrap up the actual proposal I'm presenting in fish netting and then attach sea shells and fish and I might have a big card with a big fish on it that might say, 'In a sea of magazines, success remains the ultimate catch.' It's wrapped in neat paper and when they get it, before they open what is essentially a dry proposal, they get a laugh. And

I think that makes a difference. I also have a cowboy one too. I wrap it up in burlap with a bandanna and a sheriff's badge and a six-gun and I put a tag on it that says 'Howdy partner.' Every year I try to come up with a new way to wrap proposals. People remember it."

Learn Some Humorous Stories or Jokes

Everyone who wants to be an interesting communicator needs to be able to use humor from time to time. We all should have at least three good funny stories or jokes we can tell in social situations. It's relatively easy to find them. There are lots of joke books in the bookstore, for example. An even easier way to find them is to ask people you meet if they've heard any good jokes lately.

I was recently out shopping with a friend of mine who is always loaded with funny stories and anecdotes. I discovered the source of his inspiration. When we were at a sporting goods store, he asked the check-out clerk at the cash register, a woman he had never met, what her favorite joke was. She laughed and didn't volunteer anything. At our next stop, a department store, when a clerk asked us if we needed help, he asked, "Have you heard any good jokes lately?" And this continued for the rest of the day. We heard several good stories in just a few hours of shopping, and it made the interaction with the people we came into contact with a lot of fun.

When you hear a good one, write it down and practice telling it in your car until you feel comfortable with it. Ask someone you know who tells good stories to coach you on how to tell them. They'll probably be flattered. Make a collection of the jokes you've heard and like. Using humor is a big part of the art of communication, and don't buy for one moment that you can't learn to be funny, because you can. You'll have to find your style and the kind of joke or story that suits your taste. I prefer stories that have a humorous point opposed to short jokes, but that's just my preference. You'll find your own style if you work at it a little. There are many situations where the ability to tell an appropriate funny story can really come in handy.

Increase Your Dramatic Flair

There are times when you need to be dramatic in order to be effective. A good way to develop this skill is to read dramatic plays aloud at home.

Convince your family to read aloud once a week, with everyone playing different parts, and have fun with it. Stretch yourself. Expand your range, your flair, your ability to dramatize your ideas. When you can throw yourself into the lines of great plays and exaggerate them with abandon, it will help you expand your range in day-to-day living.

"I try to make my customers feel special," explains Sharon Basile. "One time, I had a presentation to make to a company in Hawaii. I set it up so we would make the presentation right on the beach at a table by the water. I had my boss come to the meeting literally from out of the ocean. He was dressed up as King Kamehameha and he stepped off the outrigger and walked right over to the table. The customer got a kick out of it and it made a big difference. You need to be dramatic for that extra effect sometimes."

Take an Acting Class

If you're in sales, or are a person who needs to be persuasive, one of the best training classes you could ever take would be by enrolling in an acting class at your local college. Go through the communication drills and exercises that are essentially designed to help you communicate better. Stretch yourself to learn to communicate in ways you ordinarily wouldn't. Muster up the self-confidence to perform in front of others and develop the courage to be coached without being defensive.

Often when we conduct selling seminars, we will use assistants to demonstrate how a particular technique is used. One of our assistants, Bob Bogle, was absolutely fabulous every time he got on his feet and gave an example. He was natural, enthusiastic, and his communication had real punch. He told me he had gained this ability by taking acting classes, and you can too. So much of your success is dependent on your ability to be powerful in front of groups, so why not become a real master at it?

Develop a Million-Dollar Greeting

Here's one of the most powerful communication tools of all, the easiest to develop, and, remarkably, one of the most neglected. What is it? Your smile. How good is your smile? Is it fabulous? Is it genuine? Do you smile with every genuine fiber of your being? If so, great. If not, why not? Be aware as you go to work tomorrow of how often you greet people with a smile, a genuine smile. You may find that you, like many people, rarely give the people you see often a big happy smile, the kind of smile that communicates positive energy and builds rapport. Go to the mirror right now and bring the book with you. Look yourself in the mirror and put on a big full-faced smile. Smile with your eyes, your cheeks, and your teeth. How does it feel? How long has it been since you felt a smile of that size? Commit yourself to greeting everyone you meet with a big smile that lasts several soft seconds before launching into conversation. You'll be amazed at the impact it will have on people. Flash your teeth! Smile so your eyes sparkle! Smile until people start smiling back. Do you think people will think you're crazy, that you've lost your mind? Perhaps people have become so used to your monotonous expressions that a smile would seem out of place to them. So be it! Knock them down! Brighten their muted expectations of you. Express yourself through your smile and spread some good feelings around. Touch everyone you meet with your smile.

How about your handshake? Do you have a million-dollar handshake? If not, why not? Do you know the quality of your handshake? Is it warm, cheerful, and uplifting to the people you shake hands with? Why not find out? Ask someone you know and trust to judge your handshake. Give them a typical shake and ask them their reaction. Then start working on it.

Several years ago, I was visiting a colleague in Chicago. I was flying in from my home in Washington, D.C., and was a bit nervous about the meeting. The man I was meeting with, Jim, was a legend in the company I was working with. He was one of the most successful entrepreneurs in the entire system and, although I had never met him, I had heard many stories about his charisma, maverick-like and often combative ideas, and personal charm. When I arrived at his office, I was shocked to see Jim standing by the elevator bank, eager to greet me. I was not sure at that moment that he even knew who I was. To my surprise, his face lit up like a Christmas tree and he extended his hand in what was the warmest handshake I ever received. He was genuinely happy to see me, and my nervousness evaporated. The next few days revealed to me that Jim was like that with everyone, no doubt an underlying secret to his success.

When you greet someone, if you will only take a moment to concentrate on that handshake and your greeting smile and tell them they are important nonverbally that you're glad to see them, and that you feel good to be there, it's amazing how the rest of the interaction will be influenced in a positive way. When you think about it, a handshake is perhaps the most personal form of communication we have with many of the people in our lives. Touch is a very powerful sense, just as hearing and eyesight are. What we communicate through our handshake will influence the way people perceive us later. Get yourself off to a *great* start, not just an acceptable one. In my experience, I would say no more than one in five businesspeople have a truly effective greeting, which includes the handshake and greeting smile. Master it! It is a powerful, visible, memorable, and important component of your communication tool kit.

Appearance Counts

The third element that has an enormous impact on the first impression, along with your smile and your handshake, is your appearance. Simply put, it's hard to overinvest in a good appearance. Clothes and grooming communicate a ton. It's packaging, your packaging. Don't you want yourself, the most important business presentation tool you've got, to be packaged up so that you tell everyone you've arrived, you're ready to compete, and you belong in the game? You can still exhibit your own special flair while communicating a credible, dynamic, reliable, and trustworthy self through your appearance. Clothes need to be clean, pressed, and coordinated. The better the fabric and the cut, the better you feel. Wear great clothes not to impress others but for how they make you feel. When you're wearing a suit that really fits and is made of a fine fabric together with shoes that shine and a tie or scarf that is alive and accents the whole package comfortably, then you'll feel like doing something magnificent. If this is not something you are naturally good at, then take professional advice. Go to a better clothing store and ask the manager for help. Tell them where you work, the kind of environment it is, and what you would like your clothes to say about you. Then listen to their recommendation. If you don't like it, go to another store of equal or better quality until you find the right fit. Get advice from people who have an appearance you admire. Remember, your appearance is important because of the way you feel, not only for the impact it will have on others. It's hard to beat the feeling when you know you look like a million bucks. Develop a wardrobe that allows you to wear one of your favorites every day. Don't buy clothes that don't turn you on. You need to feel great in the clothes you wear. Selecting clothes is one of the true joys of being human, so make it a passion. Wear clothing that puts you in the game you want to play.

Remember People's Names

Here's another obvious skill that few people master. Remembering people's names will be an enormous advantage for you if you will only take a little time to develop the skill. Not being able to remember people's names communicates so much in a negative way. When a person you have recently met cannot remember your name, they are saying the following:

- You're not important.
- I don't care about you.
- Other people are more important to me.
- You are not memorable.
- I'm too busy to remember you.

Not long ago, Steve and I were speakers at a meeting where the company had brought in all of their division vice presidents. The room was filled with the high-powered elite of this billion-dollar company. We were there to give them a synopsis of how they could improve teamwork, and we were being introduced to them by an executive vice president, Carl, who had been working with us briefly on the project. With 50 sets of eyes on us, Carl proceeded to introduce me as Michael St. Mark (instead of St. Lawrence). The whole room was initially confused, then embarrassed, and finally laughing at Carl's mistake. Because Carl knew his colleagues so well, it turned out to be funny, but this is not always the case when you forget a person's name.

Think of all that negative energy that can be associated with you if you habitually forget people's names. Make a game of it. Focus on it and make it an important task to remember everyone's name you meet. When you go out to eat, make a point of getting the name of the hostess, your waiter, and your bartender and thank them by name on the way out. Try and remember their names the next time you go there and are served by them. They'll be shocked in a positive way!

Here are some keys to remembering names. First, you have got to hear the name correctly or you haven't got a shot of remembering it. If you didn't hear it clearly the first time, ask the person to repeat it. If you are still having trouble, ask them to spell it. Say it back to them to make sure you got it right. They'll be flattered! They will feel good that you care enough to take an interest in their name.

Next, repeat the name to yourself several times silently as you shake hands with the person. It is critical to use that person's name occasionally in your conversation with them, but don't overdo it, as this can be very annoying. You might even want to carry a few three-by-five cards in your pocket or purse and jot down the name of the person after you finish talking to them and put down a few notes about their physical appearance or features. This will help cement your memory.

Once you've heard this person's name, observe their appearance closely as you repeat their name. The best way to do this is to allow the other person to talk first. If you begin each encounter with people by starting the conversation and talking, you will find it more difficult to remember people's names. Instead, ask a question that allows them to talk and silently repeat their name, observe their physical characteristics, and listen carefully to what they are saying. This forces you to eliminate outside distractions and focus 100% of your attention on that person, another positive-vibe thrower!

The next time you are sitting in a boring meeting, make a game of it. See if you can memorize the name of everyone who is in the meeting and even how their names are spelled so that at the end of the meeting you can shake hands with everyone and say goodbye to them by name! Like all new skills, it will be a challenge at first, but through practice, you'll develop a much better ability to remember names, a skill that will serve you many times over throughout your personal and professional lives.

Call Nightingale Conent, a leading audiocassette course provider (800-323-5552) and ask them for their best title on remembering names and get it. You will find sophisticated association and word picture techniques that can make a real difference. Don't go through life conning yourself into thinking you haven't got a good memory and you just aren't good at remembering names! Huzzonga! You can be fabulous at remembering names, and it is a skill worth having if you want to make it to the highest circles of influence.

Work on Your Public Speaking Skills

A very wealthy man bought a huge ranch in Arizona and invited some of his closer associates to see it. After touring the 1,500 acres of mountains, rivers, and grasslands, he took everybody to the house. The house was as spectacular as the scenery. In the back of the house was the largest swimming pool they had ever seen. However, it was filled with alligators. The owner explained, "I value courage more than anything. It is what made me a billionaire. I value courage so much that if anyone has the courage to jump in that pool and swim to the other side, I will give them whatever they want, my land, my house, my money, anything."

Of course, everybody laughed at the challenge and turned to follow the owner into the house for lunch. Suddenly, they heard a splash. Turning around, they saw a guy splashing and thrashing in the water, swimming for his life as the alligators swarmed after him. After several death-defying seconds, the man made it unharmed to the other side. The rich billionaire was amazed but stuck to his promise. He said, "You are a man of courage; you can have anything you want. My house, land, money, whatever you want, it's yours."

The swimmer, breathing heavily, looked up, and said, "I just want to know who pushed me in the pool."

The fear the poor fellow in the story felt is similar to what millions of people feel when they are asked to speak in front of groups. No matter how hard you try to avoid it, at some point in your life you're bound to be pushed into the pool and have to express your thoughts to a group of people. Today's business environment will force you to present to teams, groups, and committees, and when you can be persuasive in those situations, you can generate impact.

Of all the ways to develop your communication skills, I know of no other avenue that will have as dramatic an impact on your overall ability to communicate than developing your public-speaking skills. Public speaking is a taxing experience. It is stressful, fearful, and loaded with risks. It puts our skills to the test. We are vulnerable, perhaps more vulnerable than in any other communication situation. Year after year, public speaking is indicated as the most common fear people have. Yet if you can become confident in front of groups, this confidence will overflow into other areas of your life and, more importantly, into all communication situations you find yourself in. What it takes to hold an audience's attention, to entertain, and to motivate them is precisely what it takes in more intimate communication situations. What happens is that public speaking is so demanding that you build an enormous reserve tank of communication power because what it takes to be effective in front of a group is simply a magnified version of what it takes one-on-one.

"I've always enjoyed speaking to groups," explains Don Graling, a top-producing salesperson and manager at a high-tech firm. "I know that some people are really nervous when it comes to public speaking, but the only way to overcome it is to do it. I think public speaking helps you on a one-on-one situation as well. It helps you organize your ideas and think on your feet quickly. It helps you deal with pressure. Because I'm good at public speaking, I can go into a meeting with our senior executives and handle tough questions because I'm used to the pressure."

The first step to becoming an effective public speaker is to commit yourself to getting in front of groups. One alternative is to join Toastmasters, a public-speaking organization that has chapters in most cities in the United States. Or join a service organization in your industry or community and volunteer to be a part of a committee that makes reports to the members. Join the PTA. Go to a town meeting and express your views. Volunteer to do a reading at church. Tell your boss you are eager to do group presentations at work. Take a good public-speaking course such as Dale Carnegie, Communispond, or Decker Communications. There are so many ways to get in front of groups, so go out and get in front of some of them. You can't develop group presentations skills and the enviable confidence that comes from the experience by analyzing it, by studying it, or by thinking about it; you have to get in front of groups. It's the only way to acquire the benefits that are absolutely necessary if you want to be a high impact communicator.

Androcles was whipping lions right and left, and Julius Caesar wanted to know how he was doing it. The next time Androcles was in the arena, Caesar watched him very carefully. He noticed that Androcles would sneak up behind the lion, lean over, and whisper something in the lion's ear. At that moment, the lion would lay down as meek as a lamb, put all four paws in the air, and surrender.

A little later that day, Caesar called Androcles to his palace and asked him what exactly he was whispering in the lion's ear. Androcles replied, "I say to the lion, do you realize that if you beat me, there are 50,000 people in this arena who are going to want to know how you did it. They are going to demand that you give a 10-minute oral presentation on what happened."

Are you like the lion in this story? If so, consider the opportunities that come as a result of possessing strong communication skills. When you are in front of a group, you are visible! You are the focus of attention and have an enormous opportunity to allow people to see all the value you bring to the table. It's advertising! When you have good public-speaking skills, people will admire you and see you as a self-confident person, which in turn increases your credibility. Because so many people shy away from situations where public speaking is required, you will be identified as a person to call on for those situations, and it is precisely those situations that lead to opportunities to advance in your career. The higher you go up most corporate ladders, the more public-speaking skills are needed.

We are now in a business environment in which work is organized around teams and groups. If you are effective operating in these group environments, you will move forward faster. If, however, you hold back with ideas much the way the lion in our story did, all of your talent is hidden from others. To be successful, you must be visible. And public speaking is one of the most visible activities of all!

Public speaking is a muscle builder. You need strong communication muscles to thrive in high-pressure, high-opportunity situations. Public speaking strengthens all the communication skills you use. It's like going to the gym and lifting weights. Your muscles strengthen, which enhances your performance in other athletic activities.

Sell yourself right now on overcoming your fear of speaking, whether it be one-on-one, to small groups, or to large audiences. This skill will dramatically enhance your chances for success. This skill will prepare you to compete at the highest level. This skill will build the confidence you need now and in the future. Don't put it off, get started now!

Sweep People into Your Message

The best communicators are able to sweep people into what they are saying. Through listening they are able to adapt their message and tailor it to the person or people they are talking to. Too often, communication between two people is more a logic tug-of-war than an exchange of ideas. Here's where things like handshakes, smiles, and remembering names add value. They create an environment of openness, of acceptance, and of positive energy that diminishes the resistance and combativeness that prevents influence from happening.

"I try not to overpower people," explains Paul Thomas, a successful sales manager. "I like to talk to people like they're my friends. I try to get on a personal level and talk in a manner where it's like, hey, we're both here to get a common thing done and while we do it let's have a good time doing it. I try to create a laid-back conversational atmosphere and it works for me."

Mark Ferraro, a top-performing salesperson, adds, "I find that when I really have to be persuasive, I like to get really quiet and make my point, or what I'm asking for, very simple. I try to really get to the core issue, maintain solid eye contact, and keep things simple and soft. It's like the softer you talk the more disarming it is for the other person."

When we concentrate too much on the message and concentrate too little on the environment we create for the message to be received, we make the influence process much more difficult. The environment is as important as the message. If you find that people are, in general, somewhat combative with you, then you need to focus on the environment building skills that include the following:

- Your smile
- Your handshake
- Remembering names
- Warm, accepting body language
- Listening
- The questions you ask
- Your understanding (not agreement) of the other person's message
- Eliminating interruptions
- Total, nondistracted attention
- Genuine interest in others

When these factors are working for you, it becomes much easier to sweep the listener into your message. In college, I was in an introductory psychology class being taught by a professor who had developed a very good reputation as an interesting speaker. His lectures were usually standing room only in the large auditorium. The first time I saw him, I was completely mesmerized by his lecture. After attending several more of his lectures I noticed that he started each class with about 15 minutes of talking with the students. He would ask a question and get several people to join him on stage for a conversation about some issue that all the college students could relate to, such as why we get nervous when we meet an attractive person of the opposite sex or how we will procrastinate even when we know the procrastination will cause a bigger problem than the problem we are trying to avoid. He built a fabulous rapport with his students before he got into his lecture and he would weave back many of the things that came out in the interactive opening. This was an experience I'll never forget in terms of sweeping the listener into the message.

When you make it a top priority to improve the environment-building factors when you communicate with other people, then you will build trust with the person you are talking with, a key element of the influence process.

LIFE IS A COMMUNICATION EXPERIMENT

The beauty of committing yourself to improving your communication skills is that you don't really have to go anywhere to do it. All day long you are given opportunities to experiment and improve. See if you can pull off the most extraordinary greeting tomorrow at work. The next phone conversation you have end by saying, "In summary, here's what we discussed . . ." On Monday morning, use an incident to describe to your boss what happened over the weekend. Tonight at the dinner table, have each person share an incident that points out his or her most cherished accomplishment. Tell someone how important they are by sharing with them an incident of great significance and value. Call someone right now and ask them some interesting questions so they can really open up.

Your life is a living, breathing communication experiment happening all the time. It's a laboratory in which you can continually try new methods. What we need to do is shut off the autopilot communication switch that we often have on and start flying manually and consciously—start communicating on purpose. Put the dictionary that's up on your bookshelf right on your desk and make your first task of the workday to look up a new word. The next time you are trying to persuade someone, put together an incident, a humorous story, and a quote and make your point with more dramatic flair. The next time someone asks you what's new, have an incident ready that will really illustrate it. Be ready for your next presentation with a host of stories and incidents that could illustrate a point you would like to make.

Dale Carnegie, perhaps the most famous teacher of communication skills who ever lived, when summing up in a speech what he felt were the most important keys to success, said, "The longer I live, the more convinced I am that enthusiasm is the little known secret of success." By applying the ideas in the tell it with gusto principle, you can't help but come across as a much more interesting and enthusiastic person. This happens because you are consciously working at it, while many of the people around you are not. They will notice and be impacted in a positive way by your unique approach.

Are You Improving as a Communicator?

Have your communication skills improved dramatically in the last year? In what way? Survey after survey of CEOs reveal that communication is the skill most wanted by top corporations. People who can communicate credibly, honestly, and convincingly have a huge edge.

Have you already settled in and accepted your communication skills as they currently are as the ceiling of what they can become? Is the game already over? Or are you willing to sell yourself right now on turbo-charging your message with the tell-it-with-gusto approach? Very few people have even come close to being as good a communicator as they could be. For the person who wants success in this business environment, it needs to be a top priority.

Put Communication Skills into Your Boss Plan

Becoming a better communicator will not happen by accident. There are a thousand other things to do, but there are few choices you can make, when deciding how to invest your time, that will yield better results. Get some activities right now into your calendar that will build you as a communicator. Learn to tell it with gusto all the time.

Chapter Five

To laugh often and much; to win the respect of intelligent people and affection of children; to earn the appreciation of honest critics and endure the betrayal of false friends; to appreciate beauty, to find the best in others; to leave the world a bit better, whether by a healthy child, a garden patch or a redeemed social condition; to know even one life has breathed easier because you lived. This is to have succeeded.

—Ralph Waldo Emerson

To live a life of achievement and accomplishment is not all it takes to reach success. Success is a unique blend of personal achievement and contribution back to the world. True success is as much a spirit within as it is visible, tangible accomplishments. Emerson's words point to a state of mind where lasting satisfaction exists. Finding lasting satisfaction is what we will be exploring in this chapter.

Principle number four, signed, sealed, delivered, has to do with *how* we do the activities that fill our days, *why* we do them, and our *attitude* toward them at their completion. Since we are always involved in one activity or another, this topic speaks directly to the way we experience what we do. It isn't only what we do that determines our level of happiness and fulfillment, it's the way we do it. Signed, sealed, delivered is the principle that will help you put more quality into your work and escalate the level of contribution you are making to other people's success.

Sale number five is to convince yourself to put your best into whatever you're doing and then give it away knowing that with this attitude your reward comes from doing the activity itself. It's putting everything you've got into your work, your relationships, and your contributions back to the world because it's the right thing to do. The reward is in the doing, not in what comes back. When we have completely bought the signed, sealed, delivered approach, then whatever we are doing is an opportunity to contribute, to grow, and to express our unique signature to the world.

This principle, signed, sealed, delivered is divided into two halves:

1. *Personal signature:* Our personal mark of excellence
2. *Giving it away:* The spirit in which we give and contribute to others

Before we look more closely at each half, however, we need to spend some time on why this principle is so significant.

QUALITY IS CRUCIAL

Life Is a Boomerang

All of our actions are boomerangs. They come back. Whether they float softly back and land right where we would like them to or klunk us unexpectedly when our back is turned is entirely dependent on the quality of action we take.

A popular philosophy is "what goes around, comes around" or if you do good then eventually good comes back and, conversely, if you do something bad to someone, it comes back too. It's as though there's a great accountant out there who tallies and doles out rewards and punishments accordingly. Here's a true story that illustrates this principle beautifully:

Many years ago, on a stormy night in Philadelphia, a man walked into a hotel at midnight without a reservation. The night clerk told the weary traveler that unfortunately the hotel was full. Upon seeing the frustrated look on the traveler's face, the clerk said, "Sir, please have my room this evening."

The man, moved by the act of kindness replied, "Thank you so much. To repay you I will build a hotel for you."

Two years later, the clerk received a letter and a round-trip ticket to New York City. He arrived at the address indicated on the letter to see a big new building made of reddish stone with turrets and watchtowers. The man who sent him the letter came down to greet him and said, "Remember me? I'm the person you gave your room to. I've built this hotel just for you, Mr. William Waldorf Astoria."

The clerk replied, "You must be joking." The man, George C. Boldt, pointed to the name on the hotel sign, the Waldorf Astoria.

It's great when fairy-tale rewards happen to pay back unselfish acts of kindness, but that is not the deeper meaning of "what goes around, comes around." Let's take another look at it. Perhaps the outcome from our actions is more immediate than that. Perhaps the reward for doing a job well, contributing to the success of others, of putting forth our best effort, is more sudden, and maybe, just maybe, it doesn't takes weeks, months, or, according to some people, years to come back. Maybe the real reward of the right activity is in what you become as a result. By thinking that you do these "selfless" tasks only because somehow it all comes back is not as powerful as saying, "I do my best for what it makes of me today! As I become more, I am able to contribute more and my value increases, because value given and value received are equal."

The greater rewards in life take time to build. Great buildings take planning, effort, an enormous amount of problem solving, well-executed activity, and perseverance to erect. It often takes an artist a lifetime of work to be recognized as a master. Authors often write several books before they are able to finally get one published. Improvement is time-consuming, that's just the way it is. We get frustrated when we expect more results than life seems willing to send us, and this frustration is capable of destroying the mechanism that *will* bring us results eventually. That mechanism is, of course, the quality of what we produce for others.

Remember, it all comes back. When you put excellence out there, the world throws you back nice surprises. Sloppiness is a boomerang too. Autopilot work is a boomerang. It tends to fetch back more monotonous assignments that can easily be done on autopilot.

Don't Make Slow Buildup No Buildup!

But we want results now! We want to get positive payback today, not tomorrow! Because results are difficult to predict, it is easy to settle into an approach that allows us to put forth our best effort only when we feel like it, or, even worse, only when the task is "important enough" to warrant it. The problem with this attitude is that when we do stumble into a task that offers the potential for some real rewards, our ability to execute it successfully at a very high level of performance is dependent on how much reserve power we have built up.

Tommy Lasorda, the retired manager of the Los Angeles Dodgers baseball team, turned out consistently successful teams in what many people feel to be the most successful baseball franchise. He was admired by the press, his players, the fans, and his peers. One of his philosophies that he shared with his players was that if you practice as if the next game you are playing is for the World Series every day and play each game with the intensity as if it was a World Series game, then soon you'll get to play in the World Series. And that's how it works for top performers. Thinking like this adds the necessary energy, reserve power, and potency to our actions that can transform ordinary to dos into extraordinary examples of execution.

This "reserve power" is built up through doing the ordinary activities of our day in a very consistent, high-quality way. Very few, if any, people are capable of slacking off 90% of the time, then miraculously notching up to a stellar level of performance when the situation demands it. Usually, in these critical situations, their best just isn't good enough and it yields disappointing results, even though they tried their best. Best effort isn't always enough to get results, but it is enough to increase our value slowly over time, and that's the key.

It takes time to increase our value; it's a slow buildup process. Don't make slow buildup no buildup by opting to ignore this fundamental. In a similar observation, M. Scott Peck, the author of *The Road Less Traveled,* explains that the overwhelming majority of adults have, in a sense, stopped growing because they believe they have figured out how the whole thing works. They run out of energy to get better and end up settling for a level of satisfaction and productivity that is far below what they could achieve with steady, incremental improvement over time.

Push versus Pull

One of the most important outcomes of adopting the OUTSELL principles is an effect we will be referring to several times in the next few chapters. This is the "pull" effect versus a "push" effect, which is the state most people live in. Push refers to what is happening when you have to push your way in to be heard and seen. You have to get your foot in the door, convince other people to listen, and sell yourself hard to the people with resources.

Pull is exactly the opposite. Pull happens when we have a high level of value and the world around us starts approaching us with good opportunities. Pull is when the people who know us begin to sense that we have a lot to contribute both in terms of resources and ability and they seek us out.

Vitality also creates a unique phenomenon around you we call a "pull-vibe," which gets to the heart of being an influencer. The pull-vibe is what happens when we reach a high enough level of energy, value, and influence that we don't have to push for opportunities any more: they start to seek us out instead. Paul Thomas, a successful sales manager, explains: "I developed a take-charge attitude when I first became aware of the things I really wanted to accomplish with my life. Once I started to accomplish things and started learning from my mistakes, that's when I started really stretching, setting goals, and working on myself. The neatest thing about it is that people are attracted to it. They kind of grab onto your coattails and want to go there with you."

Neglect building up your value, and you will always be pushing for results instead of enjoying the pull effect that only happens once our value increases to a critical level. When you adopt the signed, sealed, delivered approach, with the help of little extra momentum-building, the world begins to push you to where you want to go. You won't have to keep asking for opportunities, because they will start knocking on your door! Signed, sealed, delivered is specifically about how to create the pull effect in your life. The more value you build into the person you are, the more opportunities will start to hunt you down. It takes time to build real value, the kind that holds up and increases steadily.

To create the pull effect in your life, you will need to

1. Develop commitment to your job.
2. Become disciplined to focus on what is most important.
3. Steadily improve your ability to perform well on high priorities.
4. Master the skills to perform high-priority, high-value tasks.
5. Enjoy the enthusiasm that comes from mastery.

The pull effect kicks in here.

You cannot go to step two until you have done step one and so on until you reach the pull effect. To get to the pull effect, takes time, effort, and persistence. It's well worth the effort because the time is going to happen anyway, and the alternative is simply not as appealing.

Let's begin with the first half of the signed, sealed, delivered principle, personal signature.

PART I—PERSONAL SIGNATURE

Personal signature boils down to doing our best, no matter what the task, because it is the expression of who we are. Martin Luther King Jr., in *The Street Sweeper,* put it this way:

> If a man is called to be a street sweeper, he should sweep streets as Michelangelo painted, or Beethoven composed music, or Shakespeare wrote poetry. He should sweep streets so well that all the hosts of heaven and earth will pause to say, "Here lived a great street sweeper who did his job well.
>
> —Martin Luther King Jr.

There is tremendous power in our actions when we perform even the mundane tasks of our day with the intention that is alive in the words of Martin Luther King Jr. It is this power that developing your own personal signature and putting it into your work will tap for you.

Personal signature means to put your unmistakable mark of excellence on everything you do. The next time you go to an art museum, observe how painters sign their work, telling the world that this painting is their creation. In music, one of the highest compliments that can be paid to a guitarist is when he is said to possess a signature sound. Guitar players like B. B. King, Eric Clapton, and Eddie Van Halen have developed their signature to such a level of quality and distinction that within two or three notes of any guitar solo they play, the familiar listener recognizes their signature sound.

To sign your work, you need to leave these two marks on all of your tasks:

1. A unique print that is all your own.
2. A commitment to a higher standard of excellence.

The mark of excellence, or the unique print you put on the work you produce, is a powerful marketing tool—a way to stand out and be noticed.

The added value you put into all the work you produce is the way you raise your own value. More importantly, when you raise the value of all the things you touch (the Midas touch?), you raise your own ability to increase the value of the tasks and projects you touch in the future, because your ability to execute skillfully grows too. We sign our work by putting forth our best effort, raising our work to the highest level of competency we can generate and, over time, raising our level of competency so that our next task is of slightly higher quality. A few years of that kind of effort and what seemed impossible in the past becomes routine in the now.

"My parents taught me," explains Nola Beldegreen, a successful advertising professional, "that if you are going to do something, then pour your heart into it and do your best. I've tried to follow that in my career and it has always worked for me."

The most significant change that we experience and benefit from when we sign our work is the change we go through as a result of the quality of our efforts. Too often, we think change is simply a thinking thing, an attitude shift, but it's not. It's action! Real improvement happens when you combine the attitude shift with the action. Attitude is often the easy part, the first step. We all know people who put out a picture of a consistently positive attitude (often annoying) but are unable to back it up with results. It's like the person who moves from one multilevel marketing company to another, always telling people about the fabulous opportunity they've just found. But when you look a little closer, that success they keep talking about is always eluding them; they are unable to reach it themselves. It's all talk, no results. Positive attitude without the corresponding action is nothing more than a lot of smoke, but no results. If you can think in terms of changing yourself through your efforts and not just through your attitude, then you will understand the power of signing it.

What We Leave Behind Counts

After we complete a task and, in a sense, let it go, it becomes our lasting impression, our signature for others to see. It is the quality of that signature that makes all the difference. The value we added and the light we shone on it keeps on shining. This is how we leave a legacy, through the things we improve. Great effort, combined with great competence, leaves a legacy.

The only man-made landmark on the face of the earth that can be seen from space is also the structure that demanded the most effort to construct. It is the Great Wall of China. This is a perfect example of great effort combined with great competence. This 1,500-mile-long wall, which was constructed over 2,200 years ago, is still standing in good condition, a testament to the competence of the work it took to construct the wall. When you combine your best effort with a high level of competence, then you will leave a lasting impression on all the work you touch, in much the same way the Chinese did with the Great Wall.

Cal Ripken, the shortstop for the Baltimore Orioles, in 1996 left a legacy that will never be forgotten by accomplishing something every bit as remarkable as the Great Wall of China. He finished playing his 2,131st game in a row without missing a single game. Thirteen years without missing a game because of injury, sickness, or lack of performance. It was his commitment, extraordinary effort, and passion to contribute that produced one of the most emotionally powerful moments in sports history and certain acceptance to the Hall of Fame. Who could forget the tribute he received from his loving fans at Camden Yards, the Baltimore Orioles baseball park, where he was given a standing ovation that continued for 20 minutes!

What are the landmark accomplishments of your life? What significant achievements have you left behind for others to see and admire as evidence of your unique signature, commitment, and attention to detail? It is these accomplishments, these landmarks for others to see, that provide the most definitive evidence to the people who know you that you are a person worthy of the highest level of influence.

Stamp Your Work with Your Personal Mark of Excellence

Make the things you touch better. It's that simple. Don't ever settle for a second-class effort on anything that reflects the quality of your work. Our reputations are built on the quality of what we produce and can be often irreparably stained when we cut corners and overlook details. When a project frustrates us, when the work we have to do is stressful, it is primarily because we have not developed enough skill to do it competently and confidently. It is exactly the attainment of this skill, competence, and confidence that first-class effort produces in us. Do the work you do with excitement, with the knowledge that the extra effort you put into it is building your competence and value. Develop a reputation that impacts others so that they want you to help them out on the things they are doing.

It should be clear to others that the work you produced came from you because it has the mark of quality and your own personal flair. Sharon Basile, an advertising professional explains, "You have to follow up. You have to call when you say you will. If you guarantee something, you have to come through. That's it. You execute what you promise, no excuses."

There's a man named Tom whom I worked with for 12 years who mastered this principle. Every document that left his desk had a little extra something on it that made it distinctive and reflective of him. When he would sign a letter, he would always put on a handwritten P.S. wishing the person a happy birthday, anniversary, or a good wish for the kids. He did the extra stuff so well. Of course, his work was impeccable too. You could tell the projects he had been involved in because they had his distinctive mark of quality.

Make everything you touch a little better as a result of your eyes having seen it. Try to improve, if only a little, the things you touch.

The ancient Romans had a unique way of insisting that the people doing construction work would do it right the first time. Whenever an arch was near completion, the engineers who constructed it would be assembled to stand beneath it. Then, they would take apart the scaffolding step-by-step that was built around the arch to support it during construction. If the arch came crashing down because of faulty plans, materials, or construction, then the engineer in charge would be the first to know. The Roman engineer knew that the quality of his work would have a direct personal impact on his life and, therefore, it's not surprising to find that so many Roman arches have survived through the ages.

Tommy Giaimo, a top-producing car salesman, explains, "My father really drummed it into me that if you're going to do something you've got to do it right. That's the attitude I got into sales with. I went in with the attitude that I'm going to look at the big picture and do it right."

Want to know one of the keys to leaving behind the stresses of tomorrow and the misgivings and regrets of yesterday? It's to put everything you've got, all your might, into what you are doing right now. The immortal words of Thomas Carlyle are truer today than ever before: "Our main business is not to see what lies dimly at a distance, but to do what lies clearly at hand." When you put everything you've got into the task at hand, then you will lock out stress, worry, and regret. When, however, we do tasks on autopilot, with enough effort to get them done well enough but not good enough to showcase our best effort, we leave open room for doubt, worry, anxiety, and distraction to sneak in. Doing your best demands your full attention and even develops your ability to concentrate, which is the mechanism that allows us to live in the moment. We effectively lock out distraction when we focus all of our attention on the task at hand.

What About Liking What You Do?

Here's another dilemma. A lot of career philosopher-gurus write that once you truly find what you like to do most, then you are more likely to succeed. They will tell you stories about people working 16-hour days and loving it because they are doing what they really love doing most. We see and hear this and are often tempted to think, "If I could find something that I really enjoyed doing like these people have, I wouldn't mind putting forth that kind of effort either. They're lucky, I'm not. I've just got an average job. It's simply not that interesting." To that we say huzzonga! Which comes first; the passion for the work or the passion we put into the work? Most people simply don't find that "magical" path of doing what they want to do most and making a living from it until they have raised their ability to create value to a fairly high level. And how does that happen? It comes from putting 110% effort into whatever task is in front of you right now. Liking what you do is not the cure-all that many people think it is. Even when we find a profession we really like, in order to be very successful in it (as in all jobs), we will have to do a lot of distasteful activities. It is that capacity to throw ourselves into the messy stuff, the nasty details, the tasks that are unpleasant to do, that builds the kind of competence that leads to passion.

Mr. Holland's Opus is a movie that illustrates this point beautifully. Mr. Holland, a highly trained young composer, takes a job teaching music at the local high school in order to support his young family. Inwardly, he is resentful of the time constraints the job places on him, which limit his ability to compose new music, and initially he simply puts up with the job. At one point, he is told by a colleague, who is also his friend, that he is a lousy teacher. This realization angers him at first, then changes him. He begins putting more passion and effort into his teaching and the results with his students become very rewarding to him, and eventually teaching becomes his true passion. His commitment to excellence came first, skill and extraordinary results followed, and a true passion developed as his reward. At the end of the movie, which illustrates wonderfully how the pull effect works, many of the students that Mr. Holland had helped so dramatically over the years come to his retirement party to play a tribute to him through the performance of his "opus," a classical symphony he has been composing his entire life. Ironically, it is the people on stage, his students who have come back to play his opus, that are evidence of his greatest contribution.

Liking what you do more will not suddenly change your standards of competence. You can like doing a task and continue to do it in a low-quality way. When you have the ability to do your best at the task at hand, regardless of your liking for it, then you will find the work you are most suited to do. You will possess discipline, which is the only reliable method to reach lasting competence.

You will know you are signing your tasks when you concentrate without distraction, are committed to doing your best, and start getting feedback from the world around you that you made a significant contribution. This is a much surer path for success than searching far and wide for the perfect job that somehow sparks your inner desire and ignites your forgotten enthusiasm. There is absolutely nothing wrong with pursuing work that you are best-suited for and enjoy, but don't let the search for that elusive discovery distract you from what you are doing in the now.

Using the Feedback Mirror

But how do we really know if we are doing a great job and stamping our work with our own personal mark of excellence? This information comes from the "feedback mirror," a very important instrument to understand. Our personal world, the world we interact with, is constantly giving us signals about our performance and the quality of our contributions. Let's call this the feedback mirror. Facets of the feedback mirror could be any of the following:

- What our coworkers tell us about the quality of our work.
- What our friends tell us about the kind of person we've become.
- What our spouse says about the quality of our marriage.
- What our body says about the quality of its fitness.
- What our creditors and investment portfolios report to us.
- What the information we pay attention to tells us about our world.

When we look in this mirror, we can either see a crystal-clear reflection of who we really are and what we need to do or we can see a foggy, blurry image that reveals little, if any, usable information.

Whether the feedback mirror reveals the truth or a watered-down, easier-to-accept version that we prefer to see and hear depends on the way we interpret the information we get from the feedback mirror. If we are strongly biased to living only within our comfort zones, we get a distorted, overly adjusted view of the world that is tailor-made to allow us to stay in our comfort zones, free of risk and significant effort. We can become skilled at using excuses, complaints, "not fair" rationalizations, and half-effort justifications. We seek the comfort zone and not the achievement impact zone.

The comfort zone is a great place to relax but not a great place to grow, and it is the chief culprit of a foggy feedback mirror. For example, you may have a sincere desire to get into good physical condition. This desire occurs because of one or several accurate insights you have gotten from your feedback mirror:

- Your clothes feel too tight.
- You feel tired and listless.
- Your muscles and joints continually ache.
- You avoid activities involving exercise for fear of getting sore.

Perhaps you read an inspiring article or saw a show on TV that renews your interest and fires up a commitment. You wake up the next morning and get into an aerobics class, go for a jog, or hit the weights at the gym. Your enthusiasm is running high and you marvel at how easy it was that first day. This insight is driven by your feedback mirror. You wonder why you waited this long. You feel better throughout the day. You go to bed with even more enthusiasm to continue your program tomorrow.

Then you wake up. Everything hurts. The feedback mirror is screaming at full volume, but it is sending out uncomfortable information. Is the feedback mirror telling you to take the day off, to take the week off for that matter? Or is it signaling you to do something about this mess you've created today, so that a year from now you won't be in the same position? If you decide you've earned a day off to recuperate, you are opting to stay in the comfort zone. Inside the comfort zone, there is little risk and little reward. There is little change and little immediate pain, but often devastating long-term limitations.

When our need to be comfortable and insulated becomes greater than our need for the truth and growth, we can begin to spend time and energy defending why we are the way we are rather than growing, learning, and overcoming our limitations. This often causes a defensive or overly offensive attitude. These attitudes can actually block the truth from coming to us. People around us find it hard to be frank and honest because of the way we might react. We see what we want to see and not what really is.

I worked for a boss for several years who had a powerful temper and would attack whoever brought him criticism, whether the criticism was justified or not. As a result, over time, he trained everyone to bring him primarily good news. His picture of what was really going on became increasingly distorted because he was scaring away half of the information he needed to see the real picture. Eventually, a tidal wave hit him and washed him out of the organization. It was no surprise for the people around him, but it came as a complete shock to him.

To really know the value of your work and the power of your personal signature, you have got to be able to see the feedback mirror clearly and openly. You must welcome both the good news and the bad. You can use the bad news to make adjustments, improve, and overcome obstacles. To stamp your work with your own personal mark of excellence, it is critical to be open to criticism and, at times, even invite it!

Signing It Requires a High Degree of Competence

To truly sign your work, you must have a high degree of competence. This is the best way to consistently raise the quality of the things you touch. Without competence you will have a lot of great, often heroic, tries, but that isn't enough. Chip Sollins, asked what it took for American Pool Service to become the best in its industry, replied, "I think that if we're out there doing a good job and taking care of the customer, then the money just flows. Money is important, but what's more important to us is to be the best pool management company out there." Competence raises your value. It creates a sense of ease in the way you work, solve problems, and make decisions as illustrated in the following story:

A couple was having problems with their plumbing, so they called a plumber. The plumber arrived on time and got under the sink. He looked at the pipe for several minutes then grabbed his largest hammer. He swung the hammer back and hit the elbow joint on the pipe as hard as he could. Instantly, the problem was solved. The couple was overjoyed and asked him how much they owed him.

"Seventy-five dollars and twenty-five cents," the plumber replied.

"That's ridiculous," the couple replied. "All you did was hit it with a hammer! We want an itemized bill."

So the plumber took out a piece of paper and wrote out $75.25. Twenty-five cents for wear and tear on the hammer and $75 for knowing where to hit the pipe.

Competence is about knowing where to hit the pipe. When you know it, your value rises astronomically.

You Can't Fake Competence

At least not for long. Sooner or later, your competence level becomes visible to the people around you who are depending on you for a certain level of contribution. If you continuously exceed that expectation, then you are going to move forward.

In Stephen Covey's popular book, *The Seven Habits of Highly Effective People,* he restates a principle he calls the "law of the farm," which simply means that you can't force a crop to grow faster than nature will allow it to. Crops will be ready for harvest in the fall only if the preparation, planting, and tending work is done in the spring and summer. Without that preparation, the harvest will be disappointing. All the positive thinking in the world won't get those crops ready for harvest in early summer. Real competence operates according to the same principle; it takes time and you can't fake it. How could a person possibly fake the ability to do 30 push-ups? How could a surgeon fake the ability to perform delicate microsurgery? The important competence levels of your life, the ability to do your work in a special way, cannot be faked. These abilities have to be harvested over time.

Sometimes, however, in an effort to avert the law of the farm and be more convincing, we exaggerate or make claims that just don't hold up over time. You can't promise extraordinary results if you haven't done the up-front planting to be able to deliver. As David Achzet, a successful sales manager, explains, "Don't promise more than you can deliver. If there's one nasty habit that people get into, because of their desire to make the sale, it is that they will promise more than the company can deliver, and that often leads to a loss of credibility. Instead, underpromise and overdeliver."

To leave a lasting mark of excellence on your work, you need a very high level of competence. It is possible to try very hard and produce low-quality work if your competence level is not high enough. Often, when people become frustrated with the rewards and recognition they are receiving, they are overestimating their level of competence.

Sometimes we think that the ability to recognize and even explain high-quality work is a substitute for actually *producing* high-quality work. Just being able to recognize high-quality work is not the same thing as actualizing it. Unfortunately, many people settle for the ability to recognize it as opposed to being able to produce it.

When you deliver valuable results consistently, year after year, then you leave a legacy. You can only do this when you bring a high level of competence to the tasks you perform.

There is a story told about the Texas Rangers. It happened in the late-1800s. One of the wild outlaw gangs that roamed the Wild West took over a small Texas town. They shot up the bar, threatened the citizens, and drove the sheriff out of town, fearing for his life. The town's mayor telegraphed the governor, relaying the desperate circumstances. The mayor pleaded with the governor to send a pack of Texas Rangers to right the situation. The governor promised that a detachment would be on the next day's train.

The mayor himself met the train on which the Rangers were to arrive. As the train pulled to a stop, the mayor was surprised to see only one Ranger get off. "Where are the rest of the Rangers?" asked the Mayor.

"There aren't any," the Ranger replied.

"How can only one Ranger handle this whole gang?" asked the Mayor indignantly.

"Well," the Ranger replied. "There's only one gang, isn't there?"

The more competence you have, the less complicated it becomes for you to produce remarkable results.

Getting under construction as described in Chapter 3 is the quickest way to improve competence. Improving yourself on purpose and on plan will build that competence, which will eventually increase your ability to contribute significantly.

Competence Often Takes Time to Develop

High-level competence usually takes time to develop. People, however, tend to be more forgiving when they feel a person is putting forth their absolute best effort. You get a little leeway. Over time, people begin to pull for you because they see your effort. Maybe not at first, but over time the majority of people you interact with will admire you if you always put out your best effort.

Don't be impatient for your competence level to increase. It happens gradually, but it only happens when you do your best. And this is where we can cheat ourselves if we're not careful. After observing thousands of people in workshops, interviews, and performance reviews, I am convinced that a huge segment of the population has forgotten what doing their absolute best really means. They have settled for "good enough" for so long that "absolute best" has little or no meaning any more. Do your absolute best for what it makes of you, that's the key.

Day-in and day-out best effort is the quickest way to increase your competence. Giving it all you've got is the quickest way to grow and gain the precious rewards life has already planned for you. The right rewards, tailored to be exactly what suits you best, are already there if you will only go out and claim them. Giving your all means to:

- Do work with a giving attitude;
- Eliminate distractions;
- Make no compromises when it comes to quality.

Competence Does Not Stand Still

Competence is either increasing or decreasing. Our talents must increase or they will decrease. This is the secret of constantly renewing our enthusiasm. No task remains the same for long when our talents and competence increase. What gets dull is doing the same task, day in and day out, with the same level of competence, or, more likely, a decreasing level of competence, because, remember, enthusiasm is a key component of competence.

With increasing talent, we can experience life anew. We are doing something for the very first time when we do it with more skill, talent, and effectiveness. I've been observing my son learning to play the guitar. The first month of practice was not very pleasant, for us or for him. His fingers hurt, what he was playing was far from pleasurable to listen to, and he was not comfortable in this new world of chords, notes, and rhythm. He was given a few simple songs to play by his instructor, and gradually he got pretty good at playing them. As his skill increased, he enjoyed hearing what he was producing. That in turn produced more enthusiasm, which improved the quality of his playing. That's the way it works for all of us.

Shouldn't we be expected to constantly improve our competence and talent? If you feel bored with an activity you're doing, is it possible that you are not developing any more? Is it possible that you are doing that activity the same dull way, day after day? Have you leveled off, experiencing more and more autopilot living? If so, take back the controls and experience the joy of driving your life consciously. It's risky, but it's the only way to really live!

Clear the Bar Every Day

Should the world be a bit forgiving? We should be able to have an off day or two along the way, right? Take a walk through the forest one day and sit and observe what is going on around you. Become aware of the sense of alertness the animals of nature have. A "lazy" day could be catastrophic. They are on full alert all the time and they miraculously suffer from a lot less debilitating disease than we do. The gazelle crossing the Serengeti doesn't say to itself, "Gee, I don't feel like running today. I'm just gonna walk." Not if that gazelle wants to live to see another day. The bald eagle doesn't wake up in the morning saying, "I just don't want to hunt today. Maybe some other bird will come along and miraculously drop a salmon in my nest." No, they pour themselves into the day, knowing that today is all they have and that tomorrow depends on an extraordinary effort put forth today. It's instinctive.

The world's greatest high jumper can show up for the Olympics holding every conceivable world record from past events, but he steps up to the high-jump pit knowing that all his past achievements will have absolutely no bearing on today's event if he doesn't clear the bar here and now. He also knows that today offers the greatest opportunity ever to add an extra inch to his all-time best jump.

Often, however, people with less "glamorous" tasks think too long-term. They lose that short-term potency of having to clear the bar each day. They think in terms of clearing the bar each week, month, or year. When you clear the bar each day, the weeks, months, and years have a way of taking care of themselves, especially when you apply the kind of long-term planning we talked about in Chapter 2, one life, one boss.

Clear an extra inch today not because you have to but because of what it will make of you. When you gain strength, when your ability to clear the bar every day becomes more consistent, the value of your contribution increases.

A huge problem many would-be influencers face is the fact that they have little value to contribute. Influence is a direct result of who you are as a person: how credible you are, how consistent you are, how capable you are of achieving a personal best each day.

What would it take for you to have your all-time personal best today? Answer the following three questions:

1. Why bother having a personal best?
2. Why not?
3. Why not now?

If all of your rewards rested on what you accomplish today, instead of an accumulated value over time, how would that change your day-to-day performance? Isn't it a healthier outlook to think in terms of competing at the highest level each day rather than relying on past accomplishments?

If we start each day by saying, "My opportunity for promotion depends on today. If I put forth the best 10 hours I ever have, I get the promotion," then how would the quality of your work change? Sharon Basile explains: "You have to give 110% all of the time, every time, with no excuses. You can't hold back when it comes to doing that little extra something to make yourself special to your customers. Once, I arranged for a customer of mine to buy some personal items at a discount because of a relationship our company had with a vendor. It was no big deal for me, but it made a big difference to the customer. As a result, I became more than just a salesperson to them. We developed a personal bond, and that translates to business."

When you act as if your life depends on the quality of your work, then tasks take on a whole new meaning. The truth is, the quality of your life does depend on the quality of your work.

There is a tremendous sense of satisfaction that comes from doing our absolute best, putting forth our best effort. The pace of the world is making this more and more challenging to do. If we're not careful, we get caught up in the pace and start acting as though getting more done is more important than getting less done more thoroughly. Our actions begin to lose meaning because they are performed hastily at a 75% level of quality, leaving us not even knowing what our best is anymore. The rush to get things done, the continuous stream of demands that entice us to go quicker with less attention to detail, is the battle we have to fight.

There is a very cleansing feeling that comes from giving work to others that is done to the absolute best of your ability. A great sense of satisfaction, of meaning, and growth comes as a result.

Personal power is your capacity to generate valuable results right now. When you have competence and talent and a reputation for getting the job done, you will build your personal power capacity. More important, you will build that critical reserve power, that reserve tank of energy to get the job done in the future.

PART 2—BE A GIVER

"The Bridge Builder," a poem by William Allen Dromgoole, captures the spirit we need to strive for when giving our work and gifts to others.

> An old man, going a lone highway.
> Came at the evening, cold and gray.
> to a chasm, vast, and deep, and wide.
> Through which was flowing a sullen tide.
> The old man crossed in the twilight dim.
> The sullen stream had no fears for him.
> But he turned, when safe on the other side.
> And built a bridge to span the tide.
> "Old man," said a fellow pilgrim near.
> "You are wasting strength with building here.
> Your journey will end with the ending day.
> You never again must pass this way.
> You have crossed the chasm, deep and wide.
> Why build you the bridge at the eventide?"
> The builder lifted his old gray head.
> "Good friend in the path I have come," he said.
> "There followeth after me today.
> A youth whose feet must pass this way.
> This chasm that has been naught to me

To that fair-haired youth may a pitfall be.
He, too, must cross in the twilight dim.
Good friend I am building this bridge for him."

The second piece to the sign, seal, and deliver principle is the way we give, the spirit we embody when we contribute to others, give work to others, and assist other people to achieve their goals. This is what being a giver is all about. To truly create that desired pull effect in our lives, it's not enough to just produce quality work. We live in a world where the human touch, the way we do what we do and the spirit we are in when we interact with others has as much to do with our overall influence as our technical competence. In a nutshell, people are drawn to givers and repelled by takers. Givers who can contribute in a worthwhile way earn a pass to the greatest influence club of all, a club you can join if you decide to be a giver.

We need to seal our activities, our actions, our tasks with the right intentions. The right intentions means giving without expecting something in return. Mike Quindazzi, a top-producing sales manager, puts it simply, "You have to give to get. That's the entrepreneurial instinct in all successful people."

It's giving for the joy of making a contribution, knowing that everything will even out at some point. In today's world it's easy to fall into an entitlement mentality, the "I did this or that so the world owes me something back" approach. When we act as though everything we do for other people obligates them in some way or another, then we are in the fast lane toward disillusionment and disappointment. Our relationships will not grow, and we move further and further away from the pull-vibe described earlier.

Entitlement Mentality versus Being a Giver

We sign our work with our personal signature with competence, enthusiasm, and commitment. Then we need to seal and deliver our work with the right intentions, which means to give and contribute for what it makes of *you,* and for the sheer joy of contributing to the success of others, instead of thinking only about what you'll get in return.

"I believe too much entitlement thinking in a company can literally kill the organization," explains Chip Sollins. "When people continue to believe that they're entitled to more, it causes a cancer in the company. As long as you have entitlement in the organization, you have problems within and you need to get rid of that entitlement mentality. If you don't get rid of it, it will bring the rest of the organization down. I think entitlement thinking is one of the biggest problems in companies today. A lot of people are trying to figure out how to work less and make more. It simply doesn't work that way in the real world, and if a company let's it evolve to that, they're in big trouble. A lot of times when people rise up in a company, they feel they should have to do less because they're becoming a boss. In reality, it's the exact opposite. When you become the boss you probably have to do more. I work harder now than ever before, and I have a lot of employees. You have got to put the hours in. I put in more hours, generally, than my employees. If not, you become stagnant, and stagnant companies die out."

It's hard to be a sincere giver when we feel we are always entitled to rewards for everything we do. Yes, we provide service to our employer, our customer, our colleagues because we want to get a paycheck. External rewards are critical and we cannot ignore them. No one is saying we should be giving away our services for free. But when you are always thinking about what you will get back for every activity you put out, you often sour the taste of what other people receive and make them less likely in the long-term to want to contribute back to you. Even worse, they may think twice when it comes to asking you for help in the future.

When we feel we are entitled to certain rewards by virtue of seniority, minority-factoring adjustments, past accomplishments, connections, our track record, or any of a thousand other reasons, it becomes easier and easier for us to not give each day our absolute best effort. Sealing it with the right intentions means to do all the activities of your day primarily with the intention of making a contribution instead of getting something in return. Carefully plan them first so that they line up with your overall goals, but once that is done, contribute.

You're not entitled to your own version of what you think is fair or not fair. The world is going to decide that. Instead of trying to convince the world, or, even worse, developing anger towards the world about the injustices that are being heaped upon you, simply observe what is happening, understanding that it's all fair, and learn from it, grow from it, and use it as a platform to propel you to the next level.

How to Kill the Spirit of Giving

There are four classic ways to kill the giving spirit that we too often employ:

1. Unbalanced material gain focus
2. Overly selfish, "I'm more important," thinking
3. Win/lose scarcity thinking
4. Too much WII FM thinking

All four of these attitudes drive away the pull-vibe. Let's look at each one more closely.

Unbalanced material gain focus
We all need material things to get through life. We want money and the benefits that come from money. When, however, we think the only value that comes from our actions is monetary benefit, then we neglect the development of other sides of us that are perhaps more important to the actual enjoyment of our days.

A colleague of mine, whom we'll call Howard, was negotiating a contract with a printing supplier several years ago. The printer had been a long-time supplier for our company and had built up a very good relationship with us. Howard told the printer that he thought the price was too high. The printer asked why. Howard replied that he had gotten a bid from another printing company that we had never done business with that was a little lower. The printer told Howard that often times printers will bid very low on the first job just to get their foot in the door, but that they will usually skimp on quality. The printer said that although you may save a few dollars up front, you'll lose much more in the long run. Howard was determined to drive the price of the job down and really beat up on our reliable printer, who had for many years saved us many times with his first-class service. We ended up switching printers, alienating our old printer, and were never able to get the quality and service we had gotten in the past. When we finally did go back to our original printer, his feelings were hurt and the level of trust took a long time to build back up. Sometimes when we overfocus just on material gain and forget about relationships and other issues, we do just what Howard did in this situation.

Overly selfish, "I'm more important," thinking

Often, people develop a strong belief that they are inherently more important than the people around them because of their superior looks, intelligence, or one of a thousand other reasons. They often become very judgmental about others and feel entitled to more than their fair share. As a result, they often become the victims of their own bad judgment, as illustrated in this story:

> A minister, a boy scout, and a computer executive were the only passengers on a small plane. Suddenly, the pilot came back and told the three passengers that the engine was on fire and the plane was going to crash. He explained that although there were four people on the plane, there were only three parachutes, and said, "I should have one of the parachutes because I have a wife and three children." With that he grabbed one of the parachutes and jumped.
>
> The computer executive said, "I should have one of the parachutes because I am one of the smartest men in the world and the world still needs me," and he grabbed one of the parachutes and jumped.
>
> The minister turned to the boy scout and said sadly, but with a smile, "I have lived a good life and am old, so you should have the last parachute. You take it and I'll go down with the plane."
>
> The boy scout looked up at the minister and said, "Relax, minister, the smartest man in the world just picked up my knapsack and jumped out of the plane."

The world has a way of dealing with overly selfish people that is not always pleasant. Often, they end up surrounded by other selfish, critical people and spend their lives fearful of losing their comfortable insulation, as what they've built on the inside is worthless.

Win/lose scarcity thinking

When we think others have to lose in order for us to win, we end up alienating the people around us who are the bridges to our brighter future. The people around us are the clearest indication of where we need to start contributing. When we can help them win, help them get what they want most, then we are increasing our own ability to get what we want most. David Achzet sees it this way: "I always had perceived selling in the past where one person won, the salesperson, and the customer lost. My results got much better once I got past that and recognized that you can feel good about every transaction that happens out there and both people can win."

The National Football League under Pete Rozelle's leadership under-stood this principle and implemented it beautifully. As commissioner, Pete Rozelle knew that the strength of the league depended on creating a competitive environment in which all franchises had enough revenues to build competitive teams. So they worked out a revenue-sharing deal with the major networks that televised games so that small market and large metro-market teams evenly split the proceeds from all the games being televised. This stopped the individual teams from having to compete against one another for television rights and allowed the entire league to take a long-term, big-picture outlook. The NFL is thriving and is the envy of other professional sports. Much of it has to do with this "there's enough for all of us if we work together" thinking.

WII FM thinking

There's a station playing in every town across the globe 24 hours a day. It's the famous WII FM. WII FM plays only one song and they play it over and over and over, nonstop. WII FM listeners, the die-hard listeners who tune in all day long, tend to be selfish and self-centered. The song is "What's In It For Me." Mark Ferraro, a top-performing building-supplies salesperson, explains: "Since the mid-1980s, at least from a sales ap-proach, I think people have gotten a lot better. There's not as much of the "what's in it for me" mentality from the perspective of the salesperson. "What's in it for me" thinking from the salesperson is often a lack of gen-uine sincerity, and I think people really see through that now. We're inun-dated with different choices now, and customers have gotten so good at seeing through that selfish approach that they just won't buy it any more."

When we overdo it in the WII FM today area, we begin to tire the peo-ple around us. We are always negotiating, always working an angle, al-ways trying to get our fair share. Often, the people around us stop includ-ing us in their plans because of the hassle involved in dealing with us. They start to avoid us, to figure out ways to get things done without in-cluding us. Sure, you may learn to maximize the opportunities that come your way with this thinking, but you may not realize you are preventing even bigger opportunities from appearing in the first place.

Mike Finizio, a stock broker who has built his business with a "give service first" perspective, explains: "People who think in terms of 'I'll only do it when there is something in it for me' find that sooner or later they are affected negatively by that attitude. The bottom line is we have to do a lot of things up front before we'll ever get anything back. There are times when you'll be with a client and you'll have to overcome 10 or 15 obstacles that they'll want to know are taken care of before you ever get to what you want to do, and the person who's not patient will never make it to that point. I learned over the years that if I tried to do it all myself, then I would always be tired, working long hours. So I built a fabulous team around me, that I pay myself, to treat my clients like gold. They get whatever they ask for immediately because my team is that good. I have four or five people on my staff because I know that when I'm tired, they'll still be there providing service."

What's Really in It for You?

When you develop a greater giving and contributing attitude, what's really in it for you is the greatest reward of all, the development of your character. Oscar Wilde's famous fable of the happy prince illustrates this point in a special way.

> According to Wilde's story, a very special and elegant statue of a happy prince stood on a tall column high above a great city. The prince's body was covered with thin leaves of finely detailed gold, his eyes were made of huge sapphires, and on his sword hilt there was a large red ruby.
>
> A little swallow who had delayed his winter journey to Egypt much too long paused on his hurried trip south to put up for the night between the feet of the statue of the happy prince. However, the little bird could not sleep because of the sound of the prince weeping, so he flew up, landed on the prince's shoulder, and asked him why he was crying.
>
> The prince replied that although everyone called him the happy prince, he was not happy at all. How could he possibly be happy, he asked the little bird, when from his station high above the city he could see so many people who needed help, food, care, love, and tenderness? "Will you please help me, little bird?" the happy prince asked. "Will you help me to give myself away?" The little bird, moved by the prince's sadness, agreed to help.
>
> First, the swallow removed the ruby from the prince's sword and carried it down to a frightened young mother tending her sick child in a cold house. Then the little bird flew all the way back to the prince, removed one sapphire eye and carried it down to an old man in a small shack who had not eaten for two days. Then he flew all the way back to the prince once more, removed the other sapphire eye and left it in the city at the feet of a little match girl. One by one, the swallow carefully removed all the leaves

of gold from the prince's body and distributed them to the poor and help-less children of the city.

That night, the first frigid blasts of winter struck, and since the prince's body was no longer protected by the leaves of gold, his leaden heart cracked. And, unable to protect himself from the cold, the tiny swallow perished.

The next morning, God called His angels together and pointed down to the city saying, "Bring Me the two most precious things from that place." And when the angels returned, they were carrying the cracked heart of the prince and the body of a tiny dead bird. And God took care of the happy prince and the swallow.

When you are not sure what's in it for you when you are giving maybe a little more than you ordinarily would, reflect back on the happy prince and be reminded of the greatest reward of all that comes from giving, the building of your inner spirit and character. Mike Bowman, a top-performing financial services businessperson, adds, "When I walk by parking meters and I see the meter maid coming and there's someone who has run out of time, I like putting a quarter in there. It makes me feel good. I believe in doing things like that."

Your character, your ability to consistently stand strong for what you believe in and act according to your innermost convictions will grow when you seal your actions with the right intentions. Giving it away builds character, but it doesn't create obligations for others. Giving it away helps you get more meaning out of life all the while knowing that when the value of your contribution increases the rewards increase too. It's about focusing on the inside, the part of you that grows, instead of fo-cusing on what is going to come back.

It's knowing in the innermost part of your being that you will get ex-actly what you deserve and, instead of wasting time trying to convince others that you deserve more, you work hard at raising the level of your contributions so that you actually do deserve more. All the time, energy, and mental anguish we go through when we feel we're not getting our fair share stalls us from acting here and now.

When you do your activities with enthusiasm, caring, and a sense of giving back to others, then you are sealing your actions with the right in-tentions. The cumulative impact of this kind of action is hard for many people to even understand. The most important change is what happens inside of you, and when that change occurs, the way the world interacts with you changes too.

Giving It Away Creates a Positive Aura around You

When you are constantly giving your contributions unselfishly you create an aura around you, a magnetic vibe that others will find fascinating. People around you will say, "Wow, I want some of that." They won't even know what it is, it's indescribable! It is powerful. It gets to the heart of the highest level of influence.

It's so easy and so refreshing to be around people who act unselfishly. You can create a magnetic vibe around you that other people want to ride on, to be around, to tap into. People benefit just by being exposed to you. They feel better as a result of having talked to you because it is easy for them to drop their guard, drop their defenses, and just be themselves. And that is how to influence. And this is why the sign it, seal it, deliver it approach is the best approach. It cultivates the highest level of influence within you while building you to the highest level of contribution you are capable of. That is how to realize your full potential. Don't fall for short-cut gimmicks and communication tricks as the road to high-powered influence. Don't settle for less.

Ride the First-Class Vibe

There is a vibration that you create that other people can feel. This vibration can be disturbing, unsettling, anxiety or doubt producing, or it can be inspiring, uplifting, and invigorating.

I went to Michigan to meet a man who was a colleague of mine about five years ago. I had heard many stories about him as being a real motivator. The organization he runs has always been at the top of his field. He wouldn't want me to reveal his name in this book, as he is a very humble man, so I won't, but let me tell you about my first meeting with him.

I arrived at the airport in Detroit expecting to take a cab to my hotel. I was to meet him the following morning for breakfast. To my surprise, there he was at the gate smiling and waving as though I was an old friend. He was genuinely glad to see me. He shook my hand with warmth and when I expressed my surprise at his welcome, he told me he talked to my assistant earlier in the week and made her promise not to tell me that he was going to pick me up, because he had wanted to surprise me at the airport.

When I shook his hand, I put down my overnight bag and he immediately picked it up, insisting to carry it for me. He graciously loaded my bags into his spacious car and asked me a long stream of questions about myself, my family, and my experiences on our ride to the hotel. As he stopped at the hotel check-in, he jumped out of the car, opened the trunk, grabbed my bags and carried them up to the registration counter smiling at the bellhops as he passed, thanking them for their offer of help, but declining nonetheless. I was informed at the registration desk that I had been upgraded to a suite as a result of a call from a very good customer of theirs (guess who), and when I arrived in my room there was a fruit basket, compliments of a man I had shaken hands with for the first time only 45 minutes ago.

He told me he was running a little late and would love to spend more time with me that night but would have to leave and meet me back at the hotel tomorrow. I felt invigorated and astonished at how important I was to him. His positive vibration had transformed a flight-weary, somewhat anxious traveler into an invigorated person ready to go out for a five-mile run! Later that week, our rapport, which was a direct result of how we had interacted initially, produced a very high level of receptivity to new ideas in each of us. That's what a positive vibe can do for you and the people around you!

Is Anyone Grateful for You Today?

Look back over today and review the people you came into contact with, either in person, over the phone, or through the written word. How many of these people are thankful for something you did today? Any of them amazed? Any of them changed for the better from having come into contact with you?

"They kid me at work that in their next life they want to come back as one of my clients," explains Nola Beldegreen. "In my office, I keep cases of jam, and when I haven't seen a customer for awhile I'll send over a jar and say, 'I don't want to jam up your schedule, but I do want to meet with you.' I always send them something on their birthdays and holiday gifts for my better clients. It helps to elevate my relationship to a friendship level. It makes business a lot more fun."

The key to impacting people positively and building that positive aura is to make unexpected contributions. Send a thank-you note to someone you wouldn't ordinarily write to. Call someone who did something for you a while ago and give them some phone appreciation. Treat a stranger like a million bucks today. Make the people around you feel important, do it sincerely, and do it to the best of your ability, knowing that you will grow from it. That is your reward.

Become a Giver, Not a Taker

The most successful people, the people you probably want to be interacting with prefer to do business with givers. You will find it much easier to gain access to influential people when you create a contributing, giving vibe around you and dismantle the selfish, "what's in it for me," aura that shields opportunities like a force field.

Givers sleep easier. They enjoy the fruits of their accomplishments every moment because their self-worth soars with every contribution. They are not selfishly waiting for rewards to arrive, for anything to come back, because they enjoy the journey more. The old saying that the joy is in the giving is true.

Givers attract other givers to them. As a result, the people they interact with begin to make a contribution back to them. Fill your life with people who reflect this philosophy by practicing it yourself.

People can sense selfishness. It's people repellent. A great way to differentiate yourself from virtually everyone around you and stand out in a positive way is to step off the selfishness plane and onto the contribution plane. Few people exist on the contribution plane, and they really stick out in a positive way.

Late in the fifteenth century, two young wood-carving apprentices in Germany confided to each other their desire to study painting. But such study would take money and both Hans and Albrecht were poor. Finally, they had a solution. They decided that one of them would stay behind and work and provide the money so that the other could go away and study. Then, when the lucky one became rich and famous, he would aid the other. They tossed a coin and Albrecht won. So, while Albrecht went to Venice, Hans worked as a blacksmith. As soon as he made money, he would send it to his friend.

Months stretched into years and, at last, Albrecht returned to his native land, an independent master. Now it was his turn to help Hans. The two men had a joyous reunion but when Albrecht looked at his friend Hans, he started to cry because he discovered the extent of Hans's sacrifice. The many years of working in a blacksmith shop had bruised and callused

Hans's hands. He could never handle a painter's brush. In gratitude to his friend Hans, Albrecht Dürer, the master artist, painted a portrait of the work-worn hands that had labored so faithfully. He presented the painting to his devoted friend. Today, this painting, *The Praying Hands,* is a masterpiece, a symbol of friendship and sacrifice, and is known to millions of people throughout the world.

Meaningful contribution is the way we leave a lasting impression on the people around us and in the world we live.

Make a Lifestyle of Adding Value

There are many opportunities to contribute to the lives of others every day. On your next phone call at work, end the conversation by asking, "Can you think of anything else I can do to help you out today?" Ask a new employee in your company out to lunch and find out if there is anything you can do to help them get adjusted to their new position. On your next walk through your neighborhood, pick up a couple of pieces of trash you see along the way. Pay a compliment to the person who pours your coffee tomorrow morning at breakfast and improve their morning a bit. Organize your tasks in the morning in order of importance and start working on the most important until you have contributed value-added work on that task. When your goal is to make everything you touch just a notch better for having come in contact with you, then the path you walk will be littered with constant improvements. It will also be visible to others because your own special mark of distinction, your mark of excellence, will permeate all of your actions.

Mark Ferraro explains: "Service is really where it's at in life. When you have a family, you're really there to serve your kids and observe your responsibility as a parent. In business it's the same thing with your customers. You're there to serve them. The bottom line is if you don't serve the customer, you're not going to get the sale. In each industry, service is what you're selling." Nola Beldegreen adds, "I love the process of selling. Don't you love it when you're buying something and they give you a little extra gift like cologne or something with your purchase? I like to surprise my clients with all kinds of surprises. It works and it's a lot more fun and interesting and creative at the same time."

Value Is about What Others Need

So how do your create real value? It's simple; you do things for other people that are honest, ethical, and what they need most. Real value is the miraculous execution of the important. What does your boss need most from you? Figure that out and you've got the most important piece of information you need to do your job effectively. It's amazing how many people, when asked, "What does your boss need most from you?" are unable to answer. The answer to this question is the path to higher value. Ask him or her. Find out so you can start to make a more valuable contribution.

"We really believe in doing extra things at our company," explains Paul Thomas. "One of my customers out in the San Fernando Valley was moving, and we sent three of our delivery trucks just to help them move. We're not in the moving business and they didn't even ask, but we did it anyway. It's one of those things that they're going to remember; that our company stepped up and did something that no one else would have done. They know there is no reason why we should have done it, and they're going to remember it."

It's what others need that counts. The more difficult the needs are to satisfy, the more valuable the service that satisfies the needs. The tough needs to satisfy are difficult because few people have the discipline, persistence, and wherewithal to solve those problems.

What Is Your Vibe?

Is your vibe positive, neutral, or negative? Some people actually sap the room of energy when they walk in. What impact do you have? If you want influence, if you want to outsell the people around you, then you have got to develop that positive vibe around you so that people are better off for your being in the room.

When you adopt this principle, you shine it on others and you won't even know it. You become an inspiration to people around you in unexpected ways. You contribute without even trying. Your value becomes unintentional. That is how you start to attract back to you extraordinary results.

Several years ago a man named Paul received an automobile from his brother as a Christmas present. On New Year's Eve Paul was leaving his office. When he got to his car, parked on the street, a poor young boy with a beaming smile was walking around the car, admiring it. "Is this your car, Mister?" he asked.

Paul nodded. "Yes it is. My brother gave it to me for Christmas." The boy was astonished. "You mean your brother gave it to you and it didn't cost you nothing? Boy, I wish . . ." he hesitated.

Of course, Paul knew what he was going to wish for. He was going to wish for a brother like that. But what the lad said next jarred Paul all the way down to his heels.

"I wish," the boy continued, "that I could be a brother like that."

Paul looked at the boy in astonishment, then impulsively he added, "Would you like to take a ride in my automobile?"

"Oh yes, I'd love that," the boy replied.

After a short ride, the boy turned with his eyes aglow and said, "Mister, would you mind driving in front of my house?"

Paul smiled a little. He thought he knew what the lad wanted. He wanted to show his neighbors that he could ride home in a big automobile. But Paul was wrong again. "Will you stop where those two steps are?" the boy asked, pointing to the front of his house.

He ran up the steps. A short while later, Paul heard him coming back, but he was not coming fast. He was carrying his little crippled brother. He sat him down on the bottom step, sort of squeezed up against him and pointed to the car.

"There she is, Buddy, just like I told you upstairs. His brother gave it to him for Christmas and it didn't cost him a cent. And some day, I'm gonna give you one just like it. Then you can see for yourself all the pretty things in the Christmas windows that I've been telling you about."

Paul got out and lifted the lad to the front seat of the car. The shining-eyed older brother climbed in beside him and the three of them began a memorable holiday ride.

Giving it away is the most valuable reward of living the OUTSELL principles because the principles will attract to you achievements and focus that will allow you to become a lighthouse to the people around you. Giving with a spirit of contributing, whether it's a report that's due on Friday or a generous gift on Christmas morning, has the potential to change you into a person who shines the path for others to follow. The greatest leaders of all are the ones who attract self-selected followers. Perhaps that is why, when you look back over history to the greatest leaders, you find that they were the ones who served and gave back to the people they lead. People like Ghandi, George Washington, and Mother Teresa were all givers.

Look at Your Blueprint

Your blueprint needs to contain plans for increasing the quality of your work. Think carefully about how you can improve the quality of the projects you touch and the work you contribute to the people you come in contact with. Make a commitment right now to clear the bar every day, to constantly produce better and better work. And when it comes time to give to others, do it with a joy-filled spirit, knowing that it all comes back somehow, knowing that the giving itself builds character and is the most valuable reward of all.

Chapter Six

This entire chapter could be summed up by saying that the people you spend time with, both personally and professionally, will either lift you up or pull you down. Business is ultimately about relationships. Selling ideas and getting them accepted and acted on is a collaborative effort that involves the cooperation of other people. When we have strong relationships with skilled and talented people who are committed to helping us get things done, we are capable of accomplishing remarkable results. In business, the quality and caliber of people that you associate with will, to a large extent, determine the opportunities that open up for you. When the people who are making things happen recognize you as a person who can get results, then they become motivated to help you succeed, because as you succeed, you help them succeed.

Most of us prefer to spend time around people who support our growth and enrich our lives. Having this preference, however, does not in any way guarantee that we will, in reality, be surrounded with the kind of people who can not only support our journey, but can help us get there a little faster.

There's been a ton of huzzonga slung left, right, forward, and backward on the topic of networking, and we intend to take a fresh look at this very important topic of who we need to meet and how to meet them.

THE OUTSELL HARVEST

What we've been suggesting so far in this book is that if you let go of the quick-fix, "easy to learn" technique approach to getting results and build yourself from the ground up to be a rock-solid results producer, then you will achieve the greatest rewards in the long-term and quite possibly the short-term as well. You will earn a place at the banquet with other champions and build relationships with the people who can really quantum-leap your business career.

We have now spent a considerable amount of time exploring the first four OUTSELL principles:

1. One life, one boss
2. Under construction
3. Tell it with gusto
4. Signed, sealed, delivered

All four of these principles have to do with taking control of your life, learning and developing new skills and attitudes that will build you into the kind of person that other people will respect and admire because you will be capable of producing results in your chosen areas of focus. You won't be bluffing your way through projects, throwing out well-timed buzzwords, dodging responsibility, or playing political games. Instead, you'll have what it takes to accept total accountability, get the job done, work effectively with other people, and speak persuasively about ideas you believe in and are willing to assume responsibility for.

Forrest Gump was a fascinating film that captured the imagination of millions of movie goers. It's the story of a man's life, a man who was not born with much intelligence as traditionally measured academically or with an IQ test. He does, however, possess three notable talents. He is a very fast runner, he is a natural at Ping-Pong, and he is absolutely loyal to his family and true friends. Forrest is thrown into situations that, because of his ability to perform these three talents when the pressure is on, lead him toward remarkable achievements. It is his ability to develop his modest gifts to their absolute highest level that creates a magical pull effect in his life. The people he attracts to him are not obvious winners, but they are, nonetheless, the people he needs in order to create overwhelming success in everything he does. In a nutshell, he makes the most of who he is, even though he is, on first glance, a mentally handicapped individual.

By following the first four OUTSELL principles, you can make the absolute most of who you are, discover your special talents and gifts, and learn to make higher and higher value contributions to the people who count on you to get the job done. Influence is about communication, but it is also about dependability, coming through in the clutch, and possessing skills, abilities, and attitudes that are hard to find. The first four OUTSELL principles lead you to develop a "come through in the clutch" ability.

Principle five, eat breakfast with champions, is one of the payoffs for all the effort you put in on these first four principles. You will win an extraordinary reward, the opportunity to spend a lot of time with winners, with people who are exciting to be around, in contact with other winners, and who are capable of bringing real resources to the table. They'll want to know you, respect your opinion, and come to you for help because when you've got the first four OUTSELL principles popping in your life, you have a lot to offer.

An army general was touring a field training camp and observed a paratrooping unit right after they had landed from a jump. The men were carrying the parachutes away from the landing target area. Curious, he walked up to three of the men, who were walking together, joking loudly.

"Why do you men like to jump?" the general asked.

"I love it," the first soldier replied. "It's the greatest feeling of freedom in the world."

The second soldier looked at the general. "It is the most exciting thing I've ever done," he exclaimed with enthusiasm and a winning smile.

The general looked at the third soldier and said, "Soldier, why do you like to jump?"

"I hate it," he replied.

Surprised, the general looked at the soldier carefully and asked, "Then why do you jump?"

"I like to be around guys who like to jump," he replied.

This is the same effect that the OUTSELL principles you're selling yourself on will have on the people who know you. People will want to spend time with you, too, because you will have something that attracts others to you. This is exactly what we were talking about when we referred to the pull effect in Chapter 5. When the winners of the world start to seek you out, you are riding a "pull" wave. Eating breakfast with champions is the way you can maximize that pull effect in your life. In business the most powerful people are the ones who can get things done, and they get things done by being associated with other people who also get results. The OUTSELL factors make you a person who can get results and, in time, a person that the people in business who have the resources will want to know and call on for help. That's real influence! Not the kind of influence that comes from a carefully scripted presentation, or a well-timed buzzword.

MEETING THE CHAMPIONS

It's Who You Know?

For our entire business careers we have heard the phrase "It's who you know" repeated over and over as a self-contained mantra, implying that if you know the right people and can get their business cards, then you've got it made. But is it really that hard to get the names of the important people you need to know? In times like these when information is so available and organized in any way imaginable, getting names, phone numbers, and addresses is relatively easy. Catchy little '90s sayings like, "The person with the fattest Rolodex wins!" imply that the more cards you go out and collect the more you are "networked." It's a crock of huzzonga! We contend that who you know is not as important as many people say it is.

It's Who Wants to Know You!

It's not who you know, it's who wants to know you! Instead of looking at how thick your Rolodex is, ask yourself, "How many Rolodexes contain a card with my name on it? With a big star by my name? Highlighted and dog-eared from use?" When people want to know you and are eager to ask for your help, then you are effectively networked. It's not how many people you can ask for a favor, it's how many high-quality achievers want you to do a favor for them!

Networking events are designed to allow people to meet, shake hands, and exchange cards in an attempt to expand the number of contacts (the network) the people attending the event will have. The philosophy behind the principle eat breakfast with champions is a very different look at how you grow and expand the group of people you interact with and, more importantly, how you build a synergistic group of high-quality people that *want* to interact with *you*.

There are a typical series of steps that most people go through in order to become a high-value champion. This is how it usually works:

1. First, the "champion-in-waiting" gets committed to a career.
2. Second, they become intense learners—they get under construction.
3. Next, they battle for several years growing and learning how to get results.
4. Then, they post consistent results and develop a track record of consistency.
5. They become eager to help others and unselfish in their willingness to contribute.
6. Other champions start to notice and value their ideas and opinions more.
7. A larger opportunity comes up and it's obvious they deserve it.
8. They now have access to greater resources.

Occasionally a person comes along with exceptional talent or a strength that is so distinct that they take another route, but for 90% of the champions we have come across, and we've met a lot of them, this is how it happens. It doesn't happen overnight and it doesn't happen by blind luck. It happens because of commitment, hard work, and consistent results.

Life Is Relationships

We experience life through our relationships. The quality of our life is the quality of our relationships. You can't have one without the other because they are the same thing. It's not that they are tied together, it's that they are the same. Think back for a moment to a time when you were having a difficult time in a relationship with someone at work whom you had to see on a frequent basis. Did it impact the way you felt from day to day? For most of us, when we are having difficulty in a relationship at work that could potentially have a big impact on our life, it can really cause stress and an often unhealthy sense of frustration. When you have the OUTSELL principles working for you, they will systematically raise the quality of your relationships and, more importantly, over time, attract quality people who bring more quality to your life.

In order to have quality relationships, you need two things:

1. To have achieved a healthy, supportive relationship with yourself that is based on honesty, achievement, discipline, and self-discovery. In

short, to raise your own quality level, which will allow you to contribute more to the people around you.

2. To have effective interactive skills that attract, encourage, and support rather than repel and alienate the people around you.

The person who looks at networking as simply a technique or a quick-fix way to meet more powerful people is settling for less. Usually, when a person is trying to network and meet new people to ask for help from, they run the risk of becoming a nuisance. Increasingly, high-value people, people who know how to get things done and who are in touch with real resources, find it annoying when someone who brings little to the table is constantly asking for favors but offering nothing of value themselves. Chip Sollins, president of American Pool Service, explains: "We're the only pool management company I know of that attends board meetings. We run pools for homeowner's associations, and they have board meetings every month. I felt that if we spent more time with them at these meetings, then we would form relationships with them and become more than just a paper contract. With this bond, I find that people are more forgiving of our mistakes when they do happen, because mistakes will always happen. When they feel you are trying hard and you have that good relationship, it is much easier to keep the repeat customer from year to year." Eating breakfast with champions is about making more significant connections with the people you do business with by being a valuable resource to them.

What we suggest is to put yourself on a level playing field with the champions. Make yourself one of them. Take the long-term view, which, we suspect, is the most effective short-term strategy too.

Who Are the Champions?

Champions are peak performers. Champions are often people who are better than you at a skill area that you would like to get better at. Champions have something to offer. They are interesting to be around because they are doers, not just talkers. They have achievements to back up their intentions. They are reliable. They can get the job done. These champions can be found inside your company or your industry or can be from professions you know very little about. David Achzet, a successful sales manager, explains: "Talking to your own peer group is critical to your self-development. Talk to the successful people, even people outside your own industry, to find out what's going on in the rest of the world. It broadens your perspective."

When I was first starting out in my business career, I had the opportunity to attend a national sales meeting our company was conducting. My boss told me that I should immediately call John, a peak-performing manager, and ask him for advice on what I needed to do to succeed in sales. When I arrived in Dallas for the convention, I called him up and John, to my surprise, invited me to meet him in the lobby right away. We talked until three in the morning and I walked away with pages of notes and insights from a real champion. Ten years later, when I was up for a big promotion in that same company, it was John who put in the recommendation that got me the job.

Champions are like that. They not only help you today, but they can attract opportunities to you in the future. Champions value and keep their word and expect the same from others. Champions are dependable. Champions are on a predictable path toward success. Their lives are going to get better. They are making it today and are probably going to make it even more in years to come.

Champions have the unique ability to attract opportunities not only to themselves but to the people they interact with. Champions are like magnets because champions attract other champions to themselves. They have better resources and contacts. They are more in tune with what is going on and have a strong sense for what will work and, more importantly, what won't. When you have a solid core of champion relationships that you are contributing to, you attract opportunities back to yourself.

One Plus One Does Not Always Equal Two

Perhaps the most powerful result you'll experience when you get together with other champions is the extra power and potential you can tap into. The synergy of champions can solve problems that are often impossible to solve alone. It's like the boy scouts in this story:

> A troop of boy scouts gathered for their annual hike in the woods. Taking off at sunrise, they began a 15-mile trek through some of the most scenic grounds in the country. About mid-morning, the scouts came across an abandoned section of railroad track. Each of the scouts tried in turn to walk along the thin, rusted, elevated rail, but after a few unsteady steps, they

each lost their balance and tumbled off. Two of the scouts, after watching the other members of the troop struggle on the rail offered a bet to the rest of the group. The two bet that they could both walk the entire length of the railroad track without falling off even once.

"No way," laughed the other scouts. "You won't even be able to walk 10 feet!"

Challenged to make good on their boast, the two boys jumped up on the parallel rails, facing one another. Then they simply reached out and held hands to balance each other and steadily walked the entire section of track with no difficulty as they leaned against one another for support.

Individually, both of the boy scouts would probably have failed in the attempt to walk the distance on the rail. Together, however, they were able to harness more potential. When you develop relationships with other champions, you will experience an ability to harness more collective potential and then have the added energy to put it to use.

This is essentially the driving force of team-based work environments. The fiercely competitive business marketplace has forced virtually every industry to adopt a team-oriented approach to creative thinking and problem solving. Cross-functional teams meet constantly in competitive companies to improve processes, streamline tasks, and improve communication. Really effective teams are made of team members in which each person on the team is making a contribution. The eat-breakfast-with-champions principle is perfectly suited for this environment because, when implemented, it allows you to make the most of team-oriented work, collaboration, and partnering.

Teamwork is accomplished through people interacting with people. A certain chemistry is generated when you interact with other people. Each team member experiences this chemistry in a way unique to his or her perspective and ability to contribute. There are three types of experiences you can have when interacting with another person. First, on the low scale, you can actually come down in mood, energy, and attitude by simply spending time around a low output person. In this interaction one plus one may only equal one or can actually equal one-half because your overall effectiveness is reduced. Second, there are other people who are neutral. They add a little, but not a lot. They can't help you much, but they can't hurt much either. They are usually pleasant and helpful but not empowered. One plus one equals two. With the third type, with champions, something special happens when they get together. It's synergy! One plus one can equal three, four, or sometimes five. There is a dynamic that occurs when champions get together that is hard to describe but extremely powerful. They challenge one another to be better, and that's when breakthroughs occur. When you are supported, you are capable of taking greater risk, and greater risk can gain greater rewards. Interacting with champions is like this.

Take a moment and grab a blank sheet of paper and divide it into thirds. Make three columns, as shown in Figure 3. In the appropriate column, write in the names of people you spend time with.

1. People you spend time with who decrease your effectiveness (negative effect).
2. People you spend time with who have little impact on your effectiveness (neutral effect).
3. People you spend time with who have a positive impact on your effectiveness (positive effect).

Become aware of what the people you interact with are contributing or taking away from you. As your awareness increases, you will be able to decide what changes you need to make in terms of who you spend the bulk of your time with.

Remember, the quality of your life escalates with the quality of the people you spend time with. When you spend significant time with people at the champion level, then the quality of your life expands in ways you cannot predict.

Deal with the Low-Energy Person Problem

There is a transfer of energy that happens when two or more people get together. When you can boost the feeling of well-being that the people you meet have as a result of having come into contact with you, it will be much easier for you to persuade and convince them. Sometimes, however, a person does just the opposite as in this story:

> Two guys used to go hunting with each other in the fall. One was positive and the other was negative. The positive guy discovered something he thought the negative guy couldn't complain about: He discovered a bird dog that could walk on water. The positive guy put his new bird dog into his truck and picked up the negative guy on the way to their favorite hunt-

NEGATIVE EFFECT	NEUTRAL EFFECT	POSITIVE EFFECT

Figure 3. Champion Analyzer Chart

ing spot. After about an hour of waiting, some ducks flew by and they shot one and it landed in the water. The dog went running out to the pond and walked right out on the water and retrieved the duck!

The positive guy was smiling but the negative guy was frowning. Several minutes later, they hit another duck and it, too, landed in the water. So the dog, once again, walked right out on the water and brought back the duck. The positive guy was elated and giggling while the negative guy was cold and sour. After they hit the third duck and the dog brought it back, the positive guy couldn't hold back any more. "Haven't you noticed anything about my new dog?" he asked.

"I have noticed only one thing," the negative guy replied. "Your dog can't swim!"

It would be fine if people with low energy could keep that low energy to themselves, but that is not the case. They transfer it to others. They bring other people down. *Acting on this knowledge* is perhaps one of the most challenging things we are suggesting in this book, yet it is the most necessary. If you are determined to make the absolute most of your career, then you must limit, really *limit*, the amount of time you spend with low-output, low-energy people who are overly critical, not very supportive, and always leave you feeling worn out or even worse, as this story points out:

A scorpion, being a very poor swimmer, asked a turtle to carry him on his back across a river. "Are you mad?" exclaimed the turtle. "You'll sting me while I'm swimming and I'll drown."

"My dear turtle," laughed the scorpion, "If I were to sting you, you would drown and I would go down with you. Now where is the logic in that?"

"You're right," cried the turtle. "Hop on!" The scorpion climbed aboard and halfway across the river it gave the turtle a mighty sting. As they both sank to the bottom, the turtle resignedly said:

"Do you mind if I ask you something? You said there'd be no logic in your stinging me. Why did you do it?"

"It has nothing to do with logic," the drowning scorpion sadly replied. "It's just my character."

And some people simply can't help it because their character is so deeply rooted in looking at the negative that they are going to bring you down whether it makes sense or not. It might sound a little rough, a little cold, a little harsh, but it's the truth; you have got to limit your time with the scorpions of the world. Mike Bowman, a top-performing financial services businessperson, explains, "Surround yourself with positive successful people. If you're surrounded by a lot of down people at work, you may have to leave because any company that is attracting a lot of down people is probably in trouble anyway. They will hold you back by not allowing you to stay in a positive mode enough of the time."

If you, yourself, are one of these people that bring the energy of other people down, you have got to change and change now. You have got to get under construction immediately!

Get Infected by the Right Bug!

Remember, the vibe that surrounds you is intermingling with the vibes that surround others, and proximity creates an exchange. When you make contact with a person in a business meeting, whether it be a conversation, a handshake, or eye contact from across the room, there is a vibe exchange. You are going to get bit by the vibe or "bug" inside of other people and your vibe is going to hit them. Since this is the case, make an effort to hit others with and get bit by the right bug. In Chapter 5 we introduced John, the man from Michigan that met me at the airport in Detroit and made me feel like a star. People like John can have the same effect on you as your favorite song—it's an uplift! People like John are the champions you want to eat breakfast with.

People Create a Wake

Not long ago, I was jet skiing with some friends in Rumsen, New Jersey. I hadn't done much jet skiing before, so for me it was a new experience. At one point, a rather large boat came roaring up the channel. As it passed, I was nearly knocked off my jet ski with the waves from its wake. The wake was literally pushing me to the side. As the boat roared up the channel, I watched the waves from its wake spread out and shake other boats and eventually roll up to the shore. People have wakes too. All human activity creates a wake. Champions create a wake that can literally push you forward, if you let it.

I went to a lecture about 10 years ago that was delivered by a very energetic presenter, a champion, no doubt, who talked for a bit about "what the hell" sales calls. "What the hell" calls are long-shot prospecting telephone cold calls you make just for the hell of it. They are low-probability calls in terms of results, but they can sharpen your skills and keep your mind alert. I had brought a new salesperson I had recently hired with me to the lecture, and when we got back to the office we were both charged up with enthusiasm. So, we went into my office and the new salesperson asked me if I thought "what the hell" calls were a worthwhile thing to do. I said, "Let's find out," and I opened up a yellow pages book randomly, closed my eyes, and pointed my finger to an electrical supplies distributor and dialed the number. Two weeks later we closed a $75,000 deal with them! It was the energy that I picked up from hearing that champion speak that created that opportunity. I was literally pushed along in the wake of his crossing the channel before me. Don Graling, a top-producing salesperson and manager, adds, "I believe that enthusiasm and excitement about where you are and what you're doing is important. I like to work with people who are excited about being there. I work out at the gym with a group of about seven people because I like to work out with people who are high energy. They actually push me to put a little more into my workout. You can have a lot of fun with those people."

Negative energy creates a wake, too. A computer database development company had asked me to work with their sales team to help them develop a strategy to reach bigger buyers. I asked if I could sit in on one of their sales meetings early in the project. The owner of the company had told me that he had been getting a lot of complaints from the account executives about the vice president of sales, Joe, and I wanted to see it for myself. I noticed that before the meeting started, the account executives were generally in a good mood, talking about business and getting ready for the meeting. The moment Joe, the vice president, walked in the room, there was a noticeable escalation in tension, which in itself is not necessarily a bad thing. Joe started the meeting by asking the account executives to report on their sales results from the previous week. When the first account executive started speaking, Joe immediately interrupted him and told him to get to the point. He then criticized him in front of his peers for not hitting one of his targets (he did hit the other four), and from that point forward, the energy level of the meeting was muted. There was no feeling of support, motivation, or team accomplishment. Although most of the account executives had a good week, everyone left feeling beat up. I was able to meet with the account executives later that day and many resented the fact that they were underappreciated by Joe. Turnover had been high in his group, despite a good pay plan. Joe was actually inhibiting his people from performing at their highest level.

Sometimes, you can take it as a personal challenge to make the best of a situation where negative people are unavoidable. Mark Ferraro, a top-performing sales professional, explains: "When dealing with a lot of down people, one of the best ways to deal with them is to try and see if you can get them up instead of worrying about them bringing you down. Remember, if there weren't a lot of those people in the world, it would be a lot harder to excel. We're successful because our competitors are downers, too aggressive, or make mistakes. I don't let downer people bother me. You've got to control them and not let them control you."

Champions Have Access to Better Resources

Your view of the world is not the only view there is. We all make decisions about the way that we think the world is based on the type of people we interact with, our disciplines, our habits, and, of course, the specific set of circumstances that we have lived our life through. These beliefs we have are not necessarily an accurate description of the way the world is in its entirety. Maybe you have had very little luck in finding truly reliable people, but they are out there. Perhaps you have never really met a person who keeps his or his word always, but they do exist. Maybe you have never been around a person who can pick up the phone and move mountains, but that doesn't mean they don't exist. And many of these achievers got to be the way they are because they have aligned themselves with powerful resources. Those resources might include other reliable champions, financial backing, powerful ideas, trusting employees who can get the job done, suppliers that get the job done, and business partners who have an even more powerful set of resources. This is why it seems that some people can so effortlessly get things done. When you earn the trust of champions and, more importantly, when you start contributing to their success, they can at times give you access to their resources and help you along. And trust is critical when you are trying to get cooperation, as illustrated in this story:

> Two somewhat unscrupulous men were hiking in the mountains when they came upon a young boy looking over the side of a cliff. "What are you looking at?" they asked.
> "Over there," the boy replied pointing. "There are two young bald eagles in the nest and the parents are gone. I haven't seen them for over an hour."
> Seeing a poaching opportunity, the men whispered to one another for a moment then turned to the young boy. "Would you like to help those young eagles?" they asked.
> "Sure," the boy replied.
> "If we can get the nest, we can take the eagles to a local agency that will take care of them and make sure they are okay."
> "That would be great," the boy replied.
> "As you can see, the nest is on a very small ledge. We'll tie this rope around your waist and slowly lower you down because we're too big to fit on it. When you get down there gently pick up the nest and we'll pull you up. Then we'll take the eagles to someone who can help them."
> The little boy looked at the two men and then at the cliff they would have to lower him from. "I'll do it," he said, and the two men smiled. Then the boy added, "If my daddy holds the rope."

Champions like doing business with people they trust because champions become champions due to their ability to be trusted. As Mike Quindazzi, a top-producing sales manager, explains, "With relationship sales the way it is in the '90s, trust is number one. All things being equal, people buy from people they like. Even when things aren't equal, people will often still do business with people they like."

About 10 years ago I read an article in the *Wall Street Journal* about a man who had been promoted to president of a large brokerage house on Wall Street. I found his biography interesting and I handwrote him a note of congratulations mentioning how inspiring I found the description of the offbeat way in which he had built such a successful career. I mentioned in a P.S. that I was sure that his schedule was very crowded but it would be a great honor if I could interview him and that I was a speaker who spoke in New York often.

I got a call from him a week later and was invited to meet him. When I walked into his office, he thanked me profusely for the letter and said it was the most thoughtful congratulations letter he had received and told me I was all his for the next half-hour. As I was saying goodbye I asked him if there was anything at all I could do to repay the favor. "Yes," he said, "I chair the United Way chapter here in New York and I would appreciate it if you would put me into contact with the president of your company." I picked up the phone and called our president's office, leaving a message that the person I was meeting with would like to speak with him.

"And is there anything I can do for you?" he asked, impressed with my immediate step of action.

"If I could take you out to breakfast in the future to hear more of your remarkable story, that would be a great favor to me," I replied. That afternoon was the first of many meetings that opened the door for several large sales for me over the next several years. Sometimes, you just have to think in terms of how you can help others and not in terms of what other people can do for you. Doug Neet, a successful insurance professional, explains: "You build trust through follow-through. You've got to call people and say 'I don't want to sell you anything today, just wanted to make sure everything was going okay. Hope you had a good birthday, anniversary, and so on. Is there anything I can do to make your life easier?' People really appreciate calls like that and it strengthens your business relationships."

As my own career developed, I was able to see firsthand what it means to have access to large amounts of resources. I was a relatively young, recently promoted vice president. My boss, the CEO, asked me to help him identify people inside the company who would be asked to take over new franchises, a privilege many people worked seven or more years to earn. I was finally in a position to really help the hardworking, talented people I had gotten to know in our field sales network. Because I had access to decision-making power, I was able to help other people move forward. This is what champions can do for you. Because they have access to greater resources, they can give you leverage to get better results.

Champions Are Everywhere

You may be saying to yourself that finding champions and meeting them is a near impossible task, that meeting with these top performers is a lot easier said than done. It isn't hard to expand your champion network, if you look at it in a fresh way.

First, if you set your sights on Michael Jordan, or Jack Welch-like champions that roam the stratosphere, then yes, you are going to have to be a very creative and persistent person to get to know them. Many people at that level (including Jordan and Welch) have books out and often videos that allow you to learn from them and be inspired by their achievements without needing to meet them in person.

Who in your company has a reputation for really getting the job done? Find out and take them out to lunch. Ask them how they've succeeded and make sure to offer to help them in any way you can.

There are many more accessible, but no less extraordinary, champions around you if you'll only pay attention. Perhaps you're going through some tough times in your marriage. Doesn't it make sense to spend some time around someone who has had a successful marriage rather than taking advice from a well-meaning friend who has a history of shaky relationships? You could talk to and get advice from someone you know or someone who knows someone you know who is in a successful marriage.

Is there someone you know of who is in the kind of physical shape you would like to be in? Why not call them up and ask for some advice, some pointers, some habits that work for them? Part of the eat breakfast with champions approach is about going to people who have earned the right to talk about a subject because of their demonstrated level of success in that area.

Earlier in this book, we talked about the article that featured Jerry Rice and his amazing physical conditioning regimen. After reading that article, Jerry Rice became a champion of mine, even though I have never met him. Years before I had injured my knee pretty badly and it had not really responded to therapy very well. I had resigned myself to the fact that it would probably limit me somewhat for the rest of my life. When I felt the determination of Jerry Rice in that article I was convinced that if I worked hard enough at it, I could restore my knee to near perfect form. I am happy to say that a year later my knee is the strongest it has been since the injury (seven years ago) and I am in better overall shape now than at any time in my life, including the years I ran track and cross-country in high school. Champions can inspire you to overcome obstacles in your life and champions are easy to find in today's world of boundary-less information.

Few People Have It All

If you're looking for the peak performer who has his or her entire life together, you may be looking for a long time. Sure, they exist, but they are rare. Many top performers in business have difficulty in other areas of their life, such as health, family, or spiritual. What we must learn to do is gain from champions in their area of expertise and not allow their shortcomings in one area to completely invalidate their achievements and expertise in another. When we have different champions for career, health, finance, relationships, spiritual, and family—champions who have achieved great proficiency in their area—then we do not have to be too demanding of any one person. Thomas Jefferson is my champion for continual learning. A great deal of evidence suggests his personal life was often in disarray, but that doesn't mean I can't learn from him in the area that he excelled in. And this is the key to filling your life with champions. Try to find in each champion an area in which they excel and relate with them on that topic, if possible. By doing this, you will be allowing them to put their best foot forward, and you will gain the most you possibly can from your interaction with them. And when they are focused on something they do particularly well, their energy level and ability to contribute increases dramatically. Don't discount what a person has to say in one area that he or she is good at just because they are not perfect in other areas. It's too demanding. All people have shortcomings.

There also exist well-balanced people who are peak performers in character and consistency but are not dramatically outstanding in any one area. They live successful, meaningful lives, but are not famous or notable in any particular way except that they are dependable, reliable, honest, trustworthy, and consistent. You need to seek these folks out, too. These people become role models and not technique teachers.

Don't Be Intimidated by Champions

Champions are not always difficult to meet. Many champions got to be who they are precisely because they are interested in helping others. Sometimes we read about a person in the paper and say, "I could never talk to that person. I'm a nobody, and look at them." But this just simply isn't the case. No one is telling you to go out and stalk the latest media star—chasing stars is not what we mean when we say eat breakfast with champions. You can, however, initiate relationships with remarkable people if you are creative and realize that most remarkable people are not famous and will be quite flattered by your interest in them if you are genuine and can prove yourself to be helpful to them, too.

STEP-BY-STEP CHAMPION-BUILDING PLAN

What follows are the essential skills you need to build that will allow you to eat breakfast with champions. Work on these skills and you will be able to attract champions, find them in the most unexpected places, and cultivate long-term, mutually beneficial relationships with them that enrich your life and theirs.

Step 1. Bring Out the Champion in You

The first step is to be the champion you already are. Champions are aware of their strengths; their confidence is rooted in these strengths. Champions are aware of their shortcomings; their goals grow from those shortcomings. Champions use their strengths and share them with others. If you are good at organizing projects, why not help someone in your company who has trouble getting organized? If you are good with children, why not coach a soccer team, lead a scout troop, or organize an after-school play group? All three of these activities can improve your leadership skills. If you love reading, why not get involved in one of the many literacy campaigns? If you're a good communicator, why not get involved in a community service club and lead a committee? If you want champions to give to you, you must begin to give more of yourself as a champion in performing your strengths. Share your strengths with others. It is in performing the activities that we do well that we experience the joy of mastery. Remember one life, one boss and how important it is to be excited about living your own life and not imitating someone else. Mark Ferraro explains: "To develop relationships with high-caliber people, you have got to first just be yourself. You can't pretend to be someone else. Sometimes, when people have a leader in their life, they are a leader because they have learned to be themselves. Unfortunately, people try and imitate leaders and it doesn't work." The champion in you will only come out when you get turned on about your life.

By finding the champion inside yourself, you are starting where you are, here and now. You don't have to wait any longer to put into play the principle of eat breakfast with champions. It's an awesome responsibility to be yourself and commit to being a champion. Paul Thomas, a successful sales manager, explains, "You have one reputation, and it's the most important commodity you have. Once you burn that reputation, it's hard to get it back. If you want to talk the talk, you'd better walk the walk. If you make a mistake, it's okay, just don't make it twice."

Step 2. Find the Champion in Others

Here's a shocker for you. Everyone you meet is a champion in one way or another. Everyone. No exceptions. Everyone has valuable experience and insight into something that could add to your understanding. There are "champion compartments" in all underachievers. When you are spending time with people who are low energy and not very strong contributors, then you need to look hard for some strength they possess and pull it out of them. "To be a motivator," begins David Achzet, "you have to build a relationship with the person you want to motivate. They have to feel that you're on their side. If it's someone you manage, you want them to see you as their personal coach or trainer. You don't need an intimate friendship, but more like a player-coach relationship. When you develop this you can challenge people to rise to higher levels of expectation. You give them reinforcement, build them up, and make them feel that they can achieve higher goals. You have to put challenging goals out there so they stretch themselves. However, one of the worst things you can do is build people up too much simply because they are able to reach *small* goals. That's how you build mediocrity. If you don't put stretch goals out there, then they won't be able to rise up to higher expectations. When they fail, you pick them up, dust 'em off, give them some sensible advice, and encourage them to go back out and try to achieve that goal again."

Jack Kemp often tells this story of what happened to him at college, before he went on to fame as an NFL quarterback and later as a powerful politician. He played for Occidental College. At the start of the season, Kemp's coach called him in for a brief pep talk. He sat Kemp down and confided in him that each year there was one player he kept his eye on because he saw in that player a special quality. He told Kemp that if that player lived up to his true potential, he would not only hold the team together and lead the team to a championship, but would go on to greatness as a professional. Kemp said that the coach told him that this year, Kemp was that person on the team. The coach told Kemp that the fate of the team was in his hands and that if he would realize his full potential, he would be the key to the team's success. The coach made Kemp promise to keep the coach's words in the strictest confidence and not share them with anyone on or off the team. When Kemp left the coach's office he was fired up with enthusiasm and would do anything for the coach. Kemp was willing to do whatever the coach asked. Why? Because the coach had made him aware of the champion within. Kemp said that enthusiasm carried him through the entire season. Much later, Kemp found out that the coach had had a similar conversation with nearly every player on the team. The coach knew that the performance of the team was in the hands of each player and that each player would have to live up to his own highest potential for the team to win.

Kemp's coach was interested in bringing out the champion in each of his players, not only for what it would do for the team, but for what it would make of his individual players. He knew that if they wanted to go on to careers as professional football players, they would have to give it everything they had, and he motivated them to do it.

When you bring out the best in others you are encouraging the people you interact with to function at their highest possible level. You are bringing out of them their best possible self. "In growing up," begins Nola Beldegreen, a successful advertising professional, "I was brought up in an environment that if you felt something positive about somebody we were taught to share it with them. There is no point in noticing the strengths in others unless you share it with them. People grow when you make them aware of what they do well."

An easy way to find out what areas any person excels in, even your boss or spouse if you don't know what it is, is to ask. You can use questions like these:

- What is your greatest strength?
- What accomplishment are you most proud of?
- What is your most positive quality?
- What asset do you have that is your greatest attribute?
- What have you achieved as a person that you are most proud of?
- What quality that you possess are you most proud of?

Once you know what that person excels at or considers him or herself strong in, learn from them. Maybe a person has led a very dark and disappointing life, but somewhere they picked up a knack for having fun at social gatherings. Find out how they do it! That insight may really contribute to you in some way. Yes, we have to limit our time with people who bring our energy level down, but even those people can become a champion from time to time. Eating breakfast with champions requires us to find the champion in others and allow them to interact with us as champions. "I remember once," Dave Doehr, a highly successful manager, begins, "on a Friday afternoon at 4:30, the phone rings. So I picked up the phone and it was my vice president on the line. And he says, 'Dave, I was just going over some numbers and I am calling to let you know that I am really impressed with what you're doing down there.' And he reels off some numbers, and I know he's not just blowing smoke, because he's reading off some numbers that I actually did. He said, 'I really applaud you and want to know you're doing a darn good job.' I was blown away. I said to myself, 'That's the kind of leader I want to be.' I was ready to do anything for this guy. I learned from that."

With each person you meet in the next day, try and identify at least one positive quality they have and write it down. Then, under their name, write down what you could learn from them because they have more skill or knowledge than you. That is where you want to begin in your next conversation with them. Start with what they are good at. That is called building a bridge to you from their side of the river.

> Each person I meet is in some way superior to me, and in that I can learn from them.
>
> —Ralph Waldo Emerson

Discovering what that special quality is can transform ordinary encounters into extraordinary meetings. Consider the approach of Paul

Thomas, "I like to spend my time with good people that I can trust, but I also like to spend time with people like the people I play basketball with, who are less fortunate, who don't have the skills that I or the people I hang around with do, because that gives them the opportunity to step up and grow, too. I love to contribute back in any way I can."

Here's another way to bring out the champion in other is: Once you've identified the positive qualities they possess, tell them how much you admire those qualities, in a direct, honest, and evidence-reinforced way. "Evidence-reinforced" means to back up what your are saying with a concrete example or observation. It's the difference between saying, "Jane, you are so organized!" and "Jane, I admire how organized you are. The report you wrote last week that I just saw was well-thought-out and reflected a logical, well-organized presentation of your project."

People respond positively when they hear their strengths noticed and reinforced by others. They show their better side. We all have a champion inside of us. The person who can encourage this side to come out of the people they interact with will live a more joyful life filled with people eager to contribute back to their success.

Very few people feel overly appreciated. Most of us do not complain that we are being complimented, too much. When a person notices a strength we have and expresses it to us in a thoughtful way, it generally has a very positive effect.

Step 3. Find New Champions

The next step is to add new champions to the people you interact with regularly. The best way to do this is to first identify people in places you want to be or people who possess the skills and abilities you have identified as part of your under construction goals. Give them some serious recognition and praise for their achievements and ask them for help. Some will and some won't; that's the way it is. Nothing works 100% of the time, and great influencers recognize this.

Ask the people you know if they know anyone who is an expert in an area you are interested in. Just getting to know new people because of their knowledge instead of for a potential favor they could do for you will lead to results you could never predict. People are much more eager to share knowledge on areas of their own expertise with you than they are to buy things from you. One of the reasons that many "networkers" fail in building a quality contact base is that they are far too eager to get business from people and too "under eager" to learn from them and, more importantly, contribute to them in ways that would be helpful.

Ask yourself, "How can I contribute to these champions I want to meet?" Offer to be of service. As Molly Williamson, a top-producing salesperson, explains, "If you ask people you would like to know better what you can do for them, it is a good way to open the door. Not that many people do that." Find out if there is something you can do for the people you want to know better in order to get some time to visit with them.

Become a Champion Attracter Yourself

Becoming a champion attracter is really what this book all about. It's not how to connive your way into the lives of people who can buy something from you. It's about how to become the kind of person, the kind of high-power, high-impact business person that other people want to be around. Sharon Basile, a successful advertising salesperson, explains, "I'm a relationship salesperson. I know my customers. I never forget their birthdays. I try to find out what they're like. I find out where they live. I find out who they are as a person. I care more about the person than I do about their money. And they can tell the difference."

Too many people are waiting to get the position of power before they will change into the person worthy of that position rather than raising themselves to the caliber of person who is worthy of the power first. There are no tricks, no networking strategies that are going to get you the kind of results that this approach will. Most networking strategies are utterly annoying to people who are true champions. Here are the keys to creating a champion in you:

- Self discipline and motivation: one life, one boss
- Fast-paced development: under construction
- Clear, concise, and passionate communication skills: tell it with gusto
- A give-first get-later mentality: signed, sealed, delivered

It's not about shortcuts, tricks, or techniques. Become a champion yourself, then find the champion in others, and encouraging that side of them to come out by noticing their strengths. Don Graling explains: "I think the winners I've gotten to know have shown me that I can be successful in what I'm doing. They showed me that I have potential well beyond what I thought and, more importantly, they showed me how to get to it. They encouraged me to stretch, and that made a big difference in my life. I want to be able to do that for the people in my life."

Champions are attracted to people who are sincere, who do their best in all situations, and who are not always working an angle. When we don't consistently put out a best effort, people notice. Mark Ferraro explains: "You have to take a genuine interest in other people. You can't just go into a project thinking, 'I'm going to do good on this project because it will get me that next promotion.' You have to do good on the project to try and help the people on the project, and the rest will take care of itself."

Finally, be in contact with people you admire, be eager to contribute to them and learn from them, knowing that once you are of value to them, they will be eager to contribute back to you.

The Essential Interpersonal Skills

Meet and greet people with happiness and enthusiasm
We spent some time on the importance of greeting people in Chapter 4. You will experience great benefits if you can master the first impression. And the key to this is to think, "Be friendly and interested in the person I am meeting." The following are some of the keys:

- A warm genuine smile
- A friendly handshake
- The ability to remember names
- An interested, curious, and friendly attitude
- A cheerful focus on the positive

Steve Johnson is truly one of the greatest masters of the "begin in a friendly way" principle whom I have ever met. Once, we were going through an airport together, on the way to a flight. The curbside baggage check person was having a difficult day; there was a big crowd of late passengers and he was manning an understaffed station. He was stressed, rushed, and not having much fun. Steve handed him his bag and with a big smile extended his hand and said, "How are you doing today, you handsome stallion?" The baggage clerk looked up, shook off his stress, then cracked up and said, "That's the nicest thing anyone has said to me all day. After that, I really do feel like a stallion!" He gave us the royal treatment and we joked a bit before we headed over to the gate. "You two guys have a great flight," he said as we walked away. The point is, you can so easily transform another person's mood by simply making an effort to be pleasant and fun.

Dave Doehr explains: "I believe that when you're in a leadership position, you have to be aware of the shadow you are casting as you walk into the room. Is it a slouching, down-trodden, beat-up shadow that people see, or is it a lively, upright shadow that's strong and says, look, we are big and strong and happy to be here and we're on the move. I try and keep that image in my mind. I ask myself, 'What does my shadow look like? What do I leave behind when I leave a situation?' because those things are so important."

Give sincere appreciation

No one suffers from getting too much appreciation. Most people feel grossly underappreciated, and very few things you do will build more bridges between yourself and the people in your life than showing appreciation to them in a genuine way.

- Recognize the little things people do for you.
- Be thankful for each and every contribution others make to your success.
- Stop taking people for granted.
- Be grateful for the kindness and consideration that others show to you.

I learned firsthand the power of well-timed appreciation after conducting a day-long seminar up in Napa Valley with some service representatives from a large phone service provider. The program was focused on how to coach and bring out the best in the people who work for and with you. As a result, I got a chance to share a lot of personal incidents about service and coaching people to be the best they could be. At the end of the seminar, as the people were leaving the room, a woman came up to me and said, "I enjoyed today so much. If I was a kid, I'd want you to be my father."

I was so genuinely moved that I floated through the next several days. I'll never forget it, and that comment, in a subtle way, has changed my life.

Bring out the strengths in others

People become better when they are operating from a sense of confidence and self-esteem. And can put people into these positive states of mind at any time you want. Become the person that makes other people feel better about themselves.

- Recognize the strengths in everyone you know.
- Repeatedly compliment them on their strengths, and back it up with evidence and examples.
- Ask people how they achieved those strengths.
- Be eager to hear about other people's achievements and accomplishments.
- Constantly remind yourself that everyone you meet is superior to you in some way.
- Remember that no one gets tired of hearing about their strengths, especially when noticed and communicated in a unique way.

Years ago, I saw a children's book that had only four pages. On the first page was a picture of a man standing by a little girl. You could only see the man from the knees down. The caption coming from the little girl was, "My daddy is big." The next page showed the little girl stretching her hand to barely touch her dad's hand, but once again, we could only see the dad from the waist down. The girl said, "My daddy is big." On the next page was the little girl standing with her little feet in her father's shoes. She is saying, "My daddy is big." On the final page, the only page that has a full picture of the father, the little girl is sitting on his shoulders. The little girl is saying, "I love my daddy because he can make me bigger than he is."

That's exactly what you can do when you notice and communicate the positives you see in others. You can lift them up on your shoulders and let them be big for a moment. People really remember it.

Don't take yourself too seriously

The people who are easy to get along with in life and who are a joy to spend time with are people who do not take themselves or the people around them too seriously. Be light in your approach and genuine with your intentions. Realize that everyone is not going to agree with you—many will disagree, and some will even dislike you for reasons quite personal, often related to difficulties in their own lives. Let unkind words of others roll off your back.

Don't feel you have to toss back every arrow that comes your way. Realize the humor that is usually close to the situation and lighten up.

There are many people who are, deep down, wonderful people who are giving, loyal, and trustworthy, but they have one problem—people just don't like to be around them because they are so serious all the time. There are times when we have to just loosen up and be human, even in business. If you can't go out for a business dinner and have a little fun once in a while, then you are missing the whole point of what relationship building is all about. People like to have fun and enjoy their time in addition to getting results.

Appreciate the opinions of others

Truth is often relative to the way you see it. It is possible for two people to have widely varying opinions on a topic and both be right. Relationships become very strained when we feel as though the person we are talking with must agree with us. Because a person holds another opinion, it doesn't necessarily mean they think we are wrong. Be curious about other people's opinions without feeling the need to agree or disagree with them. Understand them first. The pressure you feel from constantly agreeing and disagreeing with everything you hear will turn your demeanor to one of confrontation if you let it. Instead, be interested to understand and don't feel confronted when people express opinions that contrast yours.

Over the years, I've gotten to know a businessperson named Mark in Arizona who recently took over a family business. Since he took over, the company has been shrinking a little each year. Mark is the kind of person who has to be right in every interaction. It is taxing to talk with him, whether it be in person or on the phone. Not only does he need to be right, but if you see a situation differently than he does, he needs to make you wrong. I asked him a few questions about his company, and he told me that several of his big producers have left since he took over the company. He said that he was, in fact, happy they left because they didn't see things his way. And his company continues to shrink. To be truly successful in a world that is becoming increasing complex and diverse, we have got to be able to see that there are often three sides and six answers to every problem.

Be curious and interested in others

Perhaps the greatest of all conversation talents is the ability to be genuinely curious about others. Most people enjoy talking about themselves to an interested audience. When you are able to openly listen with interest to what interests other people, you will quickly build rapport and trust, the gateway to influence. In tell it with gusto, Chapter 4, we examined a number of ways to improve in this area.

Interact with people in a constructive manner
When a person comes to you with a problem, you have a choice of many responses. One alternative is to explore in depth what went wrong, why it went wrong, what that indicates about the people involved, the implications of this disastrous situation, the wrongs that were committed, the justification at being angry, and so forth. Or you can quickly jump to a solution mode by asking, "What can be done to fix this situation?" Don Graling suggests, "When there is a problem to be solved, I try and immediately focus on the best way to solve it. It brings people down if you spend a lot of time placing blame and punishing. As a manager, you have to avoid wasting time overcriticizing good people." This kind of thinking, so obvious in its benefits, is distinctly lacking in many relationships, both personal and professional. Analyzing the problem from all sides without ever getting to the resolution alternatives brings people down. The old saying "you're either part of the problem or part of the solution" is what this is all about. When crises erupt, when problems need to be solved, challenge yourself to seek the remedy as soon as you understand the causes of the problem. Once the causes are out, move off the problem and into the solution. People will marvel at your focus and how efficient you are. Conversation usually brightens when we focus on solutions.

The People in Your Life Make All the Difference!

Paul Thomas sums up the entire experience you'll have when you adopt this new way of looking at networking: "Every once in awhile, I'll get a call out of the blue from someone who knows somebody I know. And they'll say, 'I don't know if you can help me, but so and so said you're the guy to call if you want to get something done.' And that's the biggest high you can get. That's what it's all about for me."

You need to remember two parts when it comes to eating breakfast with champions. First, you don't stand a chance of really succeeding in this area unless you have built a substantial amount of value that you can bring to your relationships. And we do that by practicing the OUTSELL principles. Second, you have to be proactive about cultivating relationships with the kind of people we call champions. Don't leave the answer to the question "Who are the people in your life?" to chance. Decide who they should be and go out and eat breakfast with champions!

Take Out Your Blueprint

Plan activities right now that are going to put you in contact with the people you want to get to know. Send some notes to champions you would like to meet. Call someone in your company whom you admire and tell them why you admire them. Communicate a strength to someone you work closely with every day. Plan it and do it. Put it right into your calendar.

Chapter Seven

> We are like blocks of stone out of which the creator carves the form of men—the blows of his chisel, which hurt us so much—are what make us perfect.
>
> —C. S. Lewis

One of my favorite stories involves the principle of life's hard; hunker down and reach higher ground. What makes this story so remarkable is that it's true:

Niccolo Paganini was a master composer and virtuoso violinist back in the 1800s. He was a unique showman and had developed the reputation of composing classical music that was so technically difficult to play that only he could play it. He had an enthusiastic following of fans that marveled at his technical skills.

He was performing in Italy one night and was playing a very difficult piece of music. The orchestra was behind him and the conductor started the symphony with Paganini, the featured soloist, at center stage. Ten minutes into the performance, the first string on Paganini's violin snapped. He had only three strings left to play this technically demanding piece of music. Paganini, up to the challenge, tightened his concentration and played on without missing a note. Ten more minutes passed and another snap! Paganini's second string had broken. Realizing he had only two strings left, even the great Paganini stumbled a bit. Quickly, he made up his mind to play on, his fingers racing up and down the neck of that violin in an effort to adjust to the now staggering challenge before him. The audience marveled at his mastery.

Five more minutes and another high pitched snap, as one of the remaining two strings broke. With the unraveling strings dangling from his violin, as if signaling defeat for Paganini's performance, the great musician and the orchestra behind him stopped playing. It looked as though he was going backstage for a new instrument. Instead, he looked up to the sky, held his violin up as if to rally all his courage, returned the violin to his chin, and bowed to the audience. He signaled to the conductor to start the orchestra and Paganini finished the symphony on that one string! The audience was ecstatic and wouldn't let him go home until he had played two encores on that same violin. It was an unforgettable performance and has become so famous that modern-day violinists, when playing that same piece of music, will often ceremoniously tear off three strings of their violins throughout their performance, simulating Paganini's great achievement.

Things do go wrong, often at the worst times imaginable. That's the way it is. In Paganini's case, just when he thought the worst possible accident had occurred, he was faced with two more surprises escalating in progressing magnitude the challenge of that night's performance. Did he complain? Did he quit? Did he say, "I can't take it; this isn't fair?" No, he was able to turn this unexpected nightmare into one of his greatest triumphs. Literally, the broken strings (which represent life's unexpected hurdles) allowed Paganini to reach higher ground, a level of extreme concentration and heightened performance. And that's what we'll be discussing in this section of the book. All that you've been learning in previous chapters will prepare you for this principle, because when you really understand life's hard; hunker down and reach higher ground, you'll be prepared not only to cope with life's proverbial curve balls but, like Paganini, to use them to unveil your greatest inner resources.

MASTER THIS PRINCIPLE

If you truly want to be a high-impact player, a great influencer, then you must master this principle. Not only do you need to master it, you've got to get to the point that you seek out the struggles that other people avoid. It is the ability to stride confidently into the messiest, nastiest challenges that distinguishes the real impact players from everyone else. High-impact persuaders can handle pressure, and the ability to handle pressure means that you have got to able to keep the lid on even when the heat is rising. Taken to its highest level, hunker down and reach higher ground is not just tolerating or coping with pressure, it's allowing pressure to elevate your performance, to boost your concentration, your energy, and your mental and physical acuity. Pressure becomes a passion instead of the dreaded evil forest! Oliver Wendell Holmes said, "If I had a formula for bypassing trouble, I would not pass it around. Trouble creates a capacity to handle it. I don't embrace trouble, that's as bad as treating it as an enemy. But I do say meet it as a friend, for you'll see a lot of it and had better be on speaking terms with it."

Very early in my business career, my boss, Joanne, gave me an essay called "The Common Denominator of Success." The author, who had been the president of a very large insurance company and had observed thousands of people in his company over the years, stated that what really distinguishes the successful people from everyone else is actually very simple to understand—successful people make a habit of doing what unsuccessful people do not want to do. Think about that for a moment. Successful people make a habit of doing what unsuccessful people are not able to. It is our ability to perform well on the difficult tasks that increases our value to our organizations. Usually, the difficult tasks bring with them a high degree of pressure, complexity, and communication problems. When we have the ability to perform well under difficult circumstances, when others cannot, we place ourselves in the position of creating better results, making more sales, or being recognized for promotion.

Tommy Giaimo, a top-producing car salesperson, explains how it works in his business: "When things are really slow, I start doing the things that other people don't do to keep busy, and I find that it starts coming back. When times are tough, the worst thing you can do is sit around and twiddle your thumbs, which is what I see a lot of guys doing. You can sit around and complain about how bad business is but all it does is slow you down."

What Is "Hunker Down"?

"Life is difficult" are the first three words of M. Scott Peck's *The Road Less Traveled.* He goes on in that breakthrough book to explain that a great deal of human suffering is caused by our inability to accept this simple, but profound truth. "Life is difficult," and it certainly can be at times. Hunker down means that we face what's in front of us without

- Wishing we were somewhere else;
- Complaining that life's not fair;
- Thinking, "I don't deserve to be here";

- Thinking, "How can I put this situation off until later?";
- Debilitating our effectiveness with fear and anxiety;
- Pretending the situation doesn't exist.

What is difficult in your life is often made more difficult when you try somehow to avoid the situation. When we rationalize that we shouldn't be having a particular problem or say to ourselves that life isn't fair, we are not accepting life as life presents itself to us. It is accepting that difficulty is there for our own good, custom-designed to help us become the best we can be, that transforms "life is difficult" to life is a magnificent challenge. Chip Sollins, president of American Pool Service, explains: "There's no secret to success from my perspective. Number one, you have to believe in what you're doing and your product or it will show through and people will notice. Number two is hard work. It doesn't come easy."

The age of convenience
We live in a world where convenience has been brought to an art form. We have computers, automatic document printers, faxes, e-mail, voice mail, and every imaginable service to do the routine stuff we don't want to do. In our personal lives, we have bread makers, dishwashers, clothes washers, and even more services that allow us to *not* do the tedious, messy stuff and to enjoy more and more "free" time. With all this convenience, we start thinking that there should be an easy way to handle everything. Is it possible that for some of us, this convenience has led to a decreasing tolerance for pressure? Perhaps our ability to handle tangled-up messes is not where it needs to be.

Think of how different the results of your career would be if you simply stopped asking yourself, "How can I make my life easier?" Replace it with a better question such as, "How can I lead a life that puts me in big-game moments more often?" That shift in attitude can dramatically alter the way you see the work you do and the way you deal with adversity. When you look for challenges rather than an easier way out, you will become more persuasive, convincing, and forceful when you need it. You will outsell the people around you and you will be where the action is in the closing minutes of the game, with the ball in your hands, relishing every moment of it.

"I made it because I don't quit," admits David Achzet, a successful sales manager. "I'm extremely hard working. I worked 12 hours a day when I first started out and was just being asked to work five. I had to do that to get established. I think in order to really make it, we have to go through a period where we're totally consumed with what we're doing at work. I'm not advocating everyone become a workaholic, but at first, that total focus makes a big difference in getting you established. I once heard at a sales seminar that you have to be on fire yourself to get someone else smoking, and I really use that philosophy. You have to be the most enthusiastic, the most participative, and the hardest working to make it to the top and to be considered for promotions and better jobs."

Old mule Kate knows

My dad grew up on a farm in Kansas. I'll never forget a story he told me about his life on the farm when he was a young boy:

A storm was headed for the farm his family lived on, and his mom and dad were scurrying around, getting prepared. The kids were putting the animals in the barn, bolting down the storm doors and battening down the hatches, getting ready for what looked like a real pounding, headed right for them.

Sure enough, a few minutes later, the storm unleashed a fury of rain, hail, wind, and thunder on the farm. My dad, Al, went to the living room window and looked at the ferocity of the storm. He listened to the hail bombard that old tin roof. It sounded like a relentless pounding of golf balls. Suddenly, he noticed Kate, the family's plow mule standing in the storm. "Look," he said. "We forgot to put Kate in the barn!" Sure enough, the old mule, Kate, was standing in the middle of her outdoor pen, unprotected. Young Al ran for the front door, determined to rescue Kate from the storm. His father met him at the door and stopped him. "Al, where are you going?" he asked.

"I've got to put Kate back in the barn. She's out there all alone," young Al replied, and suddenly a lightening bolt crashed behind the house. "Son," his dad replied, "I don't want you going out there in the storm. You'd best stay inside until this thing is over."

"But, Dad," Al protested, "what about Kate?" The young boy ran back to the window and his father put his arm around his shoulder.

"Son, old Kate's gonna have to just hunker down and take it." And that's just what she did. Moments later, as the storm subsided, Kate lifted her head up, shook her shoulders, throwing off the hail balls that had accumulated on her back, and started walking around, knowing the worst had passed. Then she went back to grazing. Kate didn't have a support group, anyone to feel sorry for her, or anyone to give her a big hug and kiss, because, generally, people don't kiss mules. She stood firm, braced for the worst, withstood it, and got on with her business.

The ability to be able to handle moments of extreme anxiety, pressure, and conflict without caving in is critical. Often the person who is seen as the most influential, is the person who possesses what Kate had. The ability to stand firm, even when hurricane force winds are blowing, and to hunker down and take it is an attribute of character. It's easy to find well-educated, training-seminar-coached, technically brilliant communicators who just can't win over other people's confidence and trust. It's usually because something is lacking. Often, what's missing is grace under pressure.

If, when things go wrong, you must talk it over with five different people, sit and think about it, walk around the block to shake it off, and stew over it for days and days, then your effectiveness is limited. There is absolutely nothing wrong with having a support mechanism in your life; it's just that to really make it to higher levels of influence, you have got to be able to operate relatively efficiently. You can't do that if every time something goes wrong you fall to pieces.

What Is Higher Ground?

Higher ground is the reward for hunkering down. It's an unexpected treasure and it is different for each person.

In business, there are times when the fate of the organization comes down to a critical decision. The right decision will bring success, while the wrong decision will cost revenues, profitability, and, ultimately, jobs. These decisions can be absolutely wrenching and many executives put them off, electing to wait and see. The pressure of these decisions can literally cause health problems, mental confusion, and debilitating stress to some executives, while others perform at their best when high-pressure decisions need to made. It's as if their ability to analyze and find solutions increases as the intensity of the situation escalates.

In athletics, they often attribute the term *clutch-player* to the athlete who plays well at critical moments where the momentum of the game could go either way. Great athletes do great things at the greatest possible moment in the game. It's the ability to sink a 24-foot jump shot at the buzzer to win the basketball playoff game. Or the ability to kick a soccer goal to tie the game in the final seconds. Maybe it's the ability to figure skate an absolutely flawless performance in the Olympic finals.

In less glamorous arenas, it's the ability to make your absolute best presentation the first time the president of your company sees you in action.

Maybe it's writing a letter to a customer you thought you had lost and saying the only thing that could possibly have changed her mind and opened her up to your ideas.

Higher ground is an elevated sense of awareness, an ability to know what to do and how to do it in pivotal moments, when pressure is high. The pressure provides the extra boost of energy, but higher ground occurs when you take that extra boost and turn it into heightened performance, as Paganini did.

UNDER CONSTRUCTION PLUS NASTY PROBLEM SOLVING IS THE FORMULA!

Let's not kid ourselves. Simply volunteering for those pressure tasks that put your butt on the line when you are not prepared to perform is a mistake, and a big one. That will lead to chronic underperformance at critical moments and a predictable loss of confidence and self-esteem. That's why under construction is so important. Your ability to perform well under pressure increases as you grow and over time develop the abilities you are likely to need. These skills don't usually magically appear without an effort to grow them first. How many tough decisions did Michael Eisner have to make in his career before he was able to make the decisions at Disncy that led to their resurgence? How many record-breaking long jumps did Carl Lewis make on the practice field before he did it in Olympic competition? How many 25-foot putts did Tiger Woods sink in practice before he started dropping them in professional golf tournaments?

The formula is to first get under construction and then dive into the difficult, often nasty problem solving that in the end leads to higher ground. In order to tackle nasty problems, we need to be able to hunker down without falling apart. This comes from accepting that, at times, life will be difficult.

Problems are fascinating. They are on one level the stepping stones to our magical future but on another level the seeming cause of stress and all forms of life anxiety. Upon examination, however, problems are not "alive," in and of themselves, although we often attribute to them human-like (or animal-like!) qualities. "That problem is a bear," or "Stay away from that hornet's nest," or "That sure is a bitter situation," are ways we describe problems, a way of articulating the emotion we feel when projecting ourselves into the problem.

On a more practical level, though, problems are problems because of these elements:

- They represent risk.
- Often unpleasant tasks or issue-facing is involved.
- The probable outcome often represents disappointment for the people involved.
- A "facing of the truth" element is usually involved.
- Judgment is often involved, meaning a judgment of right or wrong inherent in the problem's resolution.

For some reason, we often find these factors unpleasant. Similarly, when we go to the gym we find the exercises or the aftereffects of those exercises unpleasant because our muscles are being stretched beyond their present capacity. Problems demand this of us. They demand us to stretch beyond our current capacity in order to solve them.

By now, we know that this is where growing takes place. When we stretch, when we bite off a little more than we are used to, we open ourselves up to growth and, ultimately, higher ground.

Nasty Problems Build Your Value

When you resolve to do what it takes to tackle the most important problems you can find, then you are increasing your value in the most efficient way possible.

Problem solving strengthens you. Just facing the most important problems on your desk first, even if you don't completely solve them, will strengthen you. In order to do this, some of us need to take the first step, which is identifying what the important problems are in the first place.

If you don't solve problems, they keep coming back. "Life gives exams" has been a popular buzz phrase of the new age movement. There is a simple truth in this statement, which means that until you are able to solve the current problems in your life, you will not get a new set to deal with. It's something like not being able to get into college until you get a high school diploma and acceptable SAT scores. Certainly the challenge (or problem) of college is greater than that of high school, but it's set up so you don't end up with a problem you have little likelihood of solving without having solved a "preparatory" problem first.

Then, of course, you don't get into graduate school, which involves a greater set of problems to be solved, without that college diploma. And you can't get a Ph.D. without all of these preliminary steps, either.

It's not that life is intentionally cruel by shoving the same unsolved problems back at you. It's more that life would like to give you bigger problems to solve that will bring you bigger rewards. But you have to qualify for them first by dealing with stuff that is right in front of you. It's kind of like the man who wants to run a big company but can't get his own finances together. How would he have a chance of succeeding with a complex balance sheet if he doesn't know where his own paycheck goes or hasn't figured out how to spend less than he earns?

Persistence Is Another Reward

Persistence is another reward we receive from the hunker down principle. When we can handle the pressure, we can persist. Our determination is unshakable when we have mastered hunker down. This is what it takes to be truly convincing and to be a winner at the highest level of influence. Consider the immortal words of Calvin Coolidge:

> Nothing in the world can take the place of persistence. Talent will not; nothing is more common than unsuccessful men with talent. Genius will not; unrewarded genius is almost a proverb. Education will not; the world is full of educated failures. Persistence and determination alone are omnipotent.

Many years ago, in a little country schoolhouse that was heated by an old-fashioned, potbellied coal stove, a little boy named Glenn had the job of coming to school each day a little early in order to start the fire and warm the room before the teacher and his classmates arrived. One morning, the teacher arrived to find the schoolhouse engulfed in flames. They grabbed Glenn, unconscious and barely alive, out of the flaming building and took him to the nearby county hospital. From his bed, the dreadfully burned, semiconscious little boy faintly heard the doctor talking to his mother. "It is unlikely that your little boy will live," he said. "And to be honest," he continued, "it may be for the best because the fire has completely paralyzed the lower half of his body." It was then and there that Glenn determined that he would not die. He made up his mind that he would survive!

Somehow, to the amazement of the physician, he did survive. When the mortal danger was past, he again heard the doctor and his mother speaking quietly. The mother was told that since the fire had destroyed so much flesh in the lower part of his body that her young son was doomed to be a lifetime cripple with no use at all of his lower limbs. The doctor urged her to help young Glenn accept this gruesome reality.

Once more, the brave boy made up his mind. He would not be a cripple. He would walk. But from the waist down, he had no motor ability at all; he couldn't feel his legs. His thin limbs just dangled there, all but lifeless.

After he was released from the hospital, his mother would massage his little legs every day, but there was no feeling, no control, nothing. Yet his determination that he would walk was as strong as ever. When he wasn't in bed, he was confined to a wheelchair. One sunny day, his mother wheeled him out into the yard to get some fresh air. This day, instead of just sitting there, he threw himself from the chair. He pulled himself across the grass, dragging his legs behind him. He clawed his way to the white picket fence bordering their lot. With great effort, he raised himself up on the fence. Then, stake by stake, he began dragging himself along the fence, resolved that he would walk. He did this every day until he wore a smooth path all around the yard beside the fence. There was nothing he wanted more than to develop life in those legs.

Ultimately, through his daily massages, his iron persistence, and his resolute determination, he did develop the ability to stand up and then to walk haltingly, then, finally, to walk by himself. He began to walk to school, then to run to school, and finally, to run for the sheer joy of running. Later in college he made the track team.

Several years later, in Madison Square Garden, this young man, who years before was not expected to survive, let along walk, this determined young man, Dr. Glenn Cunningham, ran the world's fastest mile.

When we accept our circumstances and hunker down to work through whatever adversity that comes our way, we develop the kind of persistence that can literally work miracles in our lives. When you're serious about becoming a person who can sell yourself and your ideas, why settle for anything less than the higher ground that will be yours, just as it was Glenn Cunningham's. That is your reward and a platform from which you can literally transform the way others think instead of merely convincing them.

Sharon Basile, a successful advertising salesperson, explains: "I think in sales, or anything else for that matter, you have to be persistent to make it in the future because you have so many people flake out and tell you no, no, no. You have to stay motivated, you have to have the courage to get back in there. You have to care about the person and not just their money."

From Problem Solving to Challenge Seeking

Here's where the higher ground part kicks in. At first, when we become more assertive about solving the problems we have been avoiding, we need to muster all of our courage just to deal with the problem or tolerate it. We force ourselves to grin and bear it, however unpleasant and distasteful it may be.

Reaching higher ground occurs when we learn to seek out the challenges that flunkies run from. This attitude transforms the way we see problems. With this outlook, we don't put all the negative mental baggage into the problem; instead, we position it as a challenge. The challenge becomes the game, the final two minutes where we need to perform at our best. Some may say, "Geez, I don't want to be in that game, there's too much on the line!" If that's the way you often feel, then I say change it, because you can master every sales technique and every communication skill in the world, but if you shy away from prime-time challenges, you are not going to reach a high level of achievement.

In Carlos Castaneda's classic series about Don Juan Mateus, a Yaqui Indian practitioner of an ancient form of mystical knowledge, Castaneda, a Western anthropologist, becomes an apprentice of Don Juan. At one point, Don Juan points out how important it is for the serious apprentice to find what he calls a "petty tyrant," an individual who can create an infinite amount of annoying problems for the person under his or her control. The greater the difficulties, the better. The more pressure and risk, the greater the gains will be for the apprentice. The philosophy behind this is that the apprentice must work for a petty tyrant striving to complete all of the difficult, demanding, and often unreasonable work that this petty tyrant heaps upon him with the intent of doing it with joy and a sense of detachment. Don Juan explains that building our ability to perform under the most difficult of circumstances raises us to a higher level of awareness. He takes it one step further, though; it is not just the ability to perform, but to perform with a sense of joy, that is the real goal.

Hunker down and reach higher ground is a similar principle. It's the mental transformation from problems that we would rather avoid to challenges that, once we solve them, will lead to even greater opportunities. It's a refreshing outlook, to say the least.

It happens all the time in corporate America. A struggling company, hanging on to its practices of the past with an out-of-touch board of directors and aloof executive team is confronted by the shareholders. The dismal results, which are the product of years of problem-avoiding, cause the company to bring in an outsider, a person who is not stricken with organizational fear, stress, or inability to act. This outsider comes in and quickly makes the tough decisions and dives into the challenge. Look at what happened to IBM just a few short years ago. Lou Gerstner was hired in precisely this situation, and in just two years IBM is making money again and restoring the luster of its name. Gerstner eagerly dove into the problems that people who had been around IBM had been observing for years, and he did something about it. He took action. His sense of urgency rubbed off on the people around him and elevated the performance of the entire organization.

Viktor Frankl, in his inspiring book *Man's Search for Meaning* that retells his story of not only how he survived the World War II concentration camps in Auchwitz, but how he grew from the experience, reveals a key to this great mystery. It's not what happens to us, he teaches, but how we respond. He was able to find great meaning from this experience and considered it, though a living hell, a positive transformational experience in his life.

Mahatma Ghandi tells a similar story of how, in his early years of peaceful protest, he was often imprisoned, sometimes even in solitary confinement. He relates that these experiences in prison provided him with an unparalleled opportunity for solitary self-examination and discovery. He said that he became a stronger man with deeper convictions as a result and said, "I prize even the failures and disillusionments, which are but steps toward success."

Each of these men employed, at times under the most severe conditions imaginable, the principle of hunker down and reach higher ground. They accepted the conditions they found themselves in, decided to make the absolute best of it and grew as a result of their ability to overcome the challenge rather than hiding or denying it.

Character Is Built When Things Go Wrong

Character is, for many people, a difficult concept to fully understand. It's easy to identify people of character like Viktor Frankl, Ghandi, and Abraham Lincoln, but what character really is seems more difficult to understand.

Each person's character is determined by the decisions he or she makes in life. It's that simple. Character is what we receive as a reward or punishment for the contribution we make through the value of our decisions. Our character is shaped and rooted through our decisions.

Character is absolutely everything when it comes to being persuasive and consistently effective at selling ideas. The OUTSELL principles will help you to develop your character and, as such, become a person who can sell the right ideas, with the right intentions, so that everyone benefits. Learning how to convince (perhaps even trick) people against their will into decisions that give lopsided results to the person doing the persuading is not what the best salespeople, leaders, or professionals who sell ideas do at all.

Keeping this in mind, it becomes clear why problems are such a wonderful opportunity to build character and why people of such great character often emerge in times of struggle. The greater the problem, the greater the test of our character, because problems involve decision making. This is why a strong personal constitution, based on principles and not "whatever works now," is the most powerful decision-making tool you can have. The end does not always justify the means although, unfortunately, as our world gets more and more complex, we are often misguided by the "it's okay as long as you get what you want" set of standards.

Hunker down means that you set your principles in front of you as your vehicle and then let that vehicle take you where it will, which is higher ground if those principles are based on your most enlightened thinking. We build character when we are willing to accept the consequences of our decisions, even if a "lesser" decision, based on shakier, short-term principle compromises, could have gotten a less distasteful result. You always win if the decisions you make build your character, always!

A father took his seven-year-old boy into a toy shop, and the two of them walked up and down the aisles looking for a toy the young boy wanted most. At the end of one of the aisles was a four-foot-tall balloon, shaped and painted like a clown, with a weighted bottom. The little boy pushed the clown and it tipped to the side, but then sprang back upright. The little boy, amazed by what happened, shoved the clown a little harder this time until it tipped all the way over, but sure enough, the weighted bottom returned the clown to an upright position. The father watched the little boy punch the clown several times and laugh as the inflated clown returned upright, again and again. "I want this one," the little boy told his father.

The father took the clown to the cash register. As they were walking out of the store, he turned to his son and asked, "Why do you suppose the clown keeps coming up after you push it down?"

The little boy paused a moment to think and replied, "Gee, Dad, I don't know. I guess it is because he is standing up on the inside."

When you build your character, you build your ability to stand up on the inside, even though the situations of your life may push you out of balance. Hunkering down under tough condition builds that balanced center that always returns you to an upright position, ready for action. Usually, there are unexpected benefits to be earned when we resist the urge to give up too early. Molly Williamson, a top-producing salesperson, explains, "In a job I had in San Diego, I remember being very dissatisfied at one point and thinking, 'I can't last more than six months, this just isn't going to work.' And I don't know what kept me in it, but it ended up being a great job. I learned so much and was exposed to so many new things that I know now that if I had left after six months instead of staying three and a half years I wouldn't be the same person I am right now."

Problems Increase Our Flexibility

"You have enormous untapped power that you will probably never tap, because most people never run far enough on their first wind to ever find they have a second," said William James, a famous American philosopher. You will develop the ability to tap that second wind, when you don't give up on problems that are challenging and difficult to solve.

Problems give us an opportunity to exercise our creativity and flexibility. When you combine these two abilities with character, you have a person who is a powerful persuader. This story illustrates the enormous opportunity that even exasperating problems create for creativity and flexibility to flourish once you develop the ability to tap your "second wind."

The McIlhenny family of Avery Island, Louisiana, had a thriving perfume business before the start of the Civil War. At the end of the war, however, the Northern army destroyed their perfume factory, and the family was in financial ruin. The family did not have the resources to rebuild their perfume business. Edmund McIlhenny, stretched to the limit, decided to work with the only resources he had on his land. His property had many red capsicum pepper plants, which have a unique pepper taste. He picked the ripest peppers and mashed them with a small amount of Avery Island salt and aged the mixture for 30 days. He then added natural vinegar and aged the sauce for another 30 days to get the flavor and aroma just right. He bottled the sauce in the only bottles he could afford—the perfume bottles he found packed away in boxes left in the ruined perfume factory. Edmund McIlhenny sold his first 350 bottles in 1868 in New York. Word spread of the famous sauce that Mr. McIlhenny had made, and a loyal following began to develop around the world. In fact, the demand for his world famous Tabasco sauce was so great that in 1872 he opened up an additional office in London. Today, the McIlhenny tradition of excellence continues on Avery Island, where the aging process of Tabasco brand pepper sauce in white oak barrels has been extended to about three years. Careful precision and hard work still go into every drop of Tabasco.

It's not what happened to the McIlhenny family that counted, it's how they responded. It's how they dealt with their difficult set of circumstances that paved the way for their extraordinary success. They were flexible, they were creative, and they stuck to their principles of hard work, quality products, and making the best of the resources you have now. The conditions of your life are a perfect launching pad, tailor-made for you, if you can just be thankful not only for the blessings you have but for the unique set of problems that are right in front of you and do what our hot sauce friends have done.

There's an old saying that says when life throws you lemons, make lemonade. But that's not really what we're talking about. What we're saying is, make the best lemonade in town, open up a lemonade stand, sell it, expand, franchise, buy lemon groves to cut costs, and corner the world market on lemonade! Become the lemonade king!

The pages of history are filled with stories of undaunted men and women who triumphed over disabilities and adversities to demonstrate victorious spirits. Bury him deep in the snows of Valley Forge and you have a George Washington. Take away her sight and hearing and you set the stage for Helen Keller. Raise him in abject poverty and you have an Abraham Lincoln. Deafen a genius composer and you have a Ludwig van Beethoven. Have him born of parents who survived a Nazi concentration camp, paralyze him from the waist down when he is four, and you have an incomparable concert violinist, Itzhak Perlman. Call him a slow learner, retarded, and write him off as uneducable, and you have an Albert Einstein. Each one of these people experienced first the trial and then the triumph!

Every job, every career carries with it extraordinary challenges, routine work, and interesting distractions. When we ignore the extraordinary challenges and settle for the other stuff because it's easier, we leave the more important stuff for someone else to do. And that someone else gets the benefit of developing the ability to do important, demanding work, which is the most effective route to influence and authority. In sales, it's the person who is able to understand a complex proposal and overcome objection after objection who makes the biggest sales. In law, it's the lawyer who can overcome the most difficult legal challenges who moves up, gains influence, and reaches success. In architecture, it's the architect who can solve the most difficult technical challenges who is able to erect the most innovative buildings. Seeking tasks and work that are easy does not lead to the kind of influence we are talking about in this book.

The Loss/Gain Risk Problem

Often, we avoid facing the problems we have when we focus too much on what we will lose as a necessary result of resolving the problem. For instance, for many people the monthly task of paying bills is an anxiety-producing problem they often put off, even to the point of creating disgruntled creditors. Our bills often demand more money from us than we have, and we might think, "If I pay my bills, I'll find out I don't have any money, and I'll have to juggle these bills, or even worse, overdraw my account." We think that paying the bills will actually create a bigger problem than putting it off, or the anxiety of paying the bills is so undesirable that we just put it off, without really knowing why. And, of course, the problem gets worse. When we hunker down, we solve problems now and accept the consequences.

Instead, this person could storm head first into this bill-paying mess and determine that there are three other new problems that come out of it:

1. He's spending too much money.
2. He cannot pay all the bills today.
3. He needs to make more money.

There are three new problems to be solved for which there are some obvious solutions, which probably will demand change, flexibility, and adaptation, which are all positives. Often, we think the change that the problem represents is negative when, in fact, it is always positive, provided that we solve the problem using decisions based on sound principles. It's like the old saying, "Life is a grindstone. Whether it grinds you down or polishes you up depends on what you are made of."

Problems are usually solved using two methods:

1. Put forth more effort and focus.
2. Make better decisions.

Either way, if you use one of these two methods, you gain. Even if you lose results short-term, you win. It's when we try and avoid or, even worse, run from a problem that we often lose ground. Don Graling, a top-producing salesperson and manager explains: "Once you start looking for another job, you might as well be out of the one you're in now. Don't be too quick to jump ship. Sometimes you just need to hang in there and try to make your situation better. Too many people are eager to move around, and it can hurt you as much as help if every time the going gets tough, you look elsewhere."

Solving the problem builds skill, character, and usually improves the outcome of the situation, provided the decisions we make are based on well-thought-out principles. Here's where the personal constitution comes in!

When you stick to your core beliefs and principles, there is little risk in pressure moments. It's when you bend what you believe in to make short-term gains that the real risk enters in, because when you sacrifice who you are becoming for short-term benefit, your ability to persuade and influence suffers.

Know your principles, plan your activities, and work your plan until it becomes clear that your plan is failing. Then adjust your plan as necessary. But at all times, stand tall to the adversity. Changing and adapting the plan is not the same thing as retreating and avoiding.

The most important outcome, though, is the peace of mind we experience through the resolution of the problem. This is part of the higher ground. Here's what we get from straight-ahead problem solving:

• More self-confidence
• Possible problem solution benefits

- More personal power
- Self-development
- Self-awareness
- Access to greater potential challenges in the future
- A sense of positive movement in our lives
- Respect from the people around us

> Babe Ruth, one of the greatest baseball hitters of all time, had a problem. He was building a reputation for striking out more than anyone who had ever played the game. He struck out a historic 1,330 times. Was Babe Ruth a failure as a baseball player? Certainly his record indicates anything but that. He hit 714 home runs, and his lifetime batting average was .342! He probably struck out so many times because every time he went up to the plate he was trying to hit a home run. Babe Ruth was able to accept the fact that he was going to fail more than he would succeed if his goal was to hit as many home runs as possible. He literally transformed the teams he played on using that philosophy.

The risk was high for Babe Ruth, but the gain was even higher, and that's what hunkering down is all about. It's being able to deal with the potential for loss or gain. Ruth handled the paradox of loss/gain effectively, which is exactly what we need to do when it comes to problem solving. Accept the losses when the gains are more meaningful.

It's Not Just the Solution That Counts

Your problems are your opportunity to become more, because the decisions you make solving a problem always give you a chance to demonstrate great character. And the people you want to influence want to see that in you first. They want you to *be* the person they can believe in, not just a person who says things that are believable. It's the practice of your core beliefs and principles in action. And the beauty of it is, no matter how well you do on solving your current problem, the world will be quite eager to serve up a whole new plateful of them for you to solve tomorrow. More opportunities to build your character! It's OUTSELL in practice! It's enjoying the journey as much as the destination. It's the joy of watching yourself live a life worth living because that life is consciously pursuing principles that enlarge you, the individual. What could possibly be more rewarding?

Organizational Castration

Several years ago I was in a product development meeting with an outside consultant I had hired sitting beside me. The meeting involved making some critical decisions about a new product that could have major impact on our company's philosophy and core beliefs. As the meeting got into some of the hotter topics, I was shocked at how passive many of the people (12 of us total) in the meeting were in making a decision. Over half of the people in the meeting expressed no firm opinions on which way we should go, even though they were very experienced, well-informed, and capable of calculating the importance of the decision. They opted to stay on the sidelines.

Following the meeting, I had lunch with the consultant, the only outsider in the meeting. I was visibly disappointed, and he asked me what was wrong. "I handpicked these people to attend this meeting because I thought they had something to say. I was sure they would want to be involved in solving this problem, but obviously I was wrong."

The consultant, who had been through many situations like this in his work, picked out the people I had been disappointed in. "It appears to me," he began, "that they have been organizationally castrated." I asked him what he meant.

"It happens all the time in companies. People lose the ability to make decisions because of the risk they face in being wrong. So, they sit back and let other people, like you, face the risk. They are too scared of what will happen if they are wrong."

I thought about this for several days and realized that all the people we had identified as being organizationally castrated were stalled in their careers. They had reached roadblocks in their positions and were frustrated. I could recall, at one time or another, having had a "career-counseling" session with each of them to determine how they could get their careers back on track. Either they were afraid to stick their necks out and take a risk or they resented the company for not valuing them more. They felt they deserved better and they blamed the company.

Since then, I have had the opportunity to be the outsider looking in for many organizations and have observed, with striking frequency, this same malady afflicting many professionals from a variety of disciplines. Many of them have great excuses for holding back and letting someone else take the risk, but the reality is that problem-avoiding saps you of vitality and personality potency. The prescription each of these people needed was a nasty "gotta face it or else" problem or series of problems that would force them to come out of their protective, insulated shells and make decisions.

Develop an "I want to be involved in the tough, nitty-gritty stuff, and I want to take a position on what we should do" attitude once you're in there. Heed the words of Thomas Jefferson: "In matters of principle stand like a rock, in matters of taste, swim with the current." Be innovative, flexible, and creative, but don't compromise your core beliefs and principles.

Adversity Reactions

How do your react to adversity? Check the words that best describe your typical reaction to unexpected adversity:

- Bitterness
- Anger
- Resentment
- Unfairness
- Stress
- Avoidance
- Procrastination
- Eagerness
- Opportunity
- Excitement
- Adrenaline
- Positive anticipation

Just a little self-awareness break, that's all. Be aware of who you are today in order to evolve to who you want to be tomorrow. Become conscious of how you react when things don't go the way you planned and you will uncover a clue into some of the changes you need to make in your approach to problems and the never ending stream of challenges and hurdles your most evolved self is asking you to encounter. Don Graling looks at it this way: "When things go wrong, I like to ask myself what's the worst thing that can possibly happen? It's usually not that bad, and you can work around it. Bad news never gets better with time. It's best to tell whoever needs to be told as quickly as possible and get it over with. If you let it sit a week, it's never going to get better."

Consider the perspective of Dave Doehr, a highly successful manager: "There is always opportunity in negative situations if you look for it. I took over the worst offices our company has in the state. When I first met with the managers of those offices, they were really down, saying that the situation was terrible and how bad it was to be in last place, and so on. My reaction was, man, that's great! Because everything we do to improve it is really going to show up. If we improve sales by just 10%, people are really going to notice. Every improvement we make and every process we put in place makes us look like a star. It's the old glass of water analogy. It's either half full or half empty. I just think you're better off looking at situations in terms of how you can improve them."

At first glance, you may think that the hunker down perspective will bring more pain than gain. Let's take a look at the staggering benefits you receive from hunkering down, instead of taking the easy way out:

- Courage
- Insight
- Staying power and endurance
- Resilience
- Perspective
- Wisdom

With those six qualities, you can accomplish just about anything, but the current of the day, for some reason, is to think more about the material rewards we are getting instead of the most valuable reward, which is who we are becoming. Don't fall for it! Nothing is more important than who you are becoming. Remember the words of Benjamin Disraeli, "There is no education like adversity."

Drop the thought that situations should always go the way you want them to. You'll be much more effective if you have a basic game plan and become an outstanding improviser. People who can sell know how to improvise. The fun is in the improvising, and the OUTSELL model builds an outstanding base for improvising. We plan, the plan unfolds, we respond and improvise—that's the way it really works. People who create the illusion of always being in control and always being right about the way things work out are usually left out of big-game moments. And to be a powerful influencer, you have got to be in the game when critical moments arrive.

When You're Growing, Problems Are Less Threatening

When you value the growth you experience as you traverse life's difficult terrain as much as you do the individual outcomes along the way, then the problems themselves start to transform. We are so tuned, trained, and conditioned to judge our performance by the outcome, by the feedback from the outside world, and by the material gains, that we often forget to even consider what has happened to us as a person as a result of the struggles we just completed. You have nothing of real value to lose when you are growing, when you value the growth you experience through the problems you solve. The win or loss is important, but it is not the only factor for you to weigh. Who you are becoming, how you are growing, and the barriers you are breaking through is where the real value is. You can make problems much less personally threatening when you think this way. The little boy in the following story is growing through each failure with this outlook:

> A young boy is in his backyard with a bat and a baseball. He stands tall and says, "I'm a great hitter," and tosses the ball up, swings as hard as he can, but misses. The ball falls to the ground. He picks it up and says, "I'm the best hitter in the league," and tosses the ball into the air, swings as hard as he can, and misses again. He picks it up, looks up to the sky and says, "I'm the greatest hitter that ever lived." He tosses the ball into the air one more time, swings, and misses. He shakes his head with determination and says, "Wow, what a pitcher!"

Many of us would achieve much more and, as a result, become a more powerful influencer if we would, as our boy in the story illustrates, focus more on who we are becoming as we meet our challenges and focus less on the outcome.

Drop the Baggage

When you don't hunker down and stand your ground, you accumulate a lot of baggage that you'll carry everywhere you go: baggage like the regrets of not knowing what might have happened had you hung in there when the going got rough; baggage like the disappointments that come from quitting early. Certain phrases start creeping into your daily conversation: "what might have happened," "what should have happened," "what could have happened," and "what would have happened." When you hunker down, you become proud of *what did happen.* That makes all the difference in the world in the way you communicate, which is the key to the way you influence.

Hunker Down Invites an Interesting Life

When you hunker down when the pressure's on, you'll live a more interesting life, a life filled with more interesting peaks and valleys. A life of calm predictability, controlled avoidance, and carefully executed risklessness will yield a dull communicator. Want to be a great communicator? Then you have got to have something interesting to say. Interesting experiences, where you are out there and on the line, lead to breakthrough insights, incidents, and experiences that become yours to share forever more. When you can draw on a big reservoir of experiences based on the problems you have faced, sometimes winning, sometimes losing, then you will have the greatest power of all when it comes to communication—the ability to use the truth to be persuasive and interesting at the same time, without exaggerating.

GET OUT OF THE DRIVEWAY!

When we don't solve problems, but merely rethink them, reposition them, sidestep them, or avoid them altogether, we never get out of the driveway. The roads to the interesting places are paved with problems that need to be recognized, confronted, and solved. If we don't solve them, they come back over and over and over again. It's like driving around in circles. What often happens is that we become weaker and weaker and less able to deal with them, while our ability to avoid them grows stronger and stronger. John F. Kennedy put it this way, "There are risks and costs to a program of action, but they are far less than the long-range risks and costs of comfortable inaction." When we stand and deal with the pressure, the mistakes, and the problems, then we get out of the driveway and onto the expressway.

This Is the Path to True Leadership

A lot of books have been written about leadership over the last decade. Ninety percent of "leadership theory" proposes that the key to becoming a leader is possessing the ability to create a shared vision with the people you lead and getting them to embrace and support it. Before that, however, a leader must develop the ability to hunker down and reach higher ground. All great leaders must be willing to be in front when the nasty stuff starts flying. Incompetent leaders hide behind lawyers, task forces, and executive guards to protect themselves and, as a result, diminish their ability to persuade and convince.

Walk head first into the problems that come your way. Don't always wait for someone else to take the risk, take it yourself! Leadership is not a strategic board game, it's much more about being where the action is, taking the pressure, and elevating your performance to do what no one else is willing to do.

Winston Churchill became the pillar of strength that England leaned on when hope was all but lost in World War II. He didn't hide behind political walls. He stood up and accepted the pressure, the responsibility, and the duty of leading England to victory. As a result, he was able to persuade an entire nation to stand strong, even in moments where defeat seemed imminent. When Ghandi organized his famous nonviolent marches to oppose English rule, he was at the front of the line, the first one to meet danger. What made William Wallace in the film *Braveheart* such an endearing leader to audiences around the world was the fact that he was the first one on the battlefield, running beside the men who followed him. This is the highest form of leadership. The organizing skills are critical, too, especially when managing complex organizations. But what separates the great leaders from all the rest is the ability to hunker down and reach higher ground.

Selling ideas, products, and concepts is about being a leader. It's about being able to inspire others with your commitment and conviction. And this inspiration comes from absolute commitment even when the ground is shaking around you. Being able to hunker down and stand tall is at the absolute root of being a persuasive person!

Would-be leaders often organize a lot of huzzonga, wasting their time and, more importantly, the time of others when they are unable to face problems and deal with them. Virtually all performance problems in organizations exist because a manager somewhere was not able to effectively confront the problem when it surfaced and stand firm and enforce performance standards. When we avoid the little things, they become big things. Avoid the big things and they become monumental. Consider the words of Rudyard Kipling, "What you do when you don't have to, determines what you will be when you can no longer help it."

Successful People Solve Problems

It's easy and tempting to look at people in successful positions and speculate that they never had to face really tough problems because they were born into that success. We think, "If I was in that position, I could do what they do and an even better job at it." Don't be so certain. Most successful people make it as a result of their own achievements. Positions of power demand problem solving skills. Most of the people who get ahead do so precisely because they solve problems better than the people around them.

When the pressure's on, do the people around you consider you a good clutch player? Clutch players influence at a level that the technique-practicers can only dream of. Outselling is about developing character and internal strength that holds up under pressure and goes one step further; it allows you to rise up to a higher level of performance and excel under pressure. Influence is not just a language and words thing, it's about who you are inside. When the heat is on you need to elevate your performance, not retreat. The "heat" is the fun part.

Problem-Solving Formula

A willingness to solve the problem is critical, but we also need to do it in such a way that we do not aggravate the problem. Here is a simple but highly effective way to solve virtually any problem. There are seven steps:

1. State the problem.
2. State all the causes of the problem.
3. State the desired outcome of the problem you want to solve.
4. Determine the possible solutions to the problem.
5. Decide the best solution.
6. Plan the action steps to take.
7. Schedule the action steps and do them!

Let's take some time to understand these steps in more detail.

Step 1. State the problem

When you have decided to stride head first into a problem, it is critically important to be able to state the problem in simple to understand and concise terms. What is the real problem? Write it down so it sounds something like these examples:

- I do not spend enough time on my highest priorities.
- I am not able to influence my customers enough.
- The problem is that I am spending more money than I am making.
- My shoulder is sore from lack of consistent exercise over time.
- I am 35 pounds overweight.
- This project is late.
- My relationship with my boss is not strong enough.
- I have not gotten a raise yet this year.
- I am often tired and irritable at the end of the day.
- I am not as enthusiastic with my husband and children as I would like to be.
- I have poor writing skills.
- I consistently pay my bills late.
- I worry too much.
- My clothes do not fit properly.

No excuses, no reasons why, just a simple statement of the problem that needs to be solved so it can be looked at objectively without any rationalizations or excuses.

Take a moment and write down five problems you are having right now that you would benefit from, were you to solve them.

Step 2. State all the causes of the problem

This is a brainstorming activity. Think creatively, not judgmentally. Let it flow, and identify as many contributing factors as possible, as in this example.

> Problem: My relationship with my boss is a mess.
> Possible causes:
> - I am not sure what my boss expects from me.
> - My boss does not set clear goals for me.

- My boss and I have not been communicating clearly and directly.
- My boss does not see me as a key member of his A-team.
- I have not been very assertive in developing my relationship with my boss.
- My boss intimidates me at times.
- I have not done a good job at organizing my achievements so that my boss can see what I am contributing.
- I made a poor presentation at a meeting my boss attended that reflected poorly on him.
- My boss sometimes leaves me out of critical meetings and invites other members of my team who are my peers, and this makes me angry.
- I think my boss would like me to be able to write better proposals.

The list could go on and on. The key is to get as many real factors that have impact on causing the problem as possible before you proceed to the next step.

Step 3. State the desired outcome of the problem you want to solve
Once you zero in on a problem that you are going to solve, it is important to determine what outcome you are trying to create before you start solving it. For example:

> Once this problem is solved, I will be seen by my boss as a higher impact player because I will be a higher impact player. I must first develop a clearer picture of what my boss expects from me, then become focused on getting those results. I will develop my communication skills so I can become an asset for my boss in meetings and not a liability.

Step 4. Determine the possible solutions to the problem
Here comes another brainstorming activity. The key is to open up your creativity and hold back your judgmental side for awhile. You want to come up with as many possible solutions as you can. For example:

- Write down what I feel my goals and objectives are and ask my boss to review them and give me guidance and coaching.
- Offer to do a special project for my boss that would make her job easier.

- Practice my writing skills and possibly take a proposal writing course.
- Make it a priority to spend at least five minutes a day with my boss talking about priorities.
- Work on my presentation skills so the next time I have to present, I will do a fabulous job.

Again, the list could go on and on, but we think you get the picture. Obviously, you can't do all of these activities on the first day. This is simply a starting point, a creative list for you to use when formulating your actual plan to accomplish your goal and solve your problem.

Step 5. Decide the best solution

Usually, the actual solution is a combination of the possible solutions put together in a practical way. For instance:

> The solution is to schedule a meeting with my boss to find out what she feels I must do in order to do my job 25% better than I currently am. After the meeting, I will write up my notes and turn them into an action plan I will share with my boss. I will attend training on presentation skills, whether she pays for it or not, and review my progress on my plan with my boss at least once a week. I will ask my boss what I can do to make her job easier and turn that into a key priority of mine.

Now, it is very likely that this solution, over time, will yield very good results.

Step 6. Plan the action steps to take

This step is often missing, the reason that "next week" is always the best time to get started. Here, we carefully look at our solution, which is written down, and begin planning steps to make it happen. For instance:

- Schedule a meeting with my boss for this week.
- Meet with other members of my team to find out how I could be of more help to them.
- Write up my goals and share them with my boss.
- Determine what presentation courses I could take that would improve my writing skills.

- Practice my writing skills each night for at least a half hour by buying some books and audio tapes on the subject of writing proposals.
- Become more goal oriented by writing down my objectives and reviewing my progress toward them each day before I go home and sharing the results with my boss each week.

These to-do items get put on a list that you will see frequently. Reminding yourself of what needs to be done is a critical step to stay on track.

Schedule the action steps and do them

Here, we transfer the action steps into our calendar system once the plan is made so they can be looked at in bite-sized pieces/activities that we focus on one day at a time. It is much easier to stay on the plan when all we have to concentrate on is one day at a time. Remember, solving the most serious problems often involves a change in behavior or the building of positive habits such as those we learned in the one life, one boss action plan.

Share Your Struggles

We are all going to face tragedy from time to time in our lives. Tragedy can serve a very positive purpose creating a moment of serious self-reflection, values-assessment, and spiritual recommitment. Often, we feel paralyzed by difficult circumstances and can suffer a real setback unless we prevent it.

When we are suffering, there is a natural human urge to withdraw, pull back, and spend time alone. Although this is a tendency we all have, it is not always the healthiest of choices. It is our ability to extend ourselves to others, even in moments of personal crisis, that will generally speed up the healing process and also deepen our relationships. We gain more when we throw ourselves into a worthwhile cause rather than retreating into a protective cocoon for long. We all need time alone from time to time, but too much of it can hurt more than it helps.

When we contribute to others and share our problems, we in a sense work them out of us and improve the situation. Fight the urge to hide what you are going through from others. Sharing your struggles in a constructive way is not the same as negative complaining. Sharing your struggles is the process of being honest about what is happening without blaming. It is a very healing process.

Solve Problems Gracefully

Remember that we experience life in the journey. It's not only the resolution that counts, it's how you solve the problems that really counts. When under pressure do you get tense and drive everyone around you crazy? If so, then you are not reaching higher ground. The key to solving problems with style and grace is to take it one step at a time and stop worrying about the outcome. Just do your best; pour your best self into the activity you are working on knowing that your plan will work as you grow and develop. Sometimes all we get out of problem solving is the personal growth of striding into a messy, neglected area of our life. Remember the words of Thomas Carlyle, "The block of granite which was an obstacle in the pathway of the weak, became a stepping stone in the pathway of the strong."

What Are You Putting Off?

Right now, make a list of all the problems in your life that need attention. Consider the different areas of life:

- Financial
- Family
- Career
- Social
- Physical
- Mental
- Spiritual

Make as complete a list as possible. Then prioritize it and tackle one problem at a time. This is what hunkering down is all about. As we tackle the tough stuff of our lives, the stuff we all have a tendency to put off, we strengthen ourselves, and our natural adverse reaction to problems goes down. This is the gateway to higher ground. "Character is the ability to carry out a resolution after the mood in which it was made has left you," said Robert Cavett.

Higher ground is one of the greatest rewards you'll experience as a result of the OUTSELL principles. Spending a significant amount of time in that high-awareness place will lead to the most coveted destination of all, the impact zone!

Chapter Eight

The strategies that really work in business tend to be simple. For example, the following principles are relatively easy to understand:

- Take in more money than you put out.
- Make it easy for customers to understand your product and service and, more importantly, what it can do for them.
- Always deliver more to your customer than you promise.
- Treat employees and customers with respect and dignity.
- Find people who can get the job done and let them do it.
- Be clear and to the point in what you communicate.
- Plan your work and work your plan.

It doesn't take weeks of study to understand what these simple principles mean. Simple, however, is not the same thing as easy. A concept can be simple to understand yet difficult to consistently implement because of a variety of factors, most of which are human, such as the following:

- We let previously established bad habits get in the way.
- We lack day-in and day-out focus.
- We lack the patience for results.
- We have a poor understanding of how business cycles work.
- We opt for the quick-fix, "easier," way.

The OUTSELL principles we have presented thus far are also easy to understand and, no doubt, many of you have either thought or heard about them before. Although an understanding of these simple bedrock principles is the essential first step, understanding alone is not enough to bring about the influential characteristics you would like to have. No, understanding is not enough. It's your ability to transform understanding into a way of life that will create the level of influence you really want.

There is a tremendous tendency today to seek out new ideas, new approaches, and new strategies at such a dizzying pace that we deprive ourselves of the opportunity to truly *master* the essential attitudes and skills that can transform our results. It's as if knowing what's out there, knowing all the new guru-inspired power ideas is more important than being able to stick with them and put them to use. However, history shows, over and over, that lasting success is usually built on a very simple, but stable philosophy that holds up under pressure. And that is exactly what the OUTSELL principles will do for you if you learn to live them.

In this chapter, we will sum up what we've learned so far and tie the first six principles together so that the synergy they create in helping you influence others, sell your ideas, and get real results will become a little clearer. Next, we are going to look at what it means to thrive once you are committed to a strategy that will work. Finally, we will explore the real benefit of everything you've learned so far, coming alive in the impact zone. The impact zone is where real influence happens. It's where you are able to combine credibility, competence, and high-powered communication to make things happen. Those three ingredients, credibility, competence, and communication, are what the greatest sales professionals and professionals that sell possess. You can have them too.

THE OUTSELL SYNERGY

The real power of the OUTSELL principles is found when you reach a level of competence in all of the first six OUTSELL principles simultaneously:

1. One life, one boss
2. Under construction
3. Tell it with gusto
4. Signed, sealed, delivered
5. Eat breakfast with champions
6. Life's hard; hunker down and reach higher ground

You'll get much better results over the long-term if you commit to all six principles and develop them consistently, even if at a slightly slower pace than if you take one, for instance, eat breakfast with champions, and work exclusively on it. You could become absolutely fantastic at building a champion network, but if you don't have the other five elements working for you, you're going to find a lot of frustration. And if you don't develop your competence to a higher level as suggested in the under-construction principle, you'll have more contacts, but you won't be able to create increasing value for them. This will short-circuit your ability to turn your network into productivity.

But this is often exactly what people do. Instead of improving slowly but steadily in a variety of ways that are designed to complement one another, they focus exclusively on one area and, because of the resulting deficits in other key areas, they are inevitably sidetracked along the way. They just can't get past a series of hurdles that keep popping up to prevent their success.

One life, one boss creates the focus to put to use all of the skills, attitudes, and insights that the OUTSELL principles will bring you. Without the ability to sense how great you really could be and to seize control of where you are going, then all the business savvy, sales techniques, and powerful connections you have will not get you very far.

Under construction gives you the energy and vitality to pursue your dreams and develop into a full-featured individual. Under construction steadily increases your ability to generate value for others. It is the process by which you build a cathedral from the foundation of one boss, one life thinking, and it is the process you go through to increase your own self-worth, which is at the heart of all influence.

Tell it with gusto is the way you communicate to the world you interact with who you are and where you are going. When you have clear direction and the vitality to pursue it, you will need to communicate with others and gain their cooperation, whether they be customers, team members, or your boss. Communication is a crucial tool for the professional who must sell, and tell it with gusto is the principle that contains the elements that will make you a powerful communicator.

Signed, sealed, delivered is the principle that will build your credibility and competence level. The first three principles will attract opportunities your way, but signed, sealed, delivered is how you capitalize on those opportunities by consistently performing at a high-quality level. This is how you do your work and is the spirit you embody when working with others. This is how you build real trust with others, the kind of trust that leaves other people thinking that you are a high-quality, high-value contributor who knows how to get the job done and done right, the first time, every time. Signed, sealed, delivered is the way you market yourself, by leaving your own personal mark of excellence on everything you touch.

Eat breakfast with champions is the way you gain access to greater resources. However, this principle is nearly impossible to harvest without having a clear direction, vitality, good communication skills, and a work philosophy that allows you to deliver consistent results. Without the first five OUTSELL principles working for you, you run the risk of being simply another networker who does little more than annoy the top performers. Eat breakfast with champions is a principle that will lead you to an ever increasing series of relationships with other top performers who *will want to* do business with you.

Life's hard; hunker down and reach higher ground is the way you transform the difficulties of life into the joy of living. This is what perseverance is all about. When you have these first five principles working for you, you are going to come up against some significant problems simply because the top performers (which you'll be with the first five principles working for you) attract the difficult problems that other lesser performers can't deal with. The top performer doesn't buckle under pressure. Instead, she finds her greatest resources at moments of great difficulty. Without this principle, the transformational success opportunities can turn into stress, fear, and anxiety.

To live, thrive, and come alive in the impact zone you have first got to *live* the first six OUTSELL principles. It's not enough to just understand them. We know you want a high level of influence and you want to be able to sell your ideas today, and you will be able to do it if you commit to living with these principles over the long-term. Sure, you'll find new ideas and strategies you can plug in, but don't make the mistake of "plugging out" the OUTSELL principles. That's what typically happens. In our never ending search for the better, faster, more efficient, more cost effective way, we often lose sight of the bedrock foundation that simply should never change. The OUTSELL principles lay that foundation for you.

Because we're in the training business, we meet many people who attend seminars and often are told about other terrific training seminars and conferences that are out there. People often say, "I got a lot of terrific ideas from that conference." But when asked, "What did you learn that you are using?" the answer is often something like, "I need to go back over my notes," or "I've gotten so side-tracked lately at work because of all the new projects, that I haven't had a chance to put it into practice, but I want to." Don't let that same mistake happen to you. Make these principles a part of the way you *live*.

THRIVE ON THE OUTSELL PULL

There are several ways to approach the way we get through hurdles, challenges, and circumstances of the day:

- We can tolerate them.
- We can avoid them.
- We can grin and bear it.
- We can do our best to deal with them.
- We can pretend they don't exist.
- Or, we can thrive on them!

We suggest you stretch out for the brass ring on this one and develop a desire to thrive on the excitement that your daily business challenges create for you. Become the person who is energized with vitality at the thought of difficult problem solving.

The business environment seems to be stressing so many people out, and fewer and fewer people seem to be having fun. Often, this stress is simply a reluctance to let go of disappointments and an inability to assume responsibility for the conditions of our lives and the work environment we create around us.

When you are growing and achieving in a variety of areas, a disappointment in one area of your life will not be debilitating! You'll be able to shake it off faster and throw yourself into the challenge in front of you. That's what thriving is all about. Thriving is an eagerness to see what lies beyond the upcoming corner or fork in the road. You'll have that confidence because when you live the OUTSELL principles daily and let the synergy take hold of you, you'll feel a mysterious pull happening to you.

Aim higher than just tolerating what is going on around you. Instead, when you decide to thrive on it, you will discover one of the hidden mysteries of selling. The person with the kind of enthusiasm that comes from thriving on challenges will simply beat out the competition time after time.

The OUTSELL principles will create a jet stream that will pull you along, and that jet stream will contain opportunities that will have within them all kinds of challenges. Thrive on those challenges!

To thrive is not about merely getting by. It's about a much higher standard of excellence where you feel great, you feel powerful, and you express yourself knowing that you are in the process of discovery.

COME ALIVE IN THE IMPACT ZONE!

We've referenced the impact zone several times throughout the book. In a nutshell, the impact zone is the payoff for all the hard work, effort, and commitment you make to the OUTSELL principles.

"You can really get on a roll in sales," explains Don Graling, a top-producing salesperson and manager. "And when you do, you really have to ride it and take it as far as you can. Sometimes, when salespeople start doing well, they actually slow down. Not me. When I'm on a roll, everything I say just seems to work, and I'm a lot more convincing. When you've got that feeling, you really have to capitalize on it."

The impact zone is that state of mind where you feel like you are on a roll. That feeling often comes immediately after a series of successes. The only way to have a series of successes is to meet a series of situations that allow you to either succeed or fail. And the OUTSELL principles, if they do nothing else for you, will serve up an endless stream of challenges! And that's really what it's all about—being in the game, with chances to compete, to rack up victories, to learn from defeats, but always moving forward and steadily building your confidence. And you will come alive when you meet those challenges because you will be prepared for them with the OUTSELL principles by your side.

The impact zone is the feeling that you can accomplish whatever you put your mind to. It's the feeling that you can sell your idea, that you can convince a board to move on your proposal, that you can deliver the goods if they give you the order. When you have those beliefs working for you, people can see it in your eyes and they will be moved by it.

"You've got to have confidence in yourself," explains Chip Sollins, president of American Pool Service. "A lot of what it takes to really make it is simply having the confidence to take a risk. It's not gambling, it's taking risks that you know you have the confidence to work out. You've got to know that you can come through when you need to. And when you feel that way, you feel confident about taking bigger risks in the future that bring you bigger challenges and, obviously, bigger rewards."

You can't get to the impact zone by accident. You have to plan carefully and put in the extra effort that a lot of people are not willing to give. It's the combination of good planning and consistent effort that paves the way.

In order to spend more time in the impact zone, there are seven things you should be doing as a result of what you've learned so far:

1. Your five-step written blueprint should be finished, with your vision, personal constitution, goals, habits and activities.
2. Activities from your written blueprint should be written into your calendar every week, which will enable you to work on those important long-term priorities that we often never get to.
3. You should know what you need to learn in order to increase your ability to generate value in the marketplace in your chosen field. You need to work at developing in those areas every day of your life.
4. You need a serious vitality improvement plan under way that will give you more energy, enthusiasm, and resolve to accomplish your dreams.
5. You should be communicating in a more interesting, entertaining, and animated way. Your message is coming to life and holding the attention of your listener more effectively now. You are experimenting every day with incidents, stories, analogies, and powerful quotes to improve as a communicator.
6. You should be meeting new people and tuning into your current relationships to pull more horsepower out of them. You are finding new champions in your life.
7. You should have identified the problem areas in your life you need to address now and worked through the simple problem-solving formula to solve them with persistence and realism.

By doing these seven activities regularly, you will be taking the express lane to the impact zone. Deliberately seeking out the impact zone is simply a better way to live, and it is well worth the extra effort it takes to get there.

You'll know you've arrived at the impact zone when you have ideas that can really work, people who trust and believe in what you are saying, you are able to get the resources to make those ideas happen, and you deliver more than you promise to the people you do business with, because they tell you so. And when you can do that you are truly outselling.

We are passing by the age when the sizzle was more important than the steak. But we are also entering an age where the attention span of the average person is shrinking. People want results, but they want to deal with people who can communicate with power and excitement. Outselling is putting both style and substance together.

And perhaps the most sustaining nugget of knowledge you'll find, as you commit more and more of yourself to the principles you've just discovered, is that there is a mysterious force that begins to move with you that is hard to understand, and even more difficult to describe, but there nonetheless. This power at first will put you face to face with the areas of your life that need attention, then will bring you true clarity of thinking. Next, it will begin to work like a magnet, pulling toward you the rewards you are earning. Finally, it will turn you into a person who is able to enjoy whatever comes your way.

We admire and applaud you as you chisel away at the sculpture of success as you see it and would like to leave you with the Irish Prayer, which sums up our feelings of gratitude toward you for taking the time read our book.

The Irish Prayer
May the road always rise to meet you.
May the sun shine warmly on your face.
May the wind be always at your back.
May the rain fall soft upon your fields.
And until we meet again, may God hold you,
ever so gently, in the palm of His hands.

OUTSELL MISSION

To support, help, and assist people who sell lead more successful lives both personally and professionally through training, information, inspiration, and motivation.

OutSell offers the following services:

- Sales Training—beginning, intermediate, and advanced
- Customized train-the-trainer selling systems
- Convention keynote speeches by Michael St. Lawrence and Steve Johnson
- Sales strategy consulting
- Presentation skills training
- Sales management training
- Development and design of effective sales meetings
- Customer service training to increase sales

For more information on OutSell products and services contact:

> OutSell
> 1601 N. Sepulveda Boulevard
> Manhattan Beach, CA 90266
> Tel. 310-939-1230
> Fax. 310-939-1232
> Internet: outsell3@aol.com

Please send us any success stories, inspirational stories, or successful strategies that work for you so that we may share them with others.

Index